John Gregory Dunne

CROONING

A COLLECTION

SIMON AND SCHUSTER

NEW YORK · LONDON · TORONTO · SYDNEY
TOKYO · SINGAPORE

SIMON AND SCHUSTER
Simon & Schuster Building
Rockefeller Center
1230 Avenue of the Americas
New York, New York 10020

Copyright © 1990 by John Gregory Dunne
All rights reserved
including the right of reproduction
in whole or in part in any form.
SIMON AND SCHUSTER and colophon are
registered trademarks of Simon & Schuster Inc.
Designed by Edith Fowler
Manufactured in the United States of America

10 9 8 7 6 5 4 3 2 1

Library of Congress Cataloging in Publication Data

Dunne, John Gregory
Crooning : a collection / John Gregory Dunne.
p.   cm.
I. Title.
PS3554.U493C76   1990
814'.54—dc20

90-9404
CIP

ISBN 0-671-67236-3

All but one of these pieces appeared at various
times and in various forms in the following publications, and I would like to thank the editors of each:
Esquire, New West and The New York Review of
Books. In some cases, there has been substantial rewriting as titles were changed, cuts restored, and
pieces elided or brought up to date.

For Q
For Nora and Nick
For Susanna
And for Two-Oh-Two

Contents

MANUAL LABOR · 223

Introduction

I HAD WISHED to call this collection REMFs, after one of the pieces collected, but discretion, in the corporate person of my publisher, prevailed, on the grounds that REMFs, as a title, might be construed by reader and (perhaps more importantly) bookseller alike as too deliberately hostile and aggressive. That leads to two questions, the first being what does REMFs actually mean (and for the answer to that I can only direct you to page 150), the second being why I wanted to call this book REMFs anyway, taking at face value my contention it was not merely to flip a rather public bird at those thought police who are our arbiters of good taste.

Of course hostility and aggression are involved. Most writers—at least most writers of my acquaintance—have a liberal component of each in their makeup. The absolute self-reliance that orders any writer's day demands it. Doubt is the enemy, the cancer that can metastasize into writer's block; the best way to guard against doubt, or any perception of it, is to take a ninja's stance toward the world.

What I am saying is that any literary endeavor is an attempt to harness this hostility, an attempt, however camouflaged, to breach the reader's defenses, to make her or him capitulate and accept the writer's view, be it of the world at large or only a sliver of it. There are many different ways the writer can accomplish this end—by frontal assault or indirection, by humor or ridicule, by selection or rhetoric. Make no mistake, however: writing is an aggressive act, and he who would claim, as I once did, that he was one of life's neutrals, a human Switzerland, is perhaps the most aggressively insidious of all.

NINE OF THE PIECES in this collection were first published in *The New York Review of Books,* a journal with which I have had an association since 1979. There are a number of reasons why I like to write for the *Review,* and none have anything to do with money; an outside source of income is advised if one intends to publish there with any regularity. Robert Silvers is the editor of *The New York Review.* Writers are often asked what an editor does, and the ingrates among us usually reply, Nothing. I exempt Robert Silvers from this casual bad rap, but I still do not know exactly what he does or why it is so effective; I can only describe his modus operandi.

A piece usually begins with lunch at Patsy's, a nondescript Italian restaurant on the West Side of Manhattan whose walls are decorated with 8 × 10 glossies of has-been actors and actresses, many with handwritten messages expressing undying fealty to the management or encomiums for the rather watery clams marinara. Mr. Silvers' table, please. On the second floor, at the top of the stairs. Bob drinks Pellegrino and eats only the inside of the bread, all the while neatly brushing the crust crumbs with his knife into his left hand, and from there onto the butter plate, and sometimes the floor, with not a break in the conversation. The topic for the day is local Democratic politics in Connecticut. My turf, I think. Something I will know more about than Bob. I am from Hartford, after all, I know John Bailey and Tony Zazzarro. My mistake: so does Bob. And seemingly the name of every precinct captain in New Britain's fifth ward. And judges in

Waterbury. And the man to see in Derby. And the fellow who gets out the vote in New London. I am reeling, my putative knowledge reduced to the blustering ignorance it is. A plaintive question: How do you know all these people? Ah, yes, well, old boy (I will wager not many people who know the Sanitation Commissioner in Hartford call acquaintances "old boy"), I was Chet Bowles's press secretary the last few months he was governor. By my calculations Bob was nineteen. Of course.

What is astonishing about Robert Silvers is the amount he knows. If he doesn't know it, he will learn it. And if he knows it, and you're writing about it, you're going to get it. Books, clips, press releases, *The Wall Street Journal*, *The Washington Post*, the *Times*, magazines, desktop publishing, Suzy and Page 6 in the *Post*—when does he find time to read all this goddamn stuff? And will he stop sending it already? Of course not. It comes via fax, messenger, TWX, overnight mail, FedX: nobody at the *Review* seems to have heard of a twenty-five-cent stamp and the U.S. Postal Service; or perhaps they know it all too well. If Bob had been editing during the time of the Pony Express, God knows how many horses he would have killed to get that new set of galleys out to Los Angeles when I was living there, or the piece in *Pacific Islands Monthly*—"wrongheaded, but interesting"—to Jim Fallows when he was in Kuala Lumpur. And if the horses stop at water's edge, then swim!

And they would, which is why it is such an invigorating experience to write for the *Review*. Not that Bob is perfect. He would not permit the title "REMFs" either, when the piece was published, and he made me cut the last line as too ad hominem. It goes without saying that I restored it in this version.

RANDOM BITS from three pieces about baseball that were not good enough individually to fit into this collection:

On Baseball and Intellectuals: "Baseball," George Will once pontificated, "resembles nothing so much as the universe," a

bit of extension-school metaphysics that is a perfect example of
the kind of cosmic bullshit indulged in by intellectuals when
they try to scan the religion of the diamond for meaning. Jacques
Barzun was an early and egregious member of the "Baseball is [his-
torical metaphor of choice]" school. "Baseball *is* Greek," Barzun
wrote in 1954, "in being national, heroic, and broken up in the
rivalries of city-states." In fact, baseball is not the universe nor
is it Greek. It is simply, like sex, extremely difficult to write about.

On Baseball and Sports Writing: I think one reason baseball is so difficult to write about is that the natural language of
its practitioners is cliché. The major-league ballplayer lives at the
frontier of instinct and reflex, where the difference between success and failure can be measured incrementally in microseconds;
he will never again do anything in his life as well as what he does at
the age of twenty-five. Hand-to-eye coordination is better developed than the vocabulary to explain it.

Many sportswriters, as a result, ridicule the athlete's poverty
of expression. It should be said that the sports beat is one of the
less arduous assignments in newspapering, not excluding show
business, and what constantly surprises me, whenever I venture
into a press box, is the prevailing bunker mentality. The facts of
sports are immutable—one team wins, one team loses—so that
sportswriting is essentially the search for an angle. Among the
less talented, this breeds a kind of macho posturing. In some sections of the press box the prevailing attitude is that if it were not
for sports most ballplayers would be pumping gas—if they
weren't sticking up the gas station. For their part, ballplayers
are as clannish as cops, and as resistant to those who do not share
their profession. In major-league clubhouses there is an inchoate
sense that being a jock is a higher calling than being a jock
sniffer, that if we're so dumb and sportswriters are so smart, why
are they covering us. In this sullen truce, macho posturing becomes the lingua franca of both sides.

Of Baseball and Tom Lasorda: Tommy Lasorda, the man-

ager of the Los Angeles Dodgers, has the world view of an opening act in Vegas. The first time I met him, he was holding forth
in his office at Dodger Stadium. Automatically he reached into
his desk, removed an 8 × 10 glossy of himself from a stack in the
drawer, and without a break in the colloquy he was holding
with local and visiting sportswriters, autographed the photo with
the words "To John—You and the Dodgers—Both winners—
Tom Lasorda." To say Lasorda has a mouth like a sewer is to
pin a bad rap on the department of sanitation. Every sentence
was decorated with references to bodily waste and the orifices
from which the waste is excreted, to the male and female geni-
talia at rest and at play, to sodomy and reproduction. To a reporter's critical question, he replied without pausing for breath,
"Opinions are like assholes, everyone has one." I have since come
to believe that this piece of gutter wisdom is the most sane response to criticism I have ever run across.

OVER THE COURSE of the twenty-four years that I lived in
Los Angeles and he in New York, Calvin Trillin and I carried
on a long and spirited correspondence. I mention this only because in the age of the telephone, the fax, and the modem, long-
term correspondence between writers has become quaint, a craft
from the past, like basketry. The letters were usually short, generally abusive, and always funny. I saved his, nearly a hundred in
all, and Calvin (he claims) none of mine. I dedicated a book to
him, and his novel *Floater* carried what he called a claimer (as
opposed to a disclaimer): "The character of Andy Wolferman is
based on John Gregory Dunne, although it tends to flatter."
Flattery of course is in the eye of the beholder, and when I
asked Calvin in what way Andy Wolferman was meant to be
flattering, he replied, "I made you Jewish."

In 1981, after a picture I wrote (based on my novel *True
Confessions*) received a rapturous notice from the reviewer in a

national publication (the laws of libel compel me to keep his name in confidence), Calvin sent the following note:

> Dear J.G.,
>
> I had a strange telephone call this morning from [and here he named the reviewer]. He seemed to want me to act as a sort of middleman in some dealings he has with you. Although he was quite indirect, his request seems to come down to this: Now can he have the photos back (including the negatives)? He seems particularly anxious about one he would only refer to as "having something to do with some goats and a dwarf." Naturally, I'd be willing to do whatever I can. You may count on my discretion.
>
> Yours,
> Calvin

When my wife and I moved to New York, I asked Calvin if he would write a letter of recommendation to the board of the building in which we were trying to buy a cooperative apartment. His response was immediate:

> This is in answer to your inquiry concerning Mr. and Mrs. John Gregory Dunne.
> I have known Mr. and Mrs. Dunne for more than twenty years, and I can say they would make a splendid addition to any cooperative apartment building. As you may have learned by now from neighbors of Mr. and Mrs. Dunne in Brentwood, the role played by Mr. Dunne's temper in the incident there was greatly exaggerated in the press.
> I have known the Dunnes' daughter, Quintana, since her infancy, and I can assure you that she is an attractive and responsible young woman who is work-

ing hard day and night on the gruelling practice schedule necessary for anyone who aspires to be a successful hard-rock drummer. The dog that bit the UPS delivery man is hers.

In the event you have been concerned about the presence of the male nurse who is retained to escort Mr. Dunne home on evenings out, I would like to put your mind to rest. The male nurse in question is remarkably skilled at keeping control without making a fuss. I understand that, by a happy coincidence, he is related to your doorman, Mr. O'Leary, as is Mr. Dunne.

Mrs. Dunne is not Jewish.

Yours sincerely,
Calvin Trillin

FINALLY. A friend of mine, a novelist of note, years ago confessed to me that if he were not a writer he would like to be a postman. I understood; better mindless drudgery than the debilitating unhappiness of being what one wasn't. My sights are somewhat different. In those moments when I hate what I am doing (which is most of the time), I fantasize that I could be a crooner, a job description that dates me, a Johnny Mathis, say, or a Buddy Clark (always referred to after his death as "the late, great Buddy Clark"), not, perish the thought, a rock-and-roller. That I am tone deaf is beside the point. Often when alone, I unknot my tie, unbutton my jacket, stand in front of the mirror and belt away: *"Who can I turn to / When nobody needs me."* My phrasing is distinctive: "nobody" comes out as "nuh-b'dee," and "needs" I pronounce as "nids," all of this sung— perhaps not the most appropriate verb—in what I can only describe as an upper nasal register. I note this only to explain why I write. "One does what one can," as Agatha Christie once replied when asked why she wrote mysteries, "not what one can't."

WEST OF THE WEST

An American Education

1

Q. So my first question is, have you at any time ever
been a member of the Communist Party?

A. I would like to answer that by saying that I am not
a member of the Communist Party. However, as
to the second part of your question I will stand on
the fifth amendment and refuse to answer this question because I feel it could incriminate me.

Q. Well, actually I asked you only one question,
whether you had ever been a member. You state
you are not a member now?

A. Yes.

Q. When did you withdraw from the Communist
Party?

A. I would have to decline, sir, on the same ground.

Testimony before the House Committee
on Un-American Activities,
Los Angeles, California,
September 19, 1951

• •

T HIS IS AN AMERICAN STORY.

The Richard and Hinda Rosenthal Foundation Award is given every year by the American Academy and Institute of Arts and Letters to one painter and to one "American work of fiction published during the preceding twelve months which, though not a commercial success, is a considerable literary achievement." Over the years, this prize has been awarded to novels by, among others, Bernard Malamud, John Updike, Thomas Pynchon, Joyce Carol Oates, and Diane Johnson. In the spring of 1984, the book chosen was *Famous All Over Town* by Danny Santiago, a novel about an indomitable young Chicano growing up in the East Los Angeles barrio. The citation for the Rosenthal Award was read by John Kenneth Galbraith at the Academy and Institute's annual ceremonial:

> *Famous All Over Town* adds luster to the enlarging literary genre of immigrant experience, of social, cultural and psychological threshold-crossing. . . . The durable young narrator spins across a multi-colored scene of crime, racial violence and extremes of dislocation, seeking and perhaps finding his own space. The exuberant mixes with the nerveracking; and throughout sly slippages of language enact a comedy on the theme of communication.

Danny Santiago did not show up at the ceremony to pick up the $5,000 check that came with his Rosenthal Award. His absence was in keeping with a long-established pattern of reclusiveness. There was no photograph of Danny Santiago on the dust jacket of *Famous All Over Town*. His agent and publisher had never laid eyes on him. Neither had they ever spoken to him on the telephone. Danny Santiago claimed to have no telephone. His address was a post office box in Pacific Grove,

California, a modest settlement on the Monterey peninsula. All communication with Danny Santiago went through this Pacific Grove post office box. Danny Santiago refused to be interviewed and therefore did no publicity on behalf of *Famous All Over Town*. It was as if Danny Santiago did not exist, and in a way he did not.

As IT HAPPENS, I have known the author of *Famous All Over Town* for the past eighteen years. He was my landlord when my wife and I lived in Hollywood. Danny Santiago, strictly speaking, is not his name. He is not a Chicano. Nor is he young. He is seventy-three years old. He is an Anglo. He is a graduate of Andover and Yale. He was the only member of the Yale class of 1933 to major in classical Greek. He is a prize-winning playwright. He is the co-author of the book of a hit musical comedy that played 654 performances on Broadway.

He was a screenwriter. He worked with Charlie Chaplin on *The Great Dictator*. He was a member of the Communist Party. He worked as a volunteer social worker in East Los Angeles. He was one of 152 people named, on September 19, 1951, by a single witness before the House Committee on Un-American Activities, which was investigating Communist infiltration of the movie industry. He was subpoenaed to appear before the Committee. He declined under oath to say whether he had ever been a member of the Party, which he had, in fact, officially left three years earlier. He was blacklisted. He wrote monster pictures under an assumed name. He continued, along with his wife, to do volunteer work in East Los Angeles through the 1950s and into the Sixties. In 1968, he showed me some stories he had written about the neighborhood where he had been a social worker for so many years. As a result, I became a reluctant co-conspirator in his establishing the identity of Danny Santiago. His name is Daniel James. "Danny Santiago," of course, is Dan James translated into Spanish.

2
___

Q. Will you state your full name, Mr. James?
A. Daniel Lewis James.
Q. When and where were you born?
A. In Kansas City, Missouri, January 14, 1911.

> *Testimony before the House Committee*
> *on Un-American Activities,*
> *Los Angeles, California,*
> *September 19, 1951*

DAN JAMES's grandfather was the first cousin of Frank and Jesse James. This grandfather went to Brown. His grandmother was in the first graduating class at Vassar. His father graduated from Yale. The Jameses of Kansas City were Midwestern gentry, importers and purveyors of fine china—Spode and Haviland—that they sold throughout the Midwest and the border states. The business—T. M. James & Sons—flourished. Daniel James's maternal grandfather purchased the home of a robber baron in Kansas City who had gone broke. I have seen a photograph of this house, which has long since been razed. It was a house of which Soames Forsyte might have approved, the house of a man of property, huge, in the convention of the day, dominated by a tower and punctuated by turrets and gables and cupolas and verandas, and it was in this house that Daniel James was born in 1911, his parents' only child.

D. L. James, his father, was himself a Galsworthy creation, a businessman-aesthete in the manner of young Jolyon Forsyte, who painted. When he was not selling china, D. L. James was a playwright, occasionally produced in stock and little theaters and foreign and amateur productions, at work at the time of his death in 1944 on a five-act play on his kinsman Jesse James, about whom his feelings were ambivalent; he could not decide, according to his son, whether Jesse was more sinned against than sinning. "My father met anybody interesting who came to Kansas City," Daniel James says. "There was a little luncheon group of all the intellectuals in Kansas City, which numbered between nine and thirteen, I think." Walter Hampden, the actor, was a friend of D. L. James, as were Karl Menninger and Thomas Hart Benton. Sinclair Lewis came to call.

It was only natural that from 1914 on D. L. James would spend his summers, with his wife and young son, in Carmel, California. A kind of manqué literary life could exist there for him as it did among the Kansas City intellectuals, because in neither venue would it be put to a reality check. There is a visual splendor about Carmel that is almost dreamlike, a soft-focus mirage of dunes and crashing white water and guano-washed rock islets and sheer cliffs falling into the surf and forests and meadows and clinging mists and wind-bent stands of cypress; the place tends to create a pervading, even comforting sense that no artistic accomplishment could ever match the landscape. Carmel was "an outpost of bohemia," Kevin Starr wrote in *Americans and the California Dream, 1850–1915*, a place of "artists, near artists and would-be artists." There was something moony about their attempt to merge art and nature. The California novelist Mary Austin (author of *The Ford*) wore long robes, rode a white horse, and worked in a tree house. It was the perfect spot to contemplate Jesse James as the fog rolled in and the years rolled by.

In 1918, D. L. James commissioned the project that was to be his monument. He had bought some property on a promontory near Point Lobos, a few miles from Carmel, and invited an acquaintance, the great California architect Charles Sumner Greene, to take a look at the site. Charles Greene was fifty, a partner with his brother Henry Mather Greene in the firm of Greene & Greene. The Greene brothers were craftsmen, virtuosos in wood and glass. For a quarter of a century in Southern California, particularly in Pasadena, they had elevated the prairie house of Louis Sullivan into a mystical idea, the bungalow as a pre-Raphaelite vision. Stone was not their usual medium, but Charles Greene was so challenged by D. L. James's wind-buffeted point that two days later, unsolicited, he submitted a set of rough preliminary sketches for a stone house of such intricate design that it would be almost impossible to tell where cliff ended and house began. D. L. James immediately engaged him to begin work.

Construction took five years. Charles Greene was always on the site, supervising the quarrying, the cutting, and the laying of the stone, all of it indigenous to Carmel. The house is U-shaped, as if fitted to the contours of the point; its granite walls are two to three feet thick and the stones are set irregularly into the facade with broken faces exposed. The effect is medieval.

Although the house has only one story, it has several levels adhering to the topography of the cliff. The ceilings in the living room and library are sixteen feet high, and every one of the house's seven rooms has an arched window opening onto the ocean a hundred feet or so below. Charles Greene revised his plans constantly, tearing out walls and replacing them if he was dissatisfied with the masonry or the workmanship. Costs escalated. In 1922, D. L. James finally called a halt before Charles Greene could complete an office on a lower elevation or put his own stamp on the interiors, as was his plan. The final cost, astonishingly, even allowing for the dollar's soundness in that period, was less than $90,000.

The house is called "Seaward," and it has been the home of Daniel James and his wife Lilith since his mother's final illness in 1968. It is a work of art, with all the baggage that phrase might carry. "This house was the answer to my father's dream of immortality, which he did not achieve in his writing," Daniel James says. The legacy would prove as well to be an enduring financial and psychological burden for the son. "Who am I to have this?" he asks rhetorically. "In my bad moments I've often felt all those tons of rock walls balancing on the back of my neck." Whatever he accomplished, he would always measure that accomplishment against the house.

3

DAN JAMES is six feet six inches tall. He was cross-eyed until he was fourteen, a condition that nourished a tendency toward introspection. He missed a year at Yale because of tuberculosis. He majored in Greek "because it was a different thing to do." He was informed more by Carmel than he was by either Yale or the mercantile Midwest. He knew Lincoln Steffens and Ella Winter and was exposed to what Kevin Starr has called Carmel's "loquacious socialism" and "posturing reformism." He was "progressive" as a matter of course, but it was not until his last year at Yale, after his sojourn in a Connecticut TB sanitorium, that he became politically active. He joined the John Reed Club and walked in a hunger march to Hartford.

He graduated into the Depression, but at least into a job, as a china salesman for T. M. James & Sons. His territory was Oklahoma and southern Missouri. The dust bowl was not the best place those days for a drummer of fine china. Dan James remembers once-flourishing stops where stores had been boarded up and the towns had ceased to exist. "I was giving away things from my sample case," he recalls. "People who used to order Haviland were asking for a cup and saucer they could sell for ten cents."

That a young man of genteel Midwestern background, his only real experience in the marketplace a family sinecure peddling Limoges in the path of a national disaster, could wind up

the 1930s a member of the Communist Party and working for
Charlie Chaplin was a not atypical story of that time. Carmel
was the stage where Dan James blocked out the major scene
changes in his life, the place to which he would always return
after his forays into the job market. From Carmel he went to
work briefly in the Oklahoma oil fields, a job secured for him by
a relative who owned an oil-drilling company. At first the Yale
man as a swamper—a colorful name for a truck driver's assistant,
loader, gofer, and handyman—was sent to fetch circle stretchers
and left-handed monkey wrenches, but in time he learned that
"this is what it felt like to make a living." Loading and unload-
ing truckloads of pipe, the Yale man began to dream that one
day he might "organize the workers." After a few months, however, he returned to Kansas City—"my own man"—to marry
for the first time. In the face of this "explosion of domesticity"
and a bout with hepatitis that doctors thought might signal a
recurrence of his tuberculosis, the allure of the working-class life
began to recede.

He retreated to Carmel, and at his father's instigation he
began to write for the first time. The two Jameses, father and
son, collaborated on a play about the 1934 West Coast long-
shoremen's strike. "It was your typical strike play," Dan James
remembers. "There was the strike. There was the Irish family of
dockworkers. And of course there was the little kid who gets
shot." When the play was finished, he and his wife went to New
York sure that one of the burgeoning new left-wing theater
groups would produce it. His exposure to the reality principle
was swift. He recalls the reaction of one producer's reader:
"After reading the play, she said, 'You're a nice young man. But
I think very possibly you should do something else besides writing.' I resented it slightly."

For a while, James and his wife stayed on in New York. He
wrote more unproduced plays and worked as an extra in John
Howard Lawson's *Marching Song*, a strike drama he considered

far inferior to his own. The experience on stage in *Marching Song* had one postscript unforeseen at the time. A few years later, Lawson (always known as "Jack") became a major functionary and dialectician of the Communist Party in Hollywood—the "Grand High Poo-Bah," in the words of one informer before the House Committee on Un-American Activities—and it was he who would vouch for Dan James and his progressivism when he joined the Party.

New York palled, and in time James returned to Carmel. He busied himself in local theatricals and inchoate political activism. His marriage foundered. Then one day in 1938, Charlie Chaplin came to call at his father's house by the sea. "My father was the kind of man Chaplin would be brought to see if he was visiting in Carmel," Dan James says. Chaplin was just beginning to work on *The Great Dictator*. Not long after this first meeting, Dan James wrote Chaplin in Hollywood and asked him for a job. He was hired for eighty dollars a week.

Last June, in Carmel, I asked him why Chaplin would hire an assistant with no experience making movies. "He wanted to meet John Steinbeck, who I knew," Dan James said. "Not that he couldn't have met Steinbeck on his own. And he had a history of hiring tall, well-bred assistants who knew what fork to use."

4
___

Q. What has been your record of employment?
A. . . . I began writing in 1935, or 1936. The first years were extremely difficult, learning my craft and so forth. In 1938, I came here to Hollywood, was employed in an independent studio as a sort of junior writer-assistant to a producer. After that I

wrote a play called *Winter Soldiers*, which was produced in New York City in the fall of 1942. This
was then sold to Edward Small. I did a screenplay
on it, but . . . the screenplay was shelved. I then
engaged with my wife in working on her original
story of what turned out to be a musical comedy,
Bloomer Girl. Since that period, my fortunes have
been rather bad. I have written a novel, which was
not published, a couple of plays, numerous short
stories, and so forth.

Dan James, testifying
before the House Committee
on Un-American Activities,
Los Angeles, California,
September 19, 1951

CHARLIE CHAPLIN was the first of what Dan James calls
his surrogate fathers. To be in Chaplin's employ was in fact to
be included in a kind of family conspiracy. "I'm sure that Chaplin felt the Nazis could capture me and pull out my fingernails,"
Dan James says, "and I would never turn against him." During
the writing and shooting of *The Great Dictator*, James was
Chaplin's shadow, taking notes on everything he said and did—
scraps of dialogue, bits of business, pieces of pantomime. He
would type up these notes, often adding dialogue and suggestions
of his own, and Chaplin would pull them apart the next day and
start over. Writing the screenplay of *The Great Dictator* was a
matter of "going forward one inch and going back three." Chaplin's half brother Syd was usually on hand. "Syd was very in-
genious with gags," James recalls. "He was terrified the picture
was going to get too heavy. 'You're a comedian,' Syd would say.
'Let's do some funny stuff here. Let's do something funny.'"

James's other surrogate father was the Communist Party.
He had joined in 1938, his membership vetted and seconded by

John Howard Lawson. Other than premature antifascism, no epiphany led him into the Party. It was more a romantic adventure, a leap that he remembered forty-six years later with detachment and I suspect a certain rue. "I was now supporting myself," he says ironically, "and it was time to join my comrades in the working class."

He was a member of the working class who lunched nearly every day with his employer. In a restaurant a few blocks from Chaplin's studio in Hollywood, James and the great dictator would argue about politics. "Chaplin called himself an anarchist," James said. "He assumed I was a member of the Party, but he never asked. He wondered how I could justify the Nazi-Soviet Pact." In fact, James had no trouble with the Party line: the pact bought time for the Soviet Union to arm itself and created in Poland a buffer zone between Germany and Russia. It was an argument that Chaplin hooted as specious and deluded.

James and his employer also talked about women. Chaplin always had girl trouble, and when he had a problem with one girl, his usual solution was to add another to his stable. In Carmel, he had become interested in the companion of one of James's closest friends, interested enough to offer the friend a job on *The Great Dictator* so that the girl might be more available. Her name was Dorothy Comingore, and she was later cast by Orson Welles as the second Mrs. Charles Foster Kane in *Citizen Kane*. Subsequently she married a screenwriter named Richard Collins, another close friend of Dan James and also a Communist. In one of those coincidences in which the period abounds, Richard Collins, in 1951, purged himself before the House Committee on Un-American Activities and in private session not only named Dan James as a Party member but also suggested that he might be a cooperative witness. Dan James and Richard Collins never spoke again.*

* Dorothy Comingore was also called to testify, an unfriendly witness, and was responsible for perhaps the only light moment in the whole sordid interlude. Questioned by the Committee, she mused about her

Those early years in Hollywood were the most productive of Dan James's life. In 1940, he was married again, to Lilith Stanward, a divorced ballerina with a small daughter he later adopted. The Party dominated their social and professional lives. For Hollywood's Communists, social activity was predicated on the raising of money—benefits and balls and fund-raisers for the Party, for the antifascist fronts, for the Anti-Nazi League, for British and Russian War Relief. Dan James remembers old czarist and White Russian emigrés meeting uneasily with Hollywood Reds at the Russian War Relief benefits, making common cause because of the danger to Mother Russia. One of James's tasks in the Party was babysitting Theodore Dreiser, a Stalinist and a raging anti-Semite, who was, James said, being fed a lot of "Trotskyite bullshit" by James T. Farrell. "I just had to hold his hand occasionally," James said. I asked why a Party member so young was given such an important job. "I expect because I wasn't Jewish," James said.

The Party meetings seemed endless. Days were spent, James recalls, on a pamphlet titled *What Means This Strike in Steel?* At another meeting, there was a Talmudic argument about whether it was worse for Louis B. Mayer, as a Jew, to own race horses than it would be for a gentile boss to do so. For screenwriters, the meetings were directed toward identifying the class struggle in the pictures they wrote. Melodrama was the approved form, James says, because the bad boss and the crooked sheriff basic to the melodramatic plot were the classic characters of agitprop.

It was a B-picture mentality, and by and large the Party attracted B-picture writers. "The Hollywood writer was a highly

past life and her two ex-husbands, both of whom had cooperated with the investigation and named names. The first was a screenwriter named Ted Strauss, "a shy, scared little man," in the words of an acquaintance who remembered him, and the second was Richard Collins. "I've been married twice," she testified. "My first husband was a mouse, my second was a rat."

paid domestic," Murray Kempton noted with cruel accuracy in his 1955 book, *Part of Our Time.* "He was that most unfortunate of craftsmen, the man of talent who once hoped to be a genius and is treated like a lackey." Kempton goes on:

> In 1941, Leo Rosten polled a group of Hollywood professionals on their attitude toward the medium. He found that 133 out of 165 scriptwriters thought the movies were terrible. No other group registered so total a revulsion to the boss's product and no other group turned up so many persons susceptible to the Communist pull.

Years later, Dan James remarked to me that writers with first-rate credentials outside Hollywood—John O'Hara, Scott Fitzgerald, Robert E. Sherwood—rarely joined the Party, however left-wing their politics. Tax returns confirmed the stigma of the second rate. "Of the seventeen scriptwriters listed by Leo Rosten as Hollywood's highest paid in 1938," Kempton reported in *Part of Our Time,* "only one has since been identified as a Communist."

Germany's invasion of Russia in 1941 eliminated the embarrassment of the Nazi-Soviet Pact for Hollywood's Communists—Stalin became Uncle Joe overnight—and six months later Pearl Harbor elevated most of the Party's antifascist fund-raising to the level of patriotic duty. Because of his tuberculosis, Dan James was 4-F, but in any case the Party's position was that its writer members could serve the cause of the proletariat more effectively at the typewriter than at the front. James's contribution to this effort was a play called *Winter Soldiers,* which in 1942 won the Sidney Howard Memorial Award, a $1,500 prize given by The Playwrights Company "to the young American playwright showing the most promise." *Winter Soldiers* was too expensive for The Playwrights Company to mount on Broad-

way—it had eleven scenes and forty-two speaking parts—but
James used his prize money to help finance a production at
New York's New School for Social Research, with a cast of
unpaid professional actors.

Winter Soldiers is a curious relic, a celebration of the "little
people" and a love song to the Soviet Union so melodious that
I was surprised, when I read it again recently, that it could have
been produced, even in 1942 when the Wehrmacht was at the
gates of both Moscow and Stalingrad; *Song of Russia* is gritty
by comparison. The play roams over Yugoslavia, Austria, Czecho-
slovakia, Poland, and Russia—five countries Dan James had
never visited—and tells the story of a united anti-Nazi underground movement, its members hiding in caves and huts all over
Central Europe, who with daring and courage and with dynamite and picks and old rifles stop the German troop train assigned to lead the assault on Moscow.

The play is all broad strokes, characterization either by caricature or sanctity. Told that a military timetable is "impossible,"
a Nazi general shouts, "In the German language, that Jewish
word no longer exists." A heavenly glow bathes the partisans. On
a Russian collective farm, Comrade Katya remembers her reward
for finishing the harvest two weeks early. "They sent me to
Moscow," she says before going out to fight the Nazis. "I saw
Comrade Stalin."

Winter Soldiers was an artifact of the revolutionary euphoria, and with the passage of time its excesses would make Dan
James cringe. "Creaky" was his later verdict. "Seedy." The play
had the good fortune to be reviewed the same day the headlines
in *The New York Times* read: RUSSIANS BREAK NAZI DON DEFENSE
LINE. SOVIETS LIST GAINS. 100,000 NAZIS ARE SAID TO HAVE BEEN
KILLED IN THE LAST TEN DAYS. Lewis Nichols, the *Times*'s reviewer, called *Winter Soldiers* "exciting and moving . . . a perfect portrait of that other column which also carries on the war
for freedom." Other reviewers praised the play as well, and Burns
Mantle selected it for *Best Plays of 1942–1943*.

Winter Soldiers played only twenty-five performances, but for the first time James felt himself a functioning professional writer. Back home in Los Angeles, he was hired to write a screenplay of *Winter Soldiers*, a project that never got off the ground. At the same time, however, Lilith James had come up with a play idea of her own, the product of a Party-endorsed workshop on women's rights. Her idea was to highlight the heroine's campaign to exchange the hoop skirt for bloomers. She and Dan collaborated on the play and brought it to Harold Arlen and E. Y. Harburg, who thought it would make a perfect libretto for a musical. Thus *Bloomer Girl* was born. The Jameses worked on several drafts of the book and then were joined by two more experienced librettists, Sig Herzig and Fred Saidy, who made more room for song and dance by planing away the dialectic. On October 4, 1944, *Bloomer Girl* opened in New York and was an instant hit.

It should have been the best of times, but it was the worst, the beginning of an unproductive period for Dan James that would last twenty-five years. He went to work on a play for Paul Robeson, adapted from a novel by Howard Fast, but the play was, in his word, "terrible." For a few months, he and Lilith, who was pregnant, returned to Kansas City, "to my bourgeois roots." The trip was research for a novel of manners, *The Hockadays*, about the upper middle class and its pleasures. *The Hockadays* did not find a publisher.

At the same time, his enthusiasm for the Communist Party had begun to wane. "We all saw a rosy future after the war," he wrote in a letter:

> A very brave and progressive new world. It seems very stupid now, but if you'd been there you'd have felt it. We even believed with fascism dead, the Soviet Union would relax its internal repression (which previously when we admitted it, we blamed on the need to prepare for war). Again history took a turn. The San Fran-

cisco conference to create the United Nations proved no better than Wilson's old League of Nations in 1919. We tried to blame it all on the U.S. of course, but we began to be very doubtful as we saw the Iron Curtain go down in Eastern Europe. And the wartime coalition of which we were a tiny part collapsed and we found ourselves isolated. . . . Our credibility in the labor movement was destroyed because of our wartime no-strike stand. Liberals and progressives were happy to give us the cold shoulder. And in Hollywood the whole movement collapsed under the weight of the poor Ten who went to Washington as heroes and came back as enemies of the people. . . . Anyway it's when I started moving away from the Party, and of course the debacle of the Wallace campaign in '48 sealed the coffin. When I left, don't get the idea that it was a purely intellectual decision. There was plenty of fear in there, really chilling fear and with some reason in view of what happened later. And shame because of that fear.

Three years after they left the Party, Dan and Lilith James were called to testify in front of the House Committee on Un-American Activities. In the interim, naming names had become a cottage industry in Hollywood. The Jameses' friend Richard Collins named them in closed session. In open session, Martin Berkeley took the trouble to spell out Dan's name: "Also in our group were Dan James, J-A-M-E-S . . ." Again in open session, Leo Townsend, who was perhaps the Jameses' closest friend in the Party, reduced hairsplitting to a fine, even comic, art:

Q. Were you acquainted with a person by the name of Dan James?
A. I know Dan James.

Q. Did you of your own knowledge know that he was a member of the Communist Party?

A. I had heard that he had left the Communist Party. I don't know whether you would consider that knowledge of membership.

Q. Well, did you hear that from him or from some outside source?

A. I heard it from him.

Q. Well, I think that is direct testimony. Now, what were the circumstances under which you heard it from him?

A. Simply that I had told him that I had been out since 1948 and that he told me he had also left the Party.

Dan and Lilith James were subpoenaed by the Committee in the summer of 1951. Dan was playing tennis on the court in the back yard of his house on Franklin Avenue in Hollywood with a producer from whom he was trying to hustle a screenplay assignment. "It was not the most propitious moment," he recalls. I asked the Jameses not long ago why they had been summoned while so many others who were named had not been called. "They thought we would snitch," Lilith James said. "They knew we had left the Party and assumed we would cooperate." Had it ever crossed their minds? Never. Their position was that while they would say they were not members of the Party, they would decline to answer that they ever had been. "I expect no applause either from this Committee, nor from the *People's World*, nor from the *Daily Worker*," Dan James stated under oath. "This is a lonely, lonely position, and I assure you that when I am saying that I am not a Communist, I am meaning it."

With his sense of the theatrical, Dan James carried in his pocket, from his father's library in Carmel, a first edition of

Candide, which he hoped to introduce into testimony with the admonition that Voltaire had published it under a pseudonym— M. Le Docteur Ralph—and if the Committee worked its will, American writers as well would have to disguise their identities. The Committee would have none of this playlet and cut him off before he could begin.

On the evidence of a photograph in the *Los Angeles Times* the next day, Lilith James wore a hat when she testified. She has always been an intensely private woman, and the witness table was for her neither a platform nor a podium. She said she was not a Communist and then simply declined to answer further questions. Asked if she had been a member of the Party "on Sunday of this past week," and then on Monday or Tuesday or in 1944, she replied only, "I decline." When it became obvious she would not cooperate, Congressman Clyde Doyle of California tried to wheedle and coax with appeals to her motherhood. "Are there some little Jameses?" he asked, and then, "You've got some young children growing up. Why don't you help us in the field of communistic influences in Hollywood?"

"I feel it is quite possible to be opposed to communism," Lilith James said, "and its principles and its alliance to the Soviet Union and to be in support of our government, our government's policy in Korea, which I certainly am, and still feel it is not an American rule to have to name names of people when it will influence their lives and their families and their children. This is not my reason for declining. I decline on the grounds of the Fifth Amendment. But this is my position."

A moment later she was excused. The Jameses remember the day of their testimony as the same day the Hollywood Freeway opened.

5
—

IN THE FALL of 1966, almost fifteen years to the day after
Dan and Lilith James testified before the Committee, my wife
and I and our infant daughter moved into their house on Franklin Avenue in Hollywood. The rent was cheap, the place vast,
on the lines of an abandoned fraternity house. The neighborhood
had known better days. Bette Davis had lived on one corner,
Preston Sturges on the other; the Canadian consulate was a block
away, the Japanese consulate at the time of Pearl Harbor across
the street. Now the pimps and junkies were beginning to take
over Hollywood Boulevard, a block south. There was a whorehouse in a brand-new high-rise down the street, Synanon owned
one house in the neighborhood, a Dr. Feelgood was dispensing
amphetamines like gumdrops in another, and the former Japanese consulate, boarded up, was a crash pad for a therapy group.

We saw a good deal of the Jameses. They also owned the
tiny bungalow next door, and when it was not rented they would
move down from Carmel. We intuited political trouble almost
immediately. In our basement there were cartons upon cartons
of *New Masses*, and Dan James, although he was only fifty-five,
was a writer who did not seem to write anymore. We made the
inductive leap. Our questioning was indirect, their answers
oblique. The implicit reserve was finally breached one day when
Dan showed us a piece in *New Masses*, written in 1946 by Albert
Maltz, later one of the Hollywood Ten. "I have come to believe
that the accepted understanding of art as a weapon is not a useful guide but a straitjacket," Maltz had written. "I have felt this
in my own work and in the work of others. In order to write at
all, it has become necessary for me to repudiate it and abandon it."

Unexceptional as Maltz's statement seemed, James said it
had caused a furor in its day. Party leaders arrived from New

York to re-educate Maltz. There were a number of meetings, kangaroo courts, as it were, to persuade him to recant. One of the sessions had taken place in what was now our living room. "On that couch," James said, "Albert Maltz made his famous recantation." I could not imagine the scene or why Maltz had submitted to such an inquisition. "Whatever happened to 'fuck off'?" I asked. "You don't understand," James replied. "That was the pull of the Party."

Politics no longer appeared to exert any pull on him at all. On May Day 1967, I took James with me to Watts to hear the leader of a Maoist splinter group speak. I had met the Maoist when I was working on a piece and found him interesting in the way fanatics often are. He was wearing camouflage fatigues and a fatigue hat crowned with a red star. None of the blacks playing in the park where he spoke paid him the slightest heed. He talked about the "ruling class" and the "workers" and how the day was nigh when the workers would "arise." James soon wanted to leave. We drove back to Hollywood in silence. He seemed sunk in depression. "I made that same speech thirty years ago," he finally explained. "Some things never change."

In time, the Jameses filled in the blanks in the preceding fifteen years. The blacklist precluded what movie work was available. When *Bloomer Girl* appeared on television in the early 1950s, it appeared without the Jameses' credit. Using a family name, Daniel Hyatt, Dan worked on the scripts of two monster pictures, *The Giant Behemoth* and *Gorgo*, each of which ended with either Gorgo or the giant behemoth trampling, eating, and generally dismantling London. They rarely saw old Party friends. "The people we knew best were either stool pigeons or had fled to Europe," Dan James recalls. There was also another reason: money was never the problem with the Jameses that it was with so many others on the blacklist, a situation they found embarrassing. "We didn't have to go out and sell insurance like others did," Lilith James remembers. "There

was a little family money. The *Bloomer Girl* money kept coming in. We owned our house. We had no mortgage."

The people the Jameses did see were increasingly on the
Hispanic east side of Los Angeles. In 1948, they spent a weekend visiting an interracial camp in Glendale; this led to an invitation to re-create the traditional Mexican Christmas posadas
on Lamar Street in Lincoln Heights. "The action, of course,"
Dan wrote in a letter not long ago, "is that Mary and Joseph
(played by eight-year-old kids) with the Christ child in arms
go from door to door looking for a night's shelter. They're
turned away from several on one absurd excuse or another till
finally the last door is opened and in they go, with all their
candle-bearing followers. We wrote various little dialog scenes
for the doorways and taught the kids the posadas songs. It grew
into a big neighborhood event. We blocked off the street (without a police permit) and from a telephone pole ended the evening with several piñatas. We got quite famous."

THUS WAS PLANTED the seed for *Famous All Over Town*.
The experience satisfied what Dan James describes now as "a
need for flight. . . . As many of the comrades took off for Eu-
ope and elsewhere, we moved into East L.A. and started making a new life for ourselves there." For the next fifteen years,
the Jameses' activities were concentrated on three square blocks
in Lincoln Heights, a neighborhood of tiny bungalows with
Gothic trim, no larger than a Mexican village and equally con-
fined, bounded on two sides by the tracks and marshaling yards
of the Southern Pacific Railroad, on a third by the dry concrete
trough called the Los Angeles River. With only the street names
changed, it was the place that James would re-create thirty years
later as Danny Santiago. The Jameses formed and worked with
various teenage clubs, "their names," Dan recalls, "a product of
total democracy." There were the Hepkitties and the Bluebirds
and the Lamar Tigers. In a letter he wrote me, he remembers

. . . football, basketball, baseball with eastside play-ground teams (we usually lost). Beach picnics, trips to snow, various interracial camps in San Bernardino mtns. After a year when the boys started inspecting the girls we started the Starlifters, coed (if you can call it ed). Mostly dancing and volleyball in Method-ist church basement. . . . Next Los Compadres Club, whose nucleus were members of the old Hepkitties now married with children. Around 12 couples. Made an old two car garage into a clubhouse with beer bar. Bowling, dancing in clubhouse and elsewhere, overnight camp-ing trips. Emphasis on keeping the boys and girls to-gether, which was revolutionary in that tradition. Once ALMOST voted a black couple into the club. The Compadres then joined with 7 other groups, mostly old-time neighborhood gang veterans, to form the Lincoln Heights Scholarship Federation, which held a largely successful dance at the Hollywood Palladium and gave out a dozen small scholarships with the proceeds. . . . But this was only part of it. This is how we met the kids. Their families came through *compadrazco*, though our friendships began in our earlier years on Lamar when we sought permission for their daughters to join the club, go on camping trips, etc. Over the years we baptized seven babies and acted as *compadres de matri-monio* to 3 couples, which gave us a special relation with some 20 families, to be asked to all celebrations from birth to death. . . . Our closest *compadre* was Lalo Rios and it was his family and his wife Connie's that we knew best. We baptized Lalo's Ruben and five years later shared 24 hour watches as Ruben died of leu-kemia. We baptized their third son Tomas and in '74 we buried Lalo who we thought would one day bury us, another agonizing vigil. And now we stay with his widow when we're in L.A. . . . In recent years it's been mostly funerals and there's only one father left of the old original Hepkitties. We've lost track of most of our club members, except the ones united to us by *compadrazco*, but at the funerals they turn up once in a while. So you can say over the past 35 years we've known four generations of Mexicanos in their best and worst of times. We even brushed elbows with the end of their great-great-grandfathers.

6
———

EARLY IN 1968, Dan James asked me to read some stories he had written about East Los Angeles. The stories were the early chapters of *Famous All Over Town* and were drawn of course from his experiences on the east side. I thought they were very good—tough, funny, unsentimental, and undogmatic—but I was not enthusiastic about his wish to send them out under the name "Danny Santiago." I had nothing against pseudonyms—I had once used the name "Algernon Hogg" because the magazine I worked for discouraged staff writers from contributing to other publications—but the idea of an Anglo presenting himself as a Chicano I found troubling. I had spent a period myself in East Los Angeles working on a book about Cesar Chavez, and my instinct was that this particular kind of literary deception could, if discovered (and presupposing the stories were successful), have unpleasant extraliterary ramifications.

James, however, was adamant. He felt that for nearly twenty years he had been unable to write under his own name both because of the blacklist and because he had lost confidence in his own ability. "I wish I could tell you how I feel about Danny Santiago," he wrote from Carmel, where he and Lilith had gone back to live permanently.

> He's so much freer than I am myself. He seems to know how he feels about everything and none of the ifs, ands, and buts that I'm plagued with. I don't plan to make a great cops and robbers bit out of him, but now at any rate I can't let him go. Maybe he'll prove a straitjacket later on. We'll see. In any event, unless you feel too guilty about this mild little deception of mine, I'd like you to send on the stories to Brandt.

Carl Brandt was then my agent, and on March 25, 1968, I sent him the stories, with an obfuscating covering letter that never once mentioned either the author's real or putative name (I assumed the title page and the return address would do the trick): "Re the enclosed: ever since *Delano* [the book I had written about Cesar Chavez and the Delano grape strike], scarcely a week goes by without my receiving something in the mail from the Mexican-American literary community. I got the same feeling of dread when I got these stories. But I can't get them out of my mind . . . and [I] think they're good. They're sad and they're funny and they're true and he has down perfectly the convoluted machinery of the Mexican mind. I contacted the author in Carmel. He apparently met me when I was working on the book [*Delano*]. He's somewhat noncommittal about what he's doing now and knowing that convoluted machinery I didn't press it." My letter delighted Dan. "I've been chuckling and whinnying at your letter to Carl Brandt ever since its arrival," he wrote when he received the copy I sent him. "And while we're on the subject of convolutions, Mexican style, how about you bloody Irishmen, who, ever since the Book of Kells, have been skipping through Purgatory on your remote-control contact with the truth."

In time, the stories began to appear, in *Redbook* and *Playboy*; in 1971, "The Somebody" was chosen for Martha Foley's annual collection, *Best American Short Stories.* ("The Somebody," in different form, became the final chapter of *Famous All Over Town.*) We corresponded fitfully with the Jameses, all too often about the rent, which they needed and we had trouble paying. "PS. Did somebody forget January rent?" Dan wrote on January 8, 1969. In December: "The mystery is partially solved. Your note arrived today with check #1333 dated November 20."

In January 1971, we moved from Franklin Avenue to the beach, where we had bought a house. Occasionally we would spend a weekend with the Jameses in Carmel or drive down to see them if we were in San Francisco. At times we would send them friends who wanted to see the house. The one they appreciated most was a Cuban diplomat from the United Nations traveling on the West Coast for the first time. The Cuban's companion was a young Spanish woman who worked for Spain's trade mission in New York. When the couple arrived in Carmel, the Jameses invited them to spend the night. The next day Dan James called to report that the woman's father was an old Falangist who had fought with Franco's Blue Division alongside the Wehrmacht on the Russian front. It would have been about the same time he was working on *Winter Soldiers.* "Imagine it," he said. "An old Stalinist, a Cuban Communist and the daughter of a Blue Division veteran getting drunk and arguing politics in Carmel."

Danny Santiago continued to work; so as not to run afoul of the Internal Revenue Service, James set up a Danny Santiago bank account, using his own Social Security number. At the suggestion of Carl Brandt (who still did not know his client's true identity), James began shaping his published and unpublished stories into a novel. After a number of rejections, the completed manuscript was finally accepted by Simon and Schuster. Editing was accomplished by mail, via the postal drop in Pacific Grove. James's letters to his agent and his publisher were in a perfectly mimetic Danny Santiago persona—slangy, contentious, touchy, defensive. *¿Quien es mas macho?* The Eastern gringos gave the benefit of the doubt to the eccentric and erratic young Chicano novelist.

Famous All Over Town was published in March 1983, to no fanfare. The world described was that three-block area of Lincoln Heights where Dan and Lilith James had been granted *compadrazco*. The novel's narrator, Chato Medina, is a fourteen-year-old street-smart kid with an IQ of 135, resisting assimilation by a voracious Anglo culture he sees as dominated by the Southern Pacific Railroad, which wants to buy up and pave over his block in the interest of better freight management. He is equally divorced from the rural Mexico of his grandparents, a Valhalla he deprecates as a place where "they milk each other's goats."

Chato lives by his considerable wits on that brink where the comic adventure can easily flip into casual violence. With quick tongue and sharp eye, he is ever the observer of his family—his spirited sister Lena (christened Tranquilina, but never tranquil), his placid, preoccupied baby-machine mother, and especially his blustery, ham-handed father: "My father is very loud in stores speaking Spanish, but in English you can barely hear him."

The Medinas exist in a secondhand way: "Day-olds from the bakery, dented tomato cans, sunburned shirts from store windows, never two chairs alike and lucky if one shoe matched the other." They buy their clothes from the "As-Is" bin at the Goodwill, "fishing through boxes raw off the trucks before anything was washed or fumigated." But Chato is never a victim of his circumstances. He is a victor, a vivid historian of his own life: "There's my cousin Cuca and my cousin Kika and Lalo and Lola and Rosario the boy and Rosario the girl and my Uncle Benedicto that the priest put a curse on him for what he done in the bell tower."

Given my rooting interest, I found *Famous All Over Town* a lunatic success, a Chicano bildungsroman by a septuagenarian ex-Stalinist aristocrat from Kansas City. There is no trace of the didacticism of *Winter Soldiers,* no hint of the author's history, either of his communism or his apostasy. This is not social realism, not a proletarian novel; James's Southern Pacific is not Frank Norris' octopus. *Famous All Over Town* takes the form of a classic novel of initiation, and Chato Medina could be read as a Hispanic Holden Caulfield. His weapons against the world are brains and humor, his language an eloquent and scrambled mixture of Spanish and English.

The Anglo characters—a Jewish teacher, a homosexual doctor with an unrequited yen for Chato—are the book's weakest, flat and obvious, and when I asked James if this was intentional, another layer of sophisticated deception to disguise his identity further, he only laughed. The novel received generally excellent notices, from Anglo and Chicano reviewers alike, and then in the spring of 1984 the Rosenthal Award. A day or so later, I received a letter from Robert Silvers, editor of *The New York Review of Books:* "This novel just got an award from the American Academy and looking through it, it seemed that you might find it worth writing on—one way of getting at our subject [a piece we had long contemplated on East Los Angeles]; and how many Mexican Americans in Los Angeles are writing about the place? Perhaps it is something of an event."

I said there were complications and, after a trip to New York to buy an apartment, sent a copy of Robert Silvers' letter to Carmel, along with a note of my own:

> Well, I knew I was going to get asked sooner or later. . . . As it happened, we were in New York last week and had lunch with Silvers. . . . Bob was quite insistent that I review the book and I was equally insistent that I could not. . . . He kept on badgering, and I finally told him why. The upshot is this: he will

absolutely honor the confidence, but if Danny would
like to come in from the cold, he would love me to do
the piece. . . . To be honest I am ambivalent. On the
one hand, I would love to do the piece. On the other,
you have steadfastly maintained, for whatever good reasons of your own, this identity for 16 years, and peeling
away the mask could open up a can of worms. . . . If
you feel I have violated a confidence in telling Silvers,
please feel free to chastise me. He is the first person I
have told in 16 years, and then only because of his letter
and his insistence that I review the book. That, however, is not special pleading nor is it meant as an excuse. Let's talk.

7

WHEN I VISITED the Jameses in Carmel a month later, Lilith
James was clearly uncomfortable at any public acknowledgment
of their Party membership. It was not out of any sense of regret
at once having been a member. She was entirely comfortable
with her actions and her past, but she did not wish her children—now both grown women—to live with any possible burden of these actions. Her attitude, moreover, had not changed
in the thirty-three years since her appearance before the Committee: it was nobody's business then and it was nobody's business now. She finally agreed because "Danny Santiago" had long
made her uneasy and she knew that if Dan went public he could
not go public selectively.

    We talked that weekend, and over the telephone the next
few weeks, on and on, as if we were Party members discussing
what means this strike in steel. I reread the books on the blacklist. If the Jameses were mentioned at all, they were mentioned

only in passing. They were not brand-name screenwriters or celebrity informers, nor did they have the theater or literary constituencies of Lillian Hellman or Dashiell Hammett. After talking to the Jameses so often over the years, I found most of these books, especially those written by people never personally involved, irrelevant and even spurious, often vulgar in language, so flushed with secondhand outrage that they lack any real sense of the period, its social nuances, or its particular ironies.

I read the testimony of Dan and Lilith James and the testimony of their accusers. The passage of time has made them benign about those who informed on them. In the mid-1960s, they had been in touch with Leo Townsend, but, in Dan James's words, "it wasn't fun anymore." I was struck by one irony in the testimony of Richard Collins. A prodigious namer of other names besides the Jameses, Collins also made the most persuasive case of any witness I have read against the idea of Party minions poisoning the minds of moviegoers:

> Since the basic policy isn't in the hands of the writer or the director but in the hands of the owners of the studio, who are not at all interested in this propaganda, the chance of any real presentation of Communist material or what is termed Communist material in terms of the Communist Party or foreign policy are, I think, extremely unlikely.

Dan James remembered Richard Collins' testimony as "thoughtful" and wondered if he was still alive.

What struck me that weekend in Carmel was how deeply entwined, how inseparable the character of Dan James and Danny Santiago were. As one has difficulty where the rocks end and his house begins, so it is with Dan and Danny. Danny was the only persona in which Dan could write, even in his letters to my wife and me, who shared his secret all those sixteen years. I asked if he had considered the possibility of being accused of manufacturing a hoax. He shrugged and said the book itself was the only answer. If the book was good, it was good under whatever identity the author chose to use, the way the books of B. Traven were good. Nor would he consider that *Famous All Over Town* was a tour de force. "I spent thirty-five years working on this book," he said, "twenty years learning what it was all about, the last fifteen writing it. You don't spend thirty-five years on a tour de force."

When we returned to Los Angeles, my wife and I drove down to Lamar Street in Lincoln Heights. The entire three blocks had been flattened to make a parking lot for the piggyback trailers that ride the Southern Pacific flatcars. In the book, when the Southern Pacific succeeds in condemning the neighborhood, Chato Medina writes his name in Crayola on every flat surface in the area. It is the gesture that makes him "famous all over town." I had no Crayola in the car. If I had, I would have written four words on the sidewalk of Lamar Street: "Dan and Lilith James."

POSTSCRIPT

DAN JAMES died suddenly in Carmel in the spring of 1988, shortly after returning home from a stay in the hospital for a brain aneurysm. We had moved from California to New York some months earlier, and I did not learn of his death until I read his obituary in *The New York Times*. I immediately called Lilith. She said Dan had been worried that the aneurysm operation might leave him an invalid, a prospect that had filled him with dread. He came through the surgery, however, in good shape, and was home preparing for a holiday in the Caribbean with Lilith and their two daughters. It was bedtime and Dan was in the kitchen with the dog. A few moments later Lilith remembered something she wished to get from the freezer, and when she walked into the kitchen, Dan was lying on the floor, dead of a heart attack at seventy-seven.

I am not sure how much work he got done in the years after this piece appeared in *The New York Review of Books*. He worked on a screenplay of *Famous All Over Town* with the director Jonathan Demme, but it came to naught—the fate of most screenplays, I would often tell him—and said he was laboring over the further adventures of Chato Medina. Hey, he would say when he called, what do you think of this as an idea, and he would spin out another Chato tale, with all the appropriate Chicano filigree. The stories sounded bright and original, but I suspect it was easier to talk about them on the telephone than it was to get them down on paper, that the whole process was harder than he had anticipated. He was a man in his seventies, don't forget, and he no longer had the protective skin of Danny Santiago; he was Dan James playing Danny Santiago, and although we never discussed it, I expect he found his new role burdensome, an obstacle course. Had the Danny Santiago stories not worked out, no one would have known, save Dan and Lilith and to a lesser extent my wife and me. If the new stories were not successful, however, the failure would have been Dan's, not Danny's. That, I realize now, is one of the things I was trying to convey in my letter to him in the spring of 1984 by that horrid mixed metaphor to the effect that "peeling away the mask could open up a can of worms."

But that was later. In the winter of 1984, some months before Dan won the Rosenthal Award, I received a telephone call from Carmel. His publisher had nominated *Famous All Over Town* for the Pulitzer Prize in fiction, but the Pulitzer committee had insisted on a bio before they would consider the book. Dan wondered if he should make up a bio, a suggestion that horrified me. I said, one, you're not going to win, and two, in the unlikely event you do, and you've invented a bio more elaborate than the one you've got now, you'll be busted before the sun goes down, remember Janet Cooke. It might be fun, he insisted. No, I said, there is none so virtuous as the press pack on the trail of blood, they will make you out a commie fraud, bet the house on it, it's either the truth or nothing, DON'T MAKE ANYTHING UP! With some reluctance, he finally decided to keep his cover, and declined to send the Pulitzer committee the bio it had requested, thus taking *Famous All Over Town* out of prize contention.

I realize now that Dan was ready to come out, that the coincidence of the Rosenthal Award and my being asked to review the book presented the opportunity for which he had longed perhaps only in his secret heart. I think he enjoyed the fame. He was on the front page of both the New York and the Los Angeles *Times*, he was in the newsmagazines, and the television crews trooped to Carmel. He was an engaging figure, white hair, craggy face, the height of a basketball player, the kind of elegantly sloppy dress that only a peer of the realm can get away with, and with every visitor and interviewer he was nothing if not self-deprecating, a manner that seems to come with aristocratic entitlement. "You'll recognize me," he told a reporter who called from the *Los Angeles Times*. "I'm the one who doesn't look like Danny Santiago."

The reaction was generally favorable. There were, of course, those—mainly Hispanics—who professed outrage. "We were deceived," said Philip Hererra, the editor of *Nuestro*, a magazine founded as an outlet for Latino writers and one that had published an early Danny Santiago story. "We were led to believe that Danny Santiago was a Mexican-American. Clearly he was not." Alvin Poussaint, the eminent black psychiatrist at Harvard Medical School, said that the use of the Danny Santiago pseudonym was "unethical and disrespectful of the Mexican-American community. By implying it was written by a Mexican, it gave the book an authenticity it simply did not have." In *The Nation*, Alexander Cockburn, with that particular perspective of the salon Stalinist fancy man, found me at fault: "Dunne's narrative, self-regarding, contrived and conservative in the patented Didion-Dunne manner, had the whiff of the witch hunter while purporting to be something else." Most Hispanic writers, however, thought Dan's deception harmless, and in context justifiable. "I don't care who writes a book—a man, a woman, a cat or a dog," said Thomas Sanchez, author of the best-selling *Zoot Suit Murders*, a novel set in Los Angeles during the zoot suit riots of the wartime 1940s. "They say you shouldn't judge a book by its cover. Well, you shouldn't judge it by the author's ethnic or cultural background."

Dan clearly enjoyed the furor. He called on writers and editors he admired and who probably would not have received him previously, but now he was also Danny Santiago, an eminence in his own right. His new celebrity led to his name appearing in literary trivia quizzes: If Daniel James is Danny Santiago, who is Allen Stewart Königsberg? Teodor J. K. Korzeniowski? Edgar Box? It appealed to Dan that he was now showing up on the same lists as Woody Allen, Joseph Conrad, and Gore Vidal. "Among all those questions I've been asked the last few weeks," he wrote in an Op-Ed piece distributed by the Hispanic Link News Service, "here's one I want to answer in my own words: *By using a Hispanic pen name were you not climbing on the bandwagon of current interest in Chicano writing?* My answer is: What bandwagon?"

There was additional fallout. A week or so before the piece was published, it suddenly struck me that perhaps Richard Collins was not dead, as Dan had assumed. Although it was too late to make changes, I called the Writers Guild to ask if he was still an active member. The Guild said that Collins was still carried on their books and gave me the name of his agent. As it happened, he was represented by a young woman in the same agency that represented me. When I asked her if Collins was still alive, she said he was as of lunch the day before. I mentioned this to my own agent, Evarts Ziegler, who said I should call Robert Towne, a client of his and perhaps the best screenwriter in Hollywood, the author of *Chinatown*, for which he had received an Academy Award, and *Shampoo*. According to Ziggy, Bob had once called Richard Collins "the best piece of unused manpower in Hollywood," and in fact still showed him everything he wrote. And so I called Bob Towne. Collins, he said, had been producing a television series at Universal when he was breaking in as a young writer, and had essentially taught him the screenwriter's trade. "He has the best story sense of anyone I have ever known," Bob said. What about politics? I asked. "I used to go to hear Jack Lawson lecture at the Ebell Theater about screenwriting," Towne replied. "The rest of it was ancient history."

I talked to Collins a day or so later, after first reconnoitering where he lived, a small neat house on a quiet street in Brentwood, only a few blocks from my own. I told him I had written a long piece on a young Chicano novelist named Danny Santiago and the piece was being broken in both *The New York Times* and the *Los Angeles Times* and that the young Chicano was actually a contemporary of his, Daniel James. "Oh, I know Dan," he said. His tone was matter of fact, as if I had just mentioned a second cousin who was dropping into town after an absence of thirty-odd years. A moment or so later he asked: "Does he want me to do something about the book?" It flashed through my mind that perhaps he thought some help in selling the screen rights to *Famous All Over Town* might have been the reason I called. O Hollywood, I thought, some things never change. Yes, he would be willing to have lunch, and yes, he would talk about the blacklist period, he had talked about it to a number of journalists. When I next talked to Dan, he was pleased that I had made contact with Collins. "Give him the number," he said. "Have him call if he wants." Age and curiosity seemed to have dampened yesterday's furies.

I had prepared a whole list of questions (e.g.: Why was Hollywood Marxism so half-baked, especially when compared to the intellectual dialogue in New York between people of the caliber of Edmund Wilson and James Burnham?), but as I sat there with Collins in a trendy radicchio-and-goat-cheese restaurant in Venice, the questions suddenly seemed irrelevant. He was a seventy-year-old screenwriter and television producer, not so much retired as out of work. It occurred to me that had there not been a blacklist, all the Hollywood Communist screenwriters, penitent and unpenitent, would have languished in the well-paid obscurity they essentially deserved. There is a story Murray Kempton tells about William Faulkner in *Part of Our Time* that defined the paradox and the professional situation of the movie writer. On one of his screenwriting trips to Hollywood, Faulkner had listened to a terrified colleague predicting the ruin he faced if called by the Committee. "He don't have to worry none," Faulkner said after his friend left, "so long as he writes good." Few did; that was an added cruelty piled on top of their burden and torment. Perhaps the harshest irony of this dark time, and the harshest verdict on the talents of those writers caught up in its maelstrom, is that a period so rich with artistic possibilities produced only one first-rate work, *On the Waterfront*, a justification of snitching by those friendliest of friendly witnesses before the Committee, the stool pigeons, Budd Schulberg and Elia Kazan.

I asked Collins if he ever saw any friends from the old Communist days. He said there had been a falling out between him and Leo Townsend, not over politics, but because Townsend thought that Collins, as a producer, should give him more work than Collins was prepared to. Had he gone right politically? I asked. More right than when he was a Party member, he replied. Then how would he describe himself politically today? He asked if I read *The Nation*. I said yes. "I guess I'd call myself a *Nation* liberal," he said. I was reminded of a remark Dan James had made earlier that spring, to the effect that Hollywood had only a few real Communists; the rest should have belonged to the John Reed Club.

Richard Collins did call Dan and Lilith James, and they chatted without recrimination. Collins and Dan and I talked about the possibility of getting together in Los Angeles, perhaps with Leo Townsend, and talking about what it was like being a Communist in Hollywood. Dan was full of suggestions: I should get copies of the *New Masses* and *People's World* to get a feel for the times, and I should read up on the Duclos Letter. "You don't have any conception," he said, "of the urge there was for organization in those days." The prospect filled me with dread; it was the period of their epiphanies, not mine, and as a congenital non-joiner, I could not begin to understand that urge, and so for all the planning we never did get together.

I thought of Dan often in the weeks after he died. In the end, he never really was Danny Santiago, however perfect the mimicry. He was always Dan James, and that was his special grace.

Chinatowns

IN THE SUMMER of 1965, a resident of California less than a year, I had occasion to travel to the Owens Valley in Inyo County on the eastern slope of the Sierra Nevada. The purpose of the trip was the trial, in the Inyo County Seat of Independence, of a practical nurse accused by the state of California of practicing medicine without a license. That the nurse was guilty was beyond dispute; the Inyo district attorney, however, prosecuted her only under protest and was among the first to congratulate her when the jury returned an acquittal. What held my attention was less the case than the vision of a California trapped in time, an eddy uncontaminated not only by the 1960s but also by most of the twentieth century. It was as if the louche Pacific littoral where I lived, and the only California familiar to most Americans, was a foreign country.

The tiny desert community where the nurse practiced was inhabited mainly by retired talc miners, many of whom lived in a honeycomb of sandstone caves on the edge of town, and by a colony of aged Social Security pensioners drawn to this sun-baked moonscape by a putatively therapeutic hot spring. There was no indoor plumbing and but one telephone; the nearest doctor was 180 miles away, a Seventh-Day Adventist general practi-

tioner from Lone Pine, who flew his own plane in one day a
week. Suspicion of outsiders was endemic. In a bad but nonetheless scary parody of *Bad Day at Black Rock*, I was followed
by a black sedan wherever I ventured the entire week I was in
the desert. I finally asked the Seventh-Day Adventist doctor why.
"You're from Los Angeles," he explained. "You stole our water."
Thus was I introduced to the Owens Valley water war.

This was a war more in legend than in fact, a war of no
heroes and of two conflicting populist ideologies. The first is the
more romantic. At the turn of the century, the Owens Valley in
the shadow of the Sierra was lush farm and grazing land, nourished by the waters of the Owens River and presided over by
ranchers few in number but in their own minds men of the
frontier. Vigilante justice was common, and there were lynchings
in the outlying mining camps as late as 1908. Then in a giant
water swindle engineered by Los Angeles land speculators, the
river waters were siphoned off and diverted south via aqueduct
to the parched San Fernando Valley, where land prices soared
and the speculators made a killing by selling off tracts they had
previously bought at rock-bottom prices. There was deceit and
there was treachery and, on the part of public officials in cahoots
with the rapacious speculators, there was criminal malfeasance.
Their acres withering, the Inyo ranchers banded together and
blew up the aqueduct that now fertilized the City of the Angels.
But Los Angeles was too strong and too unyielding, and in the
early spring of 1927 the ranchers placed a full-page advertisement
in most of California's major newspapers, an ad that began,
"We, the farming communities of the Owens Valley, being
about to die, salute you." This is a version of the struggle for
water that lends itself both to Marxist rhetoric on the depreda-
tions of capitalism and to John Wayne movies (e.g., *New Frontier*, 1935).

The second and equally populist version also has Marxist
overtones in its praise for technocracy and progress and especially

in its elevation of the Greatest Good for the Greatest Number to a first and inflexible principle. The greatest number in this case happened to be the people of Los Angeles, at the turn of the century a boom environment destined for greatness only if its inadequate indigenous water reserves could be replenished in time to save it from dying of thirst. In their pursuit of the greater good, Los Angeles visionaries devised an aqueduct that would hook the city to the waters of the Owens River, a source so bountiful that Los Angeles could be watered in perpetuity even as the city, in its benevolence, provided for the handful of ranchers who chose to remain in their distant valley.

Emissaries of the city secured the valley's riparian lands, and with the benediction of Theodore Roosevelt and the federal government the aqueduct was built in a grand technological assault on the desert that separated Los Angeles from the Owens Valley—a ditch 233 miles long, with 142 tunnels measuring 53 miles in length. If the city was sometimes indifferent to its tenants in the Owens Valley, these were the eggs without which no omelette was ever made. But the valley ranchers chose to respond to the omelette with a campaign of violence and destruction whose only result was the devastation of the valley itself. Needless to say, this is the version most vigorously promoted by the Los Angeles Department of Water and Power.

It is one of the many considerable virtues of William L. Kahrl's *Water and Power* that he punctures both of these morality plays without diminishing the evil history of the Owens Valley. "I was brought up to love a good story," the book begins ingenuously and enchantingly. "It is a story of ideals in conflict, rich with incidents of great daring, deceit, achievement, betrayal, and faith." Clarence Darrow visits the story as it slowly unfolds over the first quarter of the twentieth century, as do Tom Mix and Teddy Roosevelt and the Wobblies and night riders and the Ku Klux Klan. Spillways are dynamited, as are the offices of the *Los Angeles Times*, whose publisher, General Harrison Gray

Otis, drove around in a limousine with a cannon on its hood. Death, disgrace, disaster, and prison terms punctuate the narrative. Here is the inspiration for *Chinatown* (which coincidentally was first titled *Water & Power*), enough plot and villainy for innumerable bad novels and terrible motion pictures. Kahrl, however, has a larger purpose, "the history of California in the twentieth century . . . the story of a state inventing itself with water."

Manifest Destiny—the way west—was essentially a journey from waterhole to waterhole. It is a peculiarity of California, most peculiar of states, that its two leading cities, in defiance of all tradition, sprang up where there was insufficient water to support future growth. Los Angeles had a further disadvantage: it was a coastal city without a port. Still the people came, floods of them, lured by a demented civic boosterism that promised nirvana in the sun. The railroads contributed to this perversion of the frontier with a series of fratricidal price wars that finally, on March 6, 1887, lowered the cost of a ticket between the Missouri Valley and Southern California to one dollar. The railroads and the boosters, of course, had land to sell, millions of acres, as did practically everyone else; the less savory speculators preyed on these bargain-basement pioneers by sticking oranges onto the branches of Joshua trees. Nothing could keep them away. Expansion, Carey McWilliams once noted, was the major business of Southern California, the very reason for its existence. The climate and the availability of reasonable real estate—an opportunity for every man to own his own castle—attracted a docile and easily replaced labor force. The population of Los Angeles doubled and trebled, increasing 1,700 percent between 1860 and 1900, increasing another 1,600 percent between the turn of the century and 1940.

The problem was water. Doomsday predictions were floated as early as 1900: in continued growth there was future calamity. But Los Angeles was a city predicated on growth, needing water

not only to boom but to support boom without end. In William
Mulholland, head of its Department of Water, Los Angeles had
a missionary of boom who, because of the unique character of
his department—it was absolutely autonomous and thus politically unassailable—could function as a Torquemada of water
politics, bringing his wrath to bear on any who did not share or,
worse, who tried to obstruct his revelation of the greater good.
Mulholland was an Irish immigrant, a ditch tender when he first
arrived in Southern California, self-taught and formidably well
read ("Damn a man who doesn't read books," he once said),
quite cheerful when asked in one of his frequent court appearances about his own lack of qualifications in the field of water
engineering: "Well, I went to school in Ireland when I was a
boy, learned the three R's and the Ten Commandments—or
most of them—made a pilgrimage to the Blarney Stone, received
my father's blessing, and here I am."

Los Angeles was where he was, but the water he had his eye
on was 200 miles to the northeast in the Owens Valley, five
miles wide and a hundred long, so rich in agricultural possibilities that the brand-new U.S. Reclamation Service had tapped it
as a prime prospect for one of its pilot irrigation projects. It was
not to be. The Reclamation Service's man in charge of the
Owens Valley project, J. B. Lippincott, also happened to be a
free-lance water consultant to Los Angeles, a friend of Mulholland, and well aware of the city's finite water supply. There
was no question that Lippincott's allegiance was to Los Angeles
and the aqueduct Mulholland envisioned, not to the service that
employed him, and certainly not to the Owens Valley. About
the only thing that can be said in Lippincott's behalf is that his
treachery was not for personal gain; he was like the mole of spy
fiction, working for one side and passing its secrets to the other—
in this case the maps and charts and hydrological surveys the
Reclamation Service had prepared to ensure the future of the
Owens Valley. Armed with this information, Fred Eaton, a

former mayor of Los Angeles and an associate of Lippincott's, appeared in the valley and began buying up options on riparian lands from ranchers who assumed he was working for the Reclamation Service. It was a fatal mistake.

Betrayal was compounded by greed. A land syndicate including General Otis and the railroad barons Henry Huntington and E. H. Harriman got wind of Mulholland's plan for an aqueduct and bought a huge tract of the San Fernando Valley, then not a part of Los Angeles. It was their not unfounded assumption that when the city ultimately absorbed the Valley, a cause they vigorously promoted, the new water would irrigate their acres, enormously increasing their value. The local newspapers—three of those whose publishers were part of the land syndicate—pledged not to blow the whistle on the city's secret activities in the Owen Valley until the trap against the ranchers was sprung. In the summer of 1905, it was. "We are going to turn that country dry," Mulholland said, and he was as good as his word.

To secure voter support for the bond issues that would buy the Owens Valley lands and build the aqueduct, Mulholland cooked the rainfall figures and fabricated a drought. (Throughout his long career as a public servant, Mulholland would prove over and again that the commandment about false witness was one he had never entirely learned.) He need not have bothered. Neither the exposure of the land syndicate nor the not-unsubstantiated imputation of a giant swindle troubled the voters; both bond issues passed by overwhelming margins. Over the protest of the ranchers, President Theodore Roosevelt anointed the aqueduct—"the Greatest Good for the Greatest Number"—and the fate of the Owens Valley was sealed; the water it once owned would now be a charitable contribution from the city of Los Angeles.

The rawness of this city was perhaps best exemplified by General Otis, who dismissed any doubts about the dealings of the land syndicate as "a stench in the nostrils of democracy." After Mulholland, Otis is the most interesting player in the Owens Valley drama. He was the model of the super-rich nineteenth-century goon, hostile to both reform and social change and violently antilabor. Never was he more in his element than when the Wobblies tried to blow up the *Times* and the Socialist Party ran a candidate for mayor who not only was, with Clarence Darrow, a member of the Wobblies' defense team but who also promised, if elected, not to allow a drop of aqueduct water in the syndicate's acreage. "Anarchic scum," General Otis railed, "the Stars and Stripes against the red flag." If Otis gave no quarter, neither did his enemies. "He sits there in senile dementia," Hiram Johnson said during his campaign for governor in 1910,

> with gangrened heart and rotting brain, grimacing at every reform, chattering impotently at all things that are decent, frothing, fuming violently, gibbering, going down to his grave in snarling infamy. He is the one thing that all California looks at when, in looking at Southern California, they see anything that is disgraceful, depraved, corrupt, crooked, and putrescent.

"There it is! Take it," Mulholland said when the spillway into Los Angeles was opened in 1913, and for the rest of the decade relations between the city and the Owens Valley were more or less circumspect. Boom in Los Angeles continued, as if by divine right. The city annexed the San Fernando Valley, the windfall anticipated by the syndicate that had bought up so much of the Valley, and also annexed a corridor to coastal San Pedro, where it had invented a harbor. But even Mulholland, the quintessential merchant of boom, had drastically underestimated the city's frenzy for growth. More water was needed, and he decided to tap the remaining ground reserves of the Owens Valley. Hit by a drought of its own, the valley was strapped for water. To Mulholland, that was just too bad. He was now in his late sixties, blinded by megalomania, his vision as tunneled as his aqueduct. He seized on "every problem as an occasion of self-righteous conflict"; his "identity was . . . so completely wrapped up in the city as a whole that he saw each challenge as a personal affront."

There were only 7,000 people living in the valley in the 1920s, and to ensure some sort of survival, valley spokesmen were willing to cut a deal with the city—a package sale of remaining water rights, a stable annual water allowance, and reparations for past abuses. Mulholland refused to bargain. This time his high-handedness was too much, and open warfare broke out. Between 1924 and 1927, there were periodic bombings of the aqueduct and its spillways; night riders warned valley dissidents to back the valley's play. But for all the guns and all the dynamite, it was not so much a war as a war game, played for newsprint and for spectators. When ranchers seized one pumping station, Tom Mix, who was making a movie nearby, sent over an orchestra to serenade them and their picnicking families. What the civil war accomplished was to bring into the open Los Angeles' plundering of the valley (the *Los Angeles Times* was sufficiently embarrassed to say that the ranchers had "a measure of justice on their side") and to create a legend—"The Rape of the Owens Valley." The devastation was there to see. By 1927, however, the ranchers were fighting not for a way of life—that was long gone—but for the highest possible price for their water rights. This was not an ignoble fight, but there are very few legends about real estate values.

In the end, no one was actually killed in the war. The only real casualties were the two valley bankers who sponsored the revolt—they stole from their own bank and went to jail—and Mulholland himself. On March 12, 1928, Mulholland certified the safety of the Saint Francis Dam, north of Los Angeles, a project he had promoted as a hedge against the Owens Valley strife, even though seventeen years earlier he had vetoed the same site as geologically unsound. That night the dam burst. Three towns were obliterated by the wall of water and over four hundred people killed. At the coroner's inquest, Mulholland, now seventy-three, said, "I envy the dead."

Water and Power is long and minutely detailed, drawing its story from three-quarters of a century of public documents, in those archives of local and state politics where the true mendacity and rapacity of the free enterprise system can best be uncovered. It is not to disparage Kahrl, a California historian, to say he would make a great city hall reporter. He sees the internal rhyming scheme of soil surveys and land records and committee reports, finding in the impenetrable diction of officialdom the broken meters that conceal collusion and fraud.

Kahrl's purpose, however, is not the raking of old muck. What happened in the Owens Valley happened over the course of a quarter of a century, with Mulholland the only major participant active both at the beginning and end. The drama of the conflict, the drama of all the novels and screenplays and popular and political accountings, is the drama of synopsis. Kahrl appreciates that no story lasting twenty-five years is as free of complexity as the demands of storytelling require. There is a claim, even an imperative, in the greater good. The history of urban growth is a history of downriver cities seeking a greater share of the water controlled by upriver communities; San Francisco's water comes from a foreign county, as does New York's. Nor is the claim of the Owens Valley unequivocal. "The ranchers who banded together in the 1920s to . . . bomb the aqueduct had no plan or program for the long-term preservation of the valley," Kahrl notes. "It was a conflict waged for immediate gain, and consideration for the valley's future had little part in it."

Even the colossal collusion and peculations were only sideshows; public thieves and civic liars have always been with us, and the aqueduct would still have been built without the grease of chicanery. In the end, the real sin of this squalid narrative was the systematic disenfranchisement of the people of the Owens Valley, making them, even to the present day, supplicants and wards of the city of Los Angeles. The valley is forever indentured. Mulholland and his successors dismissed the minimal costs of keeping it livable. Their arrogance and insensitivity bring to mind Ronald Reagan's famous dictum about the Panama Canal: "We bought it, we paid for it, it's ours."

Water and Power has an extravagantly beautiful companion volume, *The California Water Atlas*, edited by Kahrl and published by the state of California, which graphically illustrates the history and flow of all the state's water resources and water projects—its dams, its aqueducts and siphons and pumps and reservoirs and weirs, in short, California's plumbing, its most essential infrastructure. Here in the *Atlas* is the water profile of Los Angeles today—a city that draws some water from its own ground reserves, some from the Colorado River, and some from the State Water Project, but continues to obtain four-fifths of its supply from the Owens Valley, where the water comes cleaner and cheaper. Together these two volumes make clear that the history of California is in its water development. It is a complex and often tedious subject that Kahrl illuminates with meticulous detachment, bringing the drama into clear and undistorted focus. Although of small consolation to the Owens Valley, such a water war could not happen again. One legacy was the passage of legislation prohibiting the draining of one region for the development of another.

Another legacy is psychic. Like a folk song, the ballad of the Owens Valley is sung whenever a new state water project is proposed. Such was the case when the Peripheral Canal was on the June 1982 ballot. The canal, designed to carry northern water around, rather than through, the Sacramento–San Joaquin delta on its way south, divided the state politically, north versus south, as has every water project of recent memory. Once again the lyric of the Owens Valley was heard, and even the *Los Angeles Times* seemed to hear it. At the end of its editorial endorsing the building of the Peripheral Canal, the *Times* was impelled to add a parenthetical disclosure of its majority interest (with General Otis' Chandler heirs) in the Tejon Ranch Company, which was actively supporting the canal and would have been a major beneficiary of it. "The holdings of Tejon represent a minor part of Times Mirror assets," the disclosure concluded primly. "The *Times* arrives at its views on the canal, as on any other issue, utterly without regard to the views of the Tejon Ranch Co." The Peripheral Canal was beaten badly, suggesting that the *Times* had more influence when it had "gangrened heart and rotting brain."

To Live and Die in L.A.

1

THERE WAS a display of Bar-B-Q equipment in the window of the 24-hour Boys Market. Three blocks over, on South Orchard Avenue, a Sparkletts truck slowly made its way down the street and parked in front of a new Chrysler Cordoba with a bumper sticker that said, "This ain't the Mayflower, but your daughter came across in it." Down at the corner, a Mexican gardener, sweating profusely under the pale flat July sun, loaded his power lawn mower on the small flatbed attached to his pickup. The lawns on South Orchard were all closely trimmed and the small neat bungalows hedged with fuchsia and hydrangea and marigolds and petunias. It was a quiet neighborhood, a neighborhood of pride and fresh paint, a neighborhood that did not threaten. It was the neighborhood where, on the third day of January 1979, officers Edward M. Hopson, Badge No. 13541, and Lloyd W. O'Callaghan, Jr., Badge No. 21216, Los Angeles Police Department, unloaded twelve shots at Eula Mae Love, who resided at 11926 South Orchard.

Eight shots hit Eula Love—a penetrating wound of the right foot, a perforating wound of the left lower leg, a perforating wound of the left thigh, a perforating wound through the left upper arm, a penetrating wound of the right thigh, a second perforating wound of the left thigh, and a third perforating wound of the same left thigh. These seven wounds were described in Autopsy Report No. 79-00133, filed by the Los Angeles County Medical Examiner, as "not immediately life-threatening." The eighth gunshot wound, according to Report No. 79-00133, was "a penetrating wound of the chest . . . [whose] track passes through the skin, fat and muscle of the left anterior chest wall, enters the left thoracic cavity through the second intercostal space, perforates the upper lobe of the lung, enters the mediastinum and perforates the body of T5, exits the right pleural cavity through the sixth intercostal space adjacent to the spinal column and ends in the muscle of the right posterior chest wall. . . . OPINION: This gunshot wound is immediately life-threatening."

I read the autopsy report in a document entitled "Report on Fatal Shooting of Mrs. Eula Mae Love—Special Investigations Division Case No. 100-2070," which the Los Angeles County District Attorney's Office sent unsolicited to the news media. In the report, the D.A.'s office collated and interpreted the testimony of fifty-two witnesses, laid out the applicable law, and, on the basis of the evidence, reached the conclusion that "Officer O'Callaghan and Officer Hopson did not commit a criminal act when they shot Mrs. Love." There was no conclusion, however, as to the tactical judgment exercised by the two officers. "The tragic shooting of Eula Love has had a profound effect on Los Angeles," the covering letter from District Attorney John K. Van de Kamp read. "The entire community needs to be sensitized again to the value of reverence and respect for life."

This bureaucratic piety paled before the fact of Eula Mae Love on the autopsy table: "This is the well-developed, obese, unembalmed body of a 64-inch, 175-pound, 39-year-old Negro female. There is bleeding from both nostrils and pink froth in the mouth. The breasts are large and pendulous. The abdomen is convex. The extremities are unremarkable except for the effect of the gunshot wounds. No surgical scars or tattoos are noted on the body. There are no deformities. Examination of the limbs and antecubital fossae does not reveal any evidence of needle tracks."

Alive, Eula Mae Love was a widow of six months. Her late husband was a professional cook with an annual income of $15,000. When he died, she was left with his monthly Social Security checks totaling $680, a mortgage of $192.18 a month, and three daughters, the two youngest of whom lived with her in the house on South Orchard. Eula Love's gas bill was six months and $69 overdue, her water bill $80 delinquent. The Department of Water & Power wanted to shut off her lights and water that January 3, but did not have the manpower available. Not so the Southern California Gas Company. A serviceman for the gas company arrived at 11926 South Orchard and told Eula Mae Love that she would either have to pay an installment of $22.09 on her gas bill or have her service disconnected. In the words of Report No. 100-2070, "She became irrational and verbally abusive." When the serviceman went to the gas meter, Eula Love hit him with a shovel, causing, as the report continues, "an abrasion, laceration and marked swelling just below the elbow."

After the gas man retreated, Eula Love walked to the Boys Market, a three-minute trip from her house, and purchased one money order for $22.09 (the minimum amount necessary to keep her gas connected) and a second for $192.18 (the amount of her house payment); in her purse, according to the coroner's report, there was an additional $155.16 in cash and a Social Security check for $440.40 making a total of $809.83. Meanwhile, the gas man made an assault complaint against Eula Love to the Los Angeles Police Department. Two other gas company employees, in separate vehicles, were dispatched to South Orchard to attempt collection from Eula Love or to cut off her service.

The gas company, as Report No. 100-2070 indicates, also requested from the LAPD "officer assistance to insure that there
would be no further violence." At the corner of South Orchard
and 120th Street, Eula Love confronted one of the servicemen,
who remained in his truck, and when he said he was only there
to read a book, she once more became abusive. She went into
her house and emerged with a boning knife and began hacking
at a tree. Moments later, officers Hopson and O'Callaghan pulled
up, summoned by a message on their police radio: "415—business dispute. Meet the gas man at 11926 South Orchard, Code
2." In the LAPD signal manual, Code 2 means urgent but not
requiring red light and siren. Hopson and O'Callaghan exited
their black and white, guns drawn.

Consider the situation confronting Hopson and O'Callaghan. They did not know that William Love had died of sickle
cell anemia six months before. They did not know that Eula
Mae Love had a $22.09 money order for the gas company in her
purse. They saw only an enraged woman holding an eleven-inch
blade, five and a half inches of handle. Eula Love screamed at
the two officers. She said they had homosexual eating habits.
She said they fornicated with their mothers. She told them to
use their weapons. She told them to kiss her ass. Suddenly
O'Callaghan knocked the knife from Eula Love's grasp with his
nightstick. She retrieved it before he could kick it away. In the
next two and a half to four seconds, the two officers—one eight
feet from Eula Love, the other twelve feet away—squeezed off
twelve shots.

It is the shame of most of us who write that only riot or
death brings us to South Central Los Angeles: riot or death or
the ritual night ride, in the interests of research, with the officers
of the 77th Division, or that biennial ceremony in which the
white hand takes the black pulse. We bring out-of-town relatives
to the Watts Towers, pay the obligatory obeisance to the artisan-
ship of Simon Rodia, and head for the Harbor Freeway before

the sun sinks. It is my personal shame that the "whiteness" of
Eula Love's house-proud neighborhood made her death seem so
much more pertinent; this, after all, was a neighborhood where
annuals were planted and cultivated, where hibachis and char-
coal briquets were sold at the Boys, where mountain-pure bottled
water was delivered to the kitchen bubbler. The corollary was
even more shameful: Would the death of Eula Love have been
easier to swallow had she been shot in a development east of the
Harbor Freeway, where welfare and food stamps were the coin
of the realm and the wail of Code 1 was the local rhythm and
blues?

I became obsessed with Eula Love. I bought an eleven-inch
boning knife and practiced throwing it in my back yard, holding
it both by the blade, as the LAPD claimed Eula Love had, and
by the handle, as three witnesses claimed she had. I replayed an
incident of twelve years before when my wife, with cause, once
tried to kill me. She stood on the landing in our house in Hollywood with a pair of scissors in her hand, threatening to throw
them at me, promising to throw them at me. I stayed out of
range. I knew she had a bad arm. I knew she threw like a girl.
And I knew the scissors had no balance. I talked. Quietly. Reasonably. And out of range. The moment passed. The fury died.
We are still married, I like to think happily.

I kept wondering why Hopson and O'Callaghan could not
defuse the situation. I kept wondering why they perceived Eula
Love, even with a kitchen knife in her hand, as an immediate
threat. This was a short, fat, hysterical woman, an "obese . . .
64-inch, 175-pound . . . Negro female. . . . The breasts are large
and pendulous. The abdomen is convex." But the LAPD would
admit no error. In this respect, policemen are like doctors and
lawyers and writers. When under attack, draw your wagons into
a circle. There was no mistake in judgment, there was no vi-
olation of departmental firearm policy—although one deputy
chief on the three-officer shooting board issued a sharp dissent.

This momentary embarrassment did not deflect the department from its conclusion about the events on South Orchard: This was a good shoot. "She decided to solve her problem with a knife," said Chief Daryl Gates. "That's why it happened." Chief Gates seemed to see Eula Love as not unlike the James Coburn character in *The Magnificent Seven*, who could draw his blade and snap it into a gunslinger before said gunslinger could clear his six-shooter.

In fact Daryl Gates had been a public relations disaster in the sixteen months he had then been police chief, a profile in incompetence, and I suspect it was this public apprehension that accounted for the continuing fascination with Eula Love. One week after succeeding Ed Davis as chief, and in need of a bold stroke to emerge from the shadow of that loose cannon, Gates held a press conference and produced Peter Mark Jones as the Hillside Strangler. Jones was fingered by one George Shamshak, a small-time Boston hood and snitch, who was acutely uncomfortable at the prospect of doing time in a Massachusetts slammer in the company of a number of cons his squealing had helped put inside. By fingering Jones, a casual acquaintance, Shamshak hoped that California authorities would grant him a favor and let him do his time in a more congenial West Coast joint. The hitch was that Jones was clean. At a second press conference Gates was forced to announce that his case had sprung a leak; at a third, he announced that Jones had been released from custody and issued him a public apology. He maintained that Shamshak, however, remained a "prime suspect"; a few weeks later, Shamshak was cleared of Strangler involvement.

Public apology has been a feature of Gates's tenure. In a city of over a million Chicanos, he said that Mexicans had not risen in the LAPD because they were lazy; bingo—an apology to the Chicano community. Small wonder Gates fastened on Eula Love; on his terms, the incident at 11926 South Orchard was a successful operation, a chance to recoup after the joke he had made of himself and his department in the Shamshak/Jones circus. There was no one to be released on a writ of habeas corpus, no apologies for false arrest. Eula Love provided an opportunity to take the offensive. In a speech to the County Bar Association covered on local TV, Gates attacked the press for "wringing every single drop, every tear" from the Love case. His voice oozing sarcasm, he referred to Eula Love as "the poor widow trying to keep her house and home together." The "poor widow" did not owe $22, he said; "it was $64 or a $67 gas bill and it had been delinquent for six months," and what was more she had better than $700 in her purse. The implication was that Eula Love was a deadbeat and his department was not about to take a ration of guff from any deadbeat.

Gates on television that night was a man with moral athlete's foot. And he was not through. When Mayor Tom Bradley suggested that officers Hopson and O'Callaghan might have taken more time to calm Eula Love down, Gates was back at the barricades. "I don't agree with the mayor's statement that they could have tried to talk her out of it," he said. "They did that, they did that." Yes, they did. According to the D.A.'s report, Hopson and O'Callaghan arrived on the scene at 4:15 P.M.; according to Fire Department records, an ambulance was summoned at 4:21. Six minutes, including the lag time between the shooting and the call for the ambulance. Six whole minutes. Three hundred sixty seconds.

I have driven a number of times now past Eula Love's house on South Orchard. I park in the street where Hopson and O'Callaghan parked and I eat peaches and Bing cherries bought at the Boys and I keep wondering about the two officers and those six minutes. I wonder what their hurry was. Did they have a date? Was that Wednesday their bowling night? "I think they had every right and opportunity and justification to do what they did," Daryl Gates has said. His own words suggest why some people call cops pigs.

2
―――

MY FATHER's was the first dead body I ever saw. He died suddenly, of a ruptured aorta, three days after my fourteenth birthday. I kissed him goodbye in the morning, a healthy vigorous man of fifty-one, and when I came home from school that afternoon the oxygen tanks on the back porch were like a psychic barricade, Stygian signposts. I was not a stranger to the cryptograms of death. My father was a surgeon, and when he talked about his practice his words were often encoded in body English—a slight shrug, a raised eyebrow, an almost imperceptible shake of the head: the cannibal cells had taken the high ground. His wake was held in the house, and for four days I was a figure of some importance. Adults—Thomas Moylan and Terence McNulty, May Toomey, the Clarkin sisters—would grasp my hand and avoid my eyes and mumble that wonderful Irish benediction, "I'm sorry for your trouble." But late in the evening, when the mourners were gone and the drinks put away and when the only lights in the living room were the candles flickering around the casket, I would sneak downstairs in my pajamas and stare at my father's face. I tried to will him to breathe. I tried to coax movement into fingers bound with rosary beads. I listened for a heartbeat, as years later I would bend over my infant daughter's crib and listen for her heartbeat. I wonder still if I told him that last morning that I loved him. I do remember that the Brooklyn Dodgers, with Vic Lombardi pitching, beat the Pittsburgh Pirates that day.

What provoked these vivid memories of my father's death were two visits I made recently to the Los Angeles County Morgue. My guides were two homicide detectives with thirty-four years' experience between them in the department. Whenever I meet a cop, I am struck by a certain element of performance in his persona, a sense that the handcuffs hanging from the back of his heavy leather belt are the ultimate social equalizer. There is a willingness to push, a tendency to show off. In their office at Robbery-Homicide, one of the cops was wearing a dark brown tie with a pattern of beige diamonds. He pulled the tie and the polyester expanded and each diamond formed the words "Fuck You." The cop smiled. "It's my courtroom tie."

The two officers pulled out files of murders and murderers past:

"Dear Sir: With reference to the above subject, who was executed at Walla Walla on July 15, 1949 . . ."

"Dear Sir: I would greatly appreciate it if you would question Ray Dempsey Gardner who, I understand, is to be executed in Utah State Penitentiary for a similar crime."

"Dear Sir: This man is a professional hitchhiker and murderer."

A professional hitchhiker and murderer. On the road since the age of fourteen. With six known bodies left beside the highways and byways of his professional hitchhiking. Here was a true foot soldier in the armies of the night. I looked at forensic photographs as the two detectives scrutinized my face for signs of queasiness. I stared at a Polaroid photograph of a two-year-old— "30 months old, 30 inches tall, 30 pounds"—whose nipples had been pulled off with a pair of pliers. The two cops talked about the child in the photograph as if they were mechanics talking about a classic Corvette with a broken camshaft. I fell into their rhythm until it was time to go to the morgue.

The morgue on a Monday morning after a weekend during which a Santa Ana was blowing resembles an airline crash site after a jet has gone in. There had been ten murders in Los Angeles County during the preceding twenty-four hours. Bodies were undressed and weighed on a large industrial scale in an anteroom. Bodies lined both sides of the corridor outside the autopsy room. Murder victims, accident victims, suicides, ODs. Bodies that had simply died. Old people, young people, babies.

Male, female, black, white, yellow, brown. Peaceful, contorted,
resigned, smashed, battered, bruised. Wistful. Each body was
marked with a toe tag listing the victim's name (John or Jane
Doe if the name was unknown), cause of death, date, and an
identification number signifying the body's ranking in the year's
count to date; the numbers that Monday morning in the fall
had passed 12,000.

It was a festival of death. On the walls were autopsy photographs of particular or bizarre interest. I backed up into a dead
arm, moved forward and was hit by a gurney carrying yet another
body. This one was a murder victim, thrown over a cliff not a
hundred yards from a house in which I had once lived. The
bullet in his back had not passed entirely out through his chest;
when the younger of the two detectives asked me to feel the
shell protruding from the victim's sternum, I passed. I wished I
had taken the cigar the detective had offered outside. It was not
that the smell was bad; it was just constant. I looked into one
room and saw a man being embalmed. The fluid was pumping
into his body through his groin. In another room, an attendant
was having a snack; his thermos bottle was perched on the desic-
cated chest of the aged female body on the table. In yet another
room, I saw a body being prepared for viewing by next of kin;
it was strapped on a table and the table was lifted and the face
photographed by a closed-circuit television camera and the picture beamed to the next of kin in a room somewhere else in the
complex. There were no keening relatives in the morgue. It was
a place of business, and there was raucous laughter, even a Polish
joke in the corridor. Q: What do 1776, 1812, and 1914 have in
common? A: They are adjoining rooms in the Warsaw Hilton. I
heard myself laugh uproariously and then instinctively I checked
the toe tag of the body beside me to see if he was Polish, as if he
possibly could have taken offense.

The autopsy room was not like the television show *Quincy*.
There were seven autopsy tables and on each there was a body in

some stage of dismemberment; on a side table there was an infant whose skin had been cut at the base of the skull and peeled
up over its face. It was the first time I realized that the facial features are indeed a mask. There was dried blood on the floor and
there was dried blood on the telephone and there were jars full
of organs and chemical beakers filled with body fluids. And there
was noise, noise that time and distance have made me remember
as having an almost factory intensity: the noise of the electric
saw that cuts through the skull and of the chisel used to crack
the spine and of the instrument like pruning shears used to cut
the rib cage. I looked at the exposed viscera and brains and bits
of bone and cartilage and I wondered how all the pieces would fit
back into a body that would wear a suit and a tie in its casket and
perhaps have rosary beads coiled through its fingers.

The cold room, where the bodies are kept prior to their
postmortems, is the eeriest place in the morgue. It seemed immense the first time I saw it, a room shaped like a croquet wicket,
with tier after tier after tier of bodies, up one leg of the wicket,
across the arm and down the other leg. On each tier were five
plastic stretchers and each stretcher was Tiffany blue and on each
was a body, sometimes two, head to toe. What strikes me now,
weeks later, is how the room seemed to shrink between visits; I
think the reason is that the mind is simply not equipped at first
to assimilate hundreds of bodies in such a cramped surrounding;
giving it size somehow made it seem more reasonable until the
brain could adjust, to realize that this was not television or the
movies where each body in a morgue has its own wall crypt.

The temperature in the cold room was approximately 30
degrees, cold enough to keep the smell of formaldehyde and
decay bearable. Most of the bodies were wrapped in white
butcher paper (another vivid departure from television), and
when my detective hosts ripped the paper to show me a particularly choice corpse, the sound of the tearing seemed to reverberate off the walls. One tier of blue stretchers seemed to hold only

babies in what appeared to be paper bags; I was not prepared to examine them too closely. Another aisle, the sound of more paper tearing, this time to expose a bearded biker with a Harley-Davidson tattoo on his right arm and on his left a tattoo of a death's head with Mercury wings. In the exact center of his chest, there was a perfect circular hole the size of a Ping-Pong ball. The biker was a suicide; his old lady had split and he had blown himself away. With a twelve-gauge, one detective insisted, and the other said no, and the first reached into the dead biker's open wound, searched for a moment and then, triumphantly, produced a piece of wadding from the hole in the dead man's chest. "I told you it was a twelve-gauge," he said. As we left the cold room, the first detective showed me a novelty card that read "Eat a toad for breakfast and that will be as bad as you will feel all day."

There is no dignity in death: This was the litany my detective friends kept repeating in the corridors and in the decomp room and in the autopsy room and in the cold room. And of course they were right. There is no dignity when death is merely a professional by-product, when those hundreds of bodies are like so many ball bearings in a gear factory. I think that is why I thought so much about my father after I left the morgue. I tried to dredge up every memory of him that I could, good and bad. I remember once when I was ashamed of him and I remember every time I bared my backside to his strap; I remember when he told me the facts of life and how we both started to laugh when he used the slang synonym for erection; I remember insisting that I was his favorite son. In every way I pursued what Joyce Carol Oates has called "the phantasmagoria of personality." Not to do so was to visualize my father wrapped in butcher paper, and that was simply unthinkable. It is memory, after all, that gives dignity to death.

3
___

DIVISION III, Municipal Court, Santa Monica, a hot Wednesday in August. I sit and read the transcript of a vice case. I learn how to charge fellatio to a restaurant in Marina del Rey on a BankAmericard and that Greek is something other than a nationality and that the cover of a Chinese vice cop is rarely busted, because the girls never think that the fuzz will be Chinese. I learn that a "nurse call" is a john who wants an enema and that an outcall massage service called "Teenagers Who Are Terrific" offers, in outcall terms, the potential for a dynamite acronym. Department B, Superior Court, the sentencing of a prisoner convicted of multiple murders—life without possibility of parole. "He is to spend the rest of his days in prison, he is to die in prison." The judge's nasal voice is without inflection. "Society should never, be it sixty years from now, be forced to accept the risk of his presence." Department J, a family hearing: A psychiatrist testifies that a husband's masturbation fantasies were powered by his wife's infidelities. The wife is wearing a white dress, and she shapes her nails with an emery board. Department K, a custody hearing, and the tightroping of perjury:

Q. You bought cocaine for your wife?
A. No, I paid for the cocaine my wife bought.

I am drawn to the Santa Monica Courthouse the way some people are drawn to church. It is only a five-minute drive from my house, five minutes through a time warp back into the concepts of sin and retribution that were the underpinnings of my Catholic childhood. There in that antiseptic institutional pile just a few hundred yards from the sand and the sea and the Bain de Soleil I am exposed to a tapestry of transgressions scarcely imaginable to those Sisters of Mercy who were the moral arbiters of my youth, a tableau of sex and money and controlled substances, a world of the snortable, sniffable, smokable, shootable, and swallowable.

One rids himself quickly of a number of illusions in the Santa Monica Courthouse, in any courthouse. The first fancy to go is the immutability of truth. A courthouse is by definition a place where people lie; not to lie is to invite confinement in what one superior court judge calls "a structured setting." There is a presumption of perjury, and even that which is accepted as truth is pockmarked with distortion and self-interest. "I like the guy who says, 'Sure, I was in the store,'" a defense attorney tells me. "'But there was no way that bitch could've recognized me with my mask on. It was a Batman mask. Who'd she think I was? Bruce Wayne? And I didn't have no shotgun. It was a twenty-two. If she says she can recognize me, she's blowing smoke up your ass, counselor.'" The attorney smiles. "That is an easy client to defend."

The next illusion to go is the principle of innocent until proven guilty. In the Santa Monica Courthouse, in any courthouse, the criminal justice system is lubricated by a presumption of guilt, the simple reason being that most criminal defendants *are* guilty. The case backlog in every court is so huge that without plea bargaining the drains of justice would clog up irrevocably; the brokering of convictions is the Drano that keeps the system unclogged. There is little room for Perry Mason. Delay is the best defense, continuance the only strategy; memories fade, evidence goes flat, witnesses move away, address unknown; the case load backs up, nobody cares; and finally it is time to deal, to close the file. "The only cases that go to trial," a defense attorney repeats to me over lunch, "are the unimportant crimes of important people and the important crimes of unimportant people."

In Los Angeles County, the same district attorneys, the

same public defenders are assigned to the same judge and the same courtroom every day. In this cozy atmosphere, the accused are like so many markers on a board. The players feel each other out, measure the worth of felon against felony. The haggling is like a Turkish bazaar. To a defense attorney, success is measured not so much by acquittal as by the kicking of a felony down to a misdemeanor, by the agreement that time served will be counted against time; victory is talking a jury in a trial's penalty phase into life without possibility of parole instead of cyanide tablets dropped into a pail of sulfuric acid. "You don't play the game," a former public defender told me. "You play the players." It is a totally hermetic world, a world in which the most rancid view of human behavior prevails, and I find it mesmerizing.

First there are the touches, the signatures that make each crime statistic human. In the morning, I come early to watch the arrival of the black-and-white bus with the mesh bars in the windows that the sheriff's office uses to transport prisoners from the county jail to the courthouse; the prisoners are shackled and wear denims stenciled "County Jail" and file to the lockup, where they wait until their cases are called. Most of the faces are black and brown, an implicit reminder of economic determinism: Crime is the cottage industry of the underprivileged; whites make bail. In the courtrooms, the accused begin to take on separate identities. A young white male cops a plea to possession. He stands before the judge holding a soccer ball under his arm; no mention is made of the ball. Same courtroom, next case. A show business coker, Gucci handbag and blue suede loafers, no socks; case continued. A youthful black pleads guilty to armed robbery in exchange for the dropping of a murder charge; the quid pro quo is an agreement to testify against the partner who had allegedly killed the attendant in the gas station they had stuck up together. As the bailiff leads him back to the lockup, the youth blows a kiss to his mother and sister; sticking from the back pocket of his denims I see a tattered paperback copy of Richard Wright's *Black Boy*. A lawyer petitions the court for a single cell in the county jail for his client, a pale red-headed teenager. "A first offender," his lawyer whispers to me. "Fresh meat. Everyone wants a whack at him. He doesn't get a single cell, he'll get his asshole stretched." Another black in jail denims; he wants both an O.R. release and to dismiss his court-appointed attorney. "This case is getting serious, Your Honor," he says. "I need me a real lawyer. I get me on the street, I can get me some money." I think I would not want to be on the street he gets it on.

It is like watching the ultimate game show, the game being life itself. Every tactic is explored for advantage, even racism. I recall a day I spent years ago with a public defender in Clark County, Nevada. He had two black clients that day, one a prostitute who had killed a trick, the other a man accused of stealing a number of checks from a local NAACP office. The man's case was dismissed when the lawyer claimed that, for a black, stealing from the NAACP was not a robbery but a loan; the prostitute's case thrown out when he had her testify that the john, in her words, "wanted me to satisfy his dog."

In the corridors of the Santa Monica Courthouse I meet the woman attorney who one day had a professional burglar client appearing in three different courtrooms on three different charges under three different names, with no one the wiser. Over there is the attorney from the Manson case who once put a hostile witness's homosexuality on the record: "Let the record reflect that the witness winked at my client." The man in the custom-made three-piece suit with buttonholes on the sleeve is a former radical lawyer now defending a member of the Mafia. He was once the man you called if you blew up Fort Ord or if you were a rock-'n'-roller caught with ninety-seven pounds of blow. Every case that had a number at the end of it, there he was; it was said that he thought the Indianapolis 500 was an

illegal detention case. "I never saw him when he wasn't wearing a blue work shirt and sandals," an attorney says, not without admiration. "Now he's representing the wiseguys."

I watch, I listen, I learn. Department 127, the daily calen-
dar, Case No. B342076, 192.1 PC, one count. In the state penal
code, 192.1 is manslaughter. The defendant had interfered in
a domestic argument and killed a man who was beating up on
a woman. She had been released on her own recognizance. "Her
case will never get to trial," my guide says. I ask why. "Manslaughter is what you plead down to. You don't try manslaughter.
If the D.A. is only charging manslaughter, he doesn't have a
case." I begin to hear the undertones. I sit in municipal court
after three drinks and a large lunch. I am the only spectator at
the preliminary hearing. The district attorney has evasive eyes
and seems uneasy about my presence. He wonders if I am a
reporter. His eyes do not meet mine, and he mumbles something about the FBI and a potential for embarrassment. The
drinks take hold and I begin to doze. An FBI agent testifies
about an armed robbery at 1:15 A.M. on a quiet street in Beverly
Hills. Nothing extraordinary here. But when the agent steps
from the stand he and the district attorney whisper quietly. I
realize I am under discussion. The FBI agent kneels next to
me. He wonders if he might ask who it is I work for.

I am now wide awake. The victims of the armed robbery
were in fact three FBI agents, one female, two male; one of
the victims was the agent who had just testified. They had
allegedly been stuck up by the two sullen blacks at the defense
table. The three agents had been on a stakeout that had nothing to do with the two blacks. On the nation's business, as it
were. The feds were embarrassed, and their embarrassment was
a source of some quiet satisfaction in Division III. Not only
had the myth of FBI invincibility been tarnished, but the agents
had also shown some uncertainty in picking their assailants from
a sheriff's lineup. Defense counsel bored in on this uncertainty.

The suspect being staked out had in fact been arrested before the three agents came on duty. So they had gone to Lawry's and had a bottle of wine, and after that they spent a couple of hours in a bar behind Cedars-Sinai Hospital; the stickup occurred when they left the saloon. I suspect I could have conducted that cross-examination. How many drinks were consumed? Two hours in this bar and you just had coffee? I think I know now what it means to implant reasonable doubt.

When I think of the law, I do not think of Archibald Cox and Earl Warren. I do not think of Mr. Justice Cardozo or Mr. Justice Holmes. Theirs is a law of abstraction and beauty. When I think of the law I think of a morning in the Santa Monica Courthouse. I watch a judge sentence a man to two years in prison. The accused is just another hype, with a past—and probably a future—defined by a rap sheet. When sentence is passed, the defendant asks the judge if he will marry him before he is sent away. The bride is a Mexican woman, six months' pregnant with one front tooth missing. The bailiff and the public defender are the witnesses. The groom kisses the bride; the prosecutor and the public defender kiss the bride; even I kiss the bride. The judge says, "Don't write me in six months and say you want an annulment because you haven't consummated your marriage."

That is the law.

THE PUBLIC SECTOR

On the Kennedys

1

I AM TROUBLED by Chappaquiddick. I am aware of the polls indicating that the events of July 18, 1969, do not concern a large majority of American voters. I am aware that Joseph and Gwendolyn Kopechne have stated that the drowning of their daughter, Mary Jo, does not preclude supporting Edward Kennedy for the presidency. I am aware of Arthur Schlesinger's assertion that those who would make Chappaquiddick an issue use it to justify not voting for Edward Kennedy anyway. I am aware of those who maintain that mention of Chappaquiddick is an invitation to mudslinging and Kennedy-hating. I am aware of the specter of assassination. But I am still troubled by Chappaquiddick. I voted for one Kennedy and would have voted for a second. I think Chappaquiddick matters. I think Chappaquiddick has to matter.

Let us examine the record; let us examine the story as Senator Kennedy has himself told it, free of sexual speculation and conjecture about alcoholic consumption. It was the weekend of the 1969 Edgartown Regatta on Martha's Vineyard. Edward Kennedy was entered in *Victura*. On Chappaquiddick Island, five hundred feet across the channel from Edgartown, six young women who had worked without glory for Robert Kennedy's 1968 presidential campaign were preparing, with Edward Kennedy's encouragement, a reunion cookout at a cottage rented for the occasion. After sailing in a heat Friday, Edward Kennedy took the short ferry ride to Chappaquiddick and joined the party. There were five other men at the cookout—acquaintances and low-level Kennedy retainers—including Paul Markham, former U.S. attorney for Massachusetts, and Joseph Gargan, a Kennedy cousin, lawyer and factotum.

I suspect the evening was more fun in the planning than in the actuality, full of the forced jollity of people who did not after all know each other very well. Its details suggest an office party where the gang at the water cooler calls the boss by his first name; there was rum and there was vodka and there was Scotch and there were dips and food and, it being summer and the five married men having left their wives at home, I suppose there was harmless flirtation; nothing very dangerous can happen in a house without privacy, and nothing very comfortable on the sand. Shortly after eleven, in the Kennedy telling, he slipped away from the group in order to catch the last ferry back to Edgartown. He did not bother to say goodbye; he was the stellar attraction of the evening and he did not wish his departure to end the revels. Edward Kennedy was joined in his Oldsmobile by Mary Jo Kopechne, almost twenty-nine, the eldest of the six women at the party.

It is a short ride from the cottage to the ferry, three miles. There is only one paved road and it is center-lined and, where it veers left toward the ferry slip, marked with an arrow of reflecting glass. Edward Kennedy did not follow the arrow. Instead he turned right, down a dirt lane called Dike Road, which leads to the beach. Although the entrance to Dike Road is obscured by bushes and not immediately apparent to someone unfamiliar with it, Kennedy said the right turn was a mistake.

The gravel on the road causes a car to lose traction—but Edward Kennedy said he was not aware that he had driven off the asphalt and then he said there was no place to turn around; he did not see any of the half-dozen driveways visible from the lane. The Oldsmobile continued down the beach road toward Dike Bridge, a narrow and manifestly unsafe—it had no side rails—wooden structure over a tidal inlet. The bridge is set at a slight oblique angle to the road; natives brake to a stop to accommodate the angle and then proceed at scarcely more than stalling speed. The Oldsmobile did not allow for the angle; it hit the bridge at twenty miles per hour. The car flipped over, the roof caved in. Edward Kennedy swam to the surface; Mary Jo Kopechne did not.

To this point, what happened at the Dike Bridge was just another resort accident, as meaningless as a freeway crash, only here there was sun and sand and rum-and-Coke and perhaps a color of evanescent summer romance. Make no mistake about it: Whatever transpired between the two passengers, whatever their secret intentions, this was an accident, as senseless as most accidents are, the kind of accident in which everyone meant well and the survivors allow a margin of mercy for truth not quite told. It is what happened from this moment on that creates the stain of Chappaquiddick.

Edward Kennedy's account continues: He dove again and again into the water to free Mary Jo Kopechne, and when that failed, he made his way, after resting, back to the cottage where the party was still going on. He was able to summon Markham and Gargan without making the others aware of his return, or indeed of the accident. Markham and Gargan are the Rosencrantz and Guildenstern of this dark evening, servants of the legend, and they drove Edward Kennedy back to the bridge. For the better part of an hour, Markham and Gargan dove and probed for Mary Jo Kopechne; there was still the possibility she might be alive, breathing the dregs of an air bubble that could have formed inside the Oldsmobile. Finally they admitted failure and with Edward Kennedy they drove to the ferry slip. The last ferry was gone; there was no way back to Edgartown. Suddenly Edward Kennedy plunged into the water and began the five-hundred-foot swim across the channel. Here the record is unclear. His two companions either swam partway with him or they watched on shore until he disappeared into the night. Then they returned to the cottage and the party. A car had gone off a bridge, a young woman had apparently drowned, a U.S. senator with a bad back, alone and at night, had braved the treacherous channel tides and perhaps been swept out to sea, but Rosencrantz and Guildenstern kept their own counsel. Both lawyers, they brushed aside all inquiries; both lawyers, they informed no authorities; both lawyers, they spread no alarm.

Nor did Edward Kennedy. Nearly drowned, he reached the Edgartown side and at last, exhausted, his room at the Shiretown Inn. It was 2 A.M. A short time later, Edward Kennedy appeared at the desk. He was dry, he had changed into jacket and trousers, and he complained about the noise from the motel next door; he also asked the time. Exactly 2:25 A.M. For the next five hours, alone in his room, Edward Kennedy contemplated the collapsing situation. Not until morning did he go to the telephone, and then not to call the police, but to try and get the number of his brother-in-law, Stephen Smith, who was in Spain. Between 7:30 and 8, he went for a walk. He appeared composed to those who met him on the streets of Edgartown. For some minutes, he conversed with Ross W. Richards, who had won the race the day before, about sailing and the weather. In the waters off the Dike Bridge, the body in the Oldsmobile still had not been discovered.

It was eight hours after the accident when Markham and Gargan found Edward Kennedy exchanging regatta pleasantries with Richards. The three men returned to Kennedy's room in the Shiretown Inn. All lawyers, they did not report the accident. A half hour later, Edward Kennedy came downstairs and placed an order for the *Boston Globe* and *The New York Times*. He also borrowed a dime to make a telephone call. Back upstairs, the three discussed their options. All lawyers, they still did not report the accident. Then the three took the ferry to Chappaquiddick. On the ride over, the ferryman told them that a body had been recovered off the Dike Bridge. From the privacy of a pay telephone, Edward Kennedy used his borrowed dime and tried to get in touch with his friend and occasional lawyer, Burke Marshall. The attempt to reach Marshall was unsuccessful. Time was running out. Edward Kennedy then took the ferry back to Edgartown, went to the police station and reported the accident. It was, according to his own account, ten hours after the accident that had killed Mary Jo Kopechne.

"Irrational and indefensible and inexcusable and inexplicable": The words are Edward Kennedy's own evaluation of his conduct at Chappaquiddick. These many years later, the events called Chappaquiddick still seem inexcusable and indefensible, although not exactly irrational, not exactly inexplicable. What was—and is—indefensible about Chappaquiddick was never the accident itself but precisely this attempt to cosmeticize its aftermath into something "irrational" and "inexplicable," a moment of panic or trauma almost sympathetic in its suggestion of human frailty.

If there was panic at Chappaquiddick, there was calculation thereafter. From the moment Markham and Gargan appeared on the scene, through the days at Hyannis Port that followed, through the weeks before the inquest, the problem of Chappaquiddick was always how to handle it, how to contain it; it was a strategy that when later used by others not so skilled would be called "a modified limited hangout." No information was volunteered. The story came out grudgingly, if at all, riddled with contradictions and inconsistencies. Before the first sunset, the remaining partygoers were hustled off Martha's Vineyard. At Hyannis Port, Camelot's most eminent courtiers—Robert McNamara, Theodore Sorensen, Richard Goodwin, Kenneth O'Donnell—gathered to hammer out a line, a narrative, as it were, the kind that often emerges from a movie story conference. Stephen Smith suggested that lawyers be obtained for the five women at the party; it was a kindness really, an attempt to shield them from investigators and a probing press. The cost of the lawyers was over $30,000; Edward Kennedy paid it out of his own pocket. Another lawyer—William Vanden Heuvel, a former assistant to Robert Kennedy when he was attorney general—was dispatched to the Kopechne household to man the telephone and screen the calls; another kindness, another filter against crackpots and the bloodlust of the press and ambulance chasers with their whispers of civil litigation. And a final kindness: Edward Kennedy's automobile insurance policy paid only $50,000 to Mary Jo Kopechne's parents, a figure that Kennedy, in his own words, thought "unreasonably low." In a letter to the *Boston Globe*, Kennedy wrote: "Obviously a financial settlement could never compensate the Kopechne family for the loss of a daughter. . . . But if there was to be one, it should be fair." At Edward Kennedy's urging, the Kopechnes chose an independent expert who, on the basis of Mary Jo's actuarial expectations, recommended that the senator pay the family an additional $90,904; once again, Edward Kennedy reached into his own pocket.

Kindness abounded; only the facts were hard to come by. The Supreme Judicial Court of Massachusetts ordered the inquest closed after Kennedy lawyers argued that an open hearing would cause the senator and the other people at the cookout to be "publicly pilloried" by the press. "I wish I could help you," Edward Kennedy told a team of *Boston Globe* interviewers shortly after the fifth anniversary of Chappaquiddick. "I don't recall that . . . I have no recollection . . . That is the best I can give you . . . I have no memory . . . I really couldn't tell you . . ." It is the litany of Watergate.

The analogy triggers an immediate response from Edward Kennedy. Watergate, he told the *Boston Globe* interviewers, "was an attempt to corrupt the political processes of our constitutional system and to violate basic constitutional rights and liberties of individuals in a premeditated and deliberate way. The other [Chappaquiddick] was a tragic accident."

Accidents, however, like felonies, can be covered up. I try to imagine Chappaquiddick happening to any other American politician. I try to imagine that politician going ten hours without informing the authorities. I try to imagine that politician explaining away a distinguished convocation of fixers working out an alibi. I try to imagine that politician explaining away $30,000 in legal fees for potential witnesses and accessories and a $90,000 settlement to the bereaved parents of the victim and I try to imagine that politician dealing with this $120,000 when it is called hush money. I try to imagine that politician getting away with "I don't recall that" and "I have no memory" and "I wish I could help you." I think, no wonder a moral defective like Richard Nixon thought he could get away with the Watergate cover-up; Chappaquiddick was the model of the stonewall. I suspect that cartoonists would depict any other American politician in a wet suit. I suspect opponents would nickname that politician "The Swimmer." I suspect that any other American politician would forever be disqualified, by public disgust, for higher office.

Edward Kennedy, however, is running for president, and it is the consensus of his more ardent supporters that Chappaquiddick does not matter, that a man's spirit grows out of adversity and his moral fiber expands. Arthur Schlesinger takes this theme one step further: Chappaquiddick "would make [Edward Kennedy] a better president. Ever since Chappaquiddick, he has been spending his life trying to redeem himself . . . I think this ceaseless effort at self-redemption may be for Teddy Kennedy what polio was for FDR."

I suppose Edward Kennedy should not be blamed for Arthur Schlesinger. For twenty years, Schlesinger has been Camelot's resident groupie, a master of selective history who for a wink or a smile can justify any action, rationalize any obscenity, a man who has the effrontery to equate Chappaquiddick with Campobello. No need to mention in *A Thousand Days* that John Kennedy asked the publisher of *The New York Times* to remove his man in Saigon, David Halberstam, because Halberstam's injudicious pessimism about the war in Vietnam did not correspond with the rosy outlook sketched by JFK's Pentagon. If Jacqueline Onassis grimaced when kissed on the cheek by President Carter at the opening of the Kennedy Library, the reason, according to Arthur Schlesinger, was because "in the North, gentlemen do not kiss ladies on such brief acquaintance," an assessment that suggests the North he had in mind was North Korea. If Senator Edward Kennedy recommended Francis X. Morrissey, an unqualified political hack and friend of his father, for a federal judgeship, then the villain of the episode was President Lyndon Johnson. The Kennedy brothers, Robert and Edward, never meant the nomination to go forward, according to Arthur Schlesinger in *Robert Kennedy and His Times*; Lyndon Johnson only sent it to the Senate to embarrass them. This is not history; I would call it perjury.

Arthur Schlesinger is more than a mere embarrassment; he is the Lysenko of Camelot, ordering a chain of superstitions into a coherent myth. In this system, there was ample opportunity for an expansion of moral fiber. The Bay of Pigs was a legacy from the Eisenhower administration; this explanation is offered as if only an ingrate would turn down an inheritance. There were six hundred American troops in Vietnam when John Kennedy took office, twenty thousand when he was assassinated; the house historians would have us believe that he permitted the escalation so that Vietnam would not become an issue in the 1964 election, after which he planned to extricate himself and us from the quagmire. The CIA was implicated in so many attempts, successful and unsuccessful, to murder heads of state— Patrice Lumumba, Rafael Trujillo, Ngo Dinh Diem, Fidel Castro—that it almost seemed as if assassination had become an instrument of national policy, but the CIA was a rogue elephant; and if the brothers Kennedy were aware of discussions between the CIA and the Mafia to bump off Castro, it was a momentary lapse of taste, a mere sidebar to John Kennedy's roll in the feathers with Momo Giancana's girlfriend.

And then there were the federal judges John Kennedy appointed in the South: W. Harold Cox, who called blacks "niggers" and "chimpanzees" from the bench; E. Gordon West, who characterized the Warren Court's desegregation ruling as "one of the truly regrettable decisions of all time"; and Robert Elliott of Georgia, who, in 1952, said: "I don't want these pinks, radicals and black voters to outvote those who are trying to preserve our own segregation laws and other traditions." We were asked instead to remember John Kennedy's words on race, not his appointments to the bench. "We are confronted with what is primarily a moral question," he said on June 11, 1963; if an American is denied the decencies of life because of his race, "then who among us would be content to have the color of his skin changed and stand in his place?" Not, certainly, the Kennedy judges.

This same moral Muzak scores the presidential candidacy of Edward Kennedy. There has always been the sense that no misstep by any Kennedy indicates a character flaw. Instead these missteps—Edward Kennedy's cheating at Harvard, Robert Kennedy's wiring of Martin Luther King, Chappaquiddick—are presented as opportunities, chances to reflect, to put steel in the backbone, to understand suffering. Even Joan Kennedy is an opportunity. "I think we have been able to make some very good progress," Edward Kennedy told Roger Mudd on CBS. "Joan's involved in a continuing program to deal with the problems of alcoholism and she's doing magnificently well and I am immensely proud of the fact that she's shaped up to it." In other words, Joan Kennedy was choreographed into a problem the problem solver must solve, as if the problem solver was not part of the problem in the first place. It is a contemptible tactic, another example of the sexual imperialism that Edward Kennedy's more ardent women supporters cannot find it in themselves to condemn.

"I am a different person," Edward Kennedy said of Chappaquiddick in his interview with Roger Mudd. It changed his life more than even the assassinations of John and Robert Kennedy. "I am a very different person than prior to that tragedy. I know just from my own inner views or inner attitudes or views about life and people and faith in God that I am a different person." I heard those words on television and I considered the slovenly diction of image-making and I wondered exactly how many episodes of moral amnesia it would take to perfect Edward Kennedy's inner attitudes.

I am told, however, that Chappaquiddick does not matter. I am told that what matters is what one historian calls Edward Kennedy's "serious and high-minded exercise of his senatorial duties in the intervening years." I am told that he produces the best position papers in Washington, that he is better staffed than any other candidate, that he could bring the country's best minds to Washington. (I am reminded that nearly a generation ago the nation's best minds produced Vietnam.) I am finally told the bottom line: if not Edward Kennedy, then Jimmy Carter. Or Ronald Reagan. Or John Connally. This is not an argument. It is a debasement of argument, a kind of public extortion, a doctrine of indispensability that is a poisonous comment on the electorate's acquiescence in its own manipulation. The attitude that Chappaquiddick does not matter diminishes equally those who hold it and those on whom they would foist it.

2

THERE ARE no new facts about the Kennedys, only new attitudes, a literature that, like the automobile industry, puts new bodies on old chassis. First there were those huge polluting gas guzzlers, the Sorensen and the Schlesinger, useful now only insofar as their parts can be cannibalized for nuts and bolts, their gushy excesses, like tail fins, always good for sport. Conspiracy is a small but durable seller, retooled every year or so. And these days revisionism is the hottest item off the assembly line, each model sleek and economical, with a racy name, "Destroyer," say, or "Marauder."

In *The Kennedy Imprisonment*, Garry Wills flashes his Marauder across the high plains of Camelot like a night rider—burn the barn, destroy the crops, take no prisoners, scorch the myth as if it were the earth itself. The myth of the Kennedys—and the hold—was always the hold of the renegade rich, out there on the frontier beyond accountability. There are no legends about the du Ponts; the legends are about Howard Hughes. Nor do the Rockefellers quicken the pulse the way the Kennedys did, and do. The Rockefellers only have money and a foundation and a museum and a bank and suits with vests. Nelson Rockefeller supervised Diego Rivera at the beginning of his working life and at the end was supervising expensive reproductions; ironic but not the stuff of legend.

The Kennedys shared only one attitude with the traditional American rich: they assumed that the possessors of great wealth constituted a real if unacknowledged—this is a republic, after all—nobility. With the aid of the "cool media" and a gut understanding of the power that media could wield, they pushed this proposition one step further: the Kennedys were not merely noble, they were regal, and by shrewd manipulation of the media, the divine right of the sovereignty was acknowledged. They knighted what Wills calls "honorary Kennedys," and we remember the names and MOSs of these troops as we remember second cousins and family retainers—Red Fay and Kenny O'Donnell and Larry O'Brien and Dave Powers and Joe Gargan and Paul Markham, the gutter Irish NCOs who told the jokes and kept the grunts in step and did the dirty work and cleaned up afterward. The officers' mess was positively Dickensian in the breadth of its arriviste and aristocratic pretensions—the Bundys and the Rostows and McNamara and Dillon and Rusk and poor Adlai Stevenson and poor Chester Bowles. Even the gazetteers of this brigade carried colors. Joseph Alsop was William Howard Russell and Theodore H. White brevetted himself Sir Thomas Malory; Arthur Schlesinger prowled around the perimeter of the encampment like Mr. Samgrass in *Brideshead Revisited*.

Then Dallas, then the kitchen of the Ambassador Hotel in Los Angeles. The myth was lit into an eternal flame and honorary Kennedys were anointed its keepers. The thousand days of John Kennedy became Camelot, the eighty-five days of Robert Kennedy's last campaign the end of promise. Those early hagiographies, born of grief and saturated with blood, had all the elements of pop mythology. Charisma became commitment and the Kennedys' renewal each election season with a different set of values, a new set of priorities, was turned into a virtue—the pragmatic virtue of flexibility, the flexible virtue of pragmatism. There were no failures in Camelot, no warts spotted by the valet biographers.

Garry Wills buys none of it. His John Kennedy looks like the Elephant Man—a liar, a cheat, a philanderer, a war lover who waged war less successfully abroad than against the very government he was elected to lead. In Wills's view, John Kennedy was the first Green Beret—a force Kennedy commissioned—and the enemy he sought to destabilize, to terminate with extreme prejudice, was his own bureaucracy. Command was fun, power exhilarating, throw caution to the wind. Vietnam was one of the hangovers produced by this heady wine.

It was a style of leadership to which John Kennedy came naturally. He was his father's son, and that was but the first cell of the many prisons in which Wills finds the Kennedys incarcerated. Joseph P. Kennedy was a randy raider, Harvard-educated but always a parvenu on-the-make mick to classmates who booed him, this emissary from Franklin Roosevelt, at their twenty-fifth reunion. He was not so much a businessman as a predator of other men's businesses. Always traveling fast, traveling light, he struck and moved on and struck again. The running of his various enterprises was not for him or his sons; that was the chore of flunkies and sons-in-law. Joseph Kennedy had "no ideology but achievement," Wills writes, and he created "a kind of space platform out of his own career, one from which the children could fly out to their own achievements and come back for refueling."

The raider collected women as he collected companies. Rose Kennedy visited his bed often enough to produce nine children and suffered gracefully when her husband invited Gloria Swanson, for years the official mistress, and other more casual conquests to Hyannis Port. Rose Kennedy offered it up, as the Catholic women of her generation were taught to do, every mortification and every humiliation an opportunity for a plenary indulgence, markers against her time in purgatory. Her husband made passes at the daughters of his friends and at the friends of his daughters and used Arthur Krock, the conservative and seemingly punctilious resident oracle of *The New York Times*, as an ex-officio pimp who stashed discarded Kennedy girl friends in the various newsrooms of Washington. "What are you, our staff procurer?" a Washington newspaper editor asked Krock in 1941, and it took Krock nearly thirty years to realize that was indeed his role, both literally and figuratively, with his putative friends, Joseph Kennedy & Sons.

For most American Irish Catholics, the only real sins are sins of the flesh, but to Joseph Kennedy that notion was parochial school nun stuff, part of the baggage of Catholic guilt and ethnicity he jettisoned early. The Kennedys, as seen by Wills, were only "semi-Irish" and superficially Catholic. They were citizens of the world of celebrity and touched down in Palm Beach and Hyannis Port and logged in safari time on the zebra stripes of El Morocco. Not for them harp Boston politicians "with outlandish nicknames like Knocko and Onions." Massachusetts was where they were registered to vote and Mass where they went to be photographed with Cardinal Cushing.

The Kennedys were mid-Atlantic people before the term was invented, "semi-English," as Wills calls them. Father and (especially) children were absolutely moony over the virtues of the English aristocracy in that way that only rich Americans can get. John Kennedy went to England to study under Harold Laski and said that David Ormsby-Gore was the brightest man he'd ever met, a statement that makes him sound like Sebastian Flyte's teddy bear. The very model of the politician he aspired to be was Queen Victoria's Whig prime minister, Lord Melbourne— languid, horny, a man of state sustained by family and contemptuous of outsiders—and he was equally taken by John Buchan's idea of "adventurer-aristocrats, who could save the people by guiding them, sometimes without their knowledge." Democracy in spite of the people, in other words. Wills pinpoints the carcinoma inherent in this hubris:

> The world of aristocratic rakes like Melbourne has an underside, the dark area where T. E. Lawrence moves, and Richard Hannay, and James Bond, all the Green Berets and gentlemen spies of the CIA. Presiding over this potentially dangerous world is the honor of the aristocrats, their code of national service.

It is John Kennedy's honor, from those earliest days in England, that Wills finds suspect. If he was a prisoner of family, he was also a prisoner of image, one maximum-security slammer leading inevitably to another. "The whole point of being a Kennedy, in the father's scheme of things," Wills says, "was to look good." To make John Kennedy look good, his father saw to it that *Why England Slept* was published. John Kennedy's tutor thought it "much too long, wordy, repetitious," its "fundamental premise never analysed," but what did he know, he had never met a payroll. Joseph Kennedy asked the family ponce, Arthur Krock, to rewrite and retitle the book, himself supplied a hodge-podge of charts and statistics that never actually quite made any point, and got Henry Luce to attach a foreword. No stranger to this game himself, Luce saw that a book by the son of Franklin Roosevelt's ambassador to the Court of St. James offered a perfect opportunity both to push Wendell Willkie and to take a swat at Roosevelt. Only Harold Laski seemed to see through the whole charade. "In a good university, half a hundred seniors do books like this as part of their normal work in their final year," he wrote Joseph Kennedy. "I don't honestly think any publisher would have looked at that book of Jack's if he had not been your son, and if you had not been ambassador."

Perhaps because of his time in the movie business, Joseph Kennedy seemed to share the Jack Warner view that writers were "schmucks with Underwoods," and that there would always be schmucks—if not Harold Laski—available to make his boys look good. It was not enough that John Kennedy exhibited rare physical courage when PT-109 went down and he saved the life of one of his crew members. First John Hersey and then Robert Donovan buffed courage into heroism, both writers begging the essential question: How does a glorified speedboat get run over in the dark by a heavier, slower, and more ponderous enemy destroyer? John Kennedy's version was that the 109 was "attempting a torpedo attack," but the Navy's medal and citations board would not swallow that and rewrote the citation for his Navy and Marine Corps Medal, changing the "attack" into a simple "collision," adding that he had "contributed to the saving of several lives." Cliff Robertson played the part in the movie; John Kennedy's personal choice, Warren Beatty, turned it down.

Next to Arthur Krock, no writer ever made a Kennedy look better than the young Senator Kennedy's amanuensis and aide-de-camp, Theodore Sorensen. He had a way with words and (especially in *Kennedy*) a dramatically lit memory. Every Kennedy was a hero to this exemplary servant; he was Hudson to their Bellamys and he kept his trap shut. Joseph Kennedy thought books made the man—"You would be surprised how a book that really makes the grade with high-class people stands you in good stead for years to come," the ambassador once said—and he was not choosy about who wrote them as long as a son could claim authorship.

Thus *Profiles in Courage* was fabricated; "John F. Kennedy" was the nom de plume used by Sorensen and Georgetown historian Jules Davids, who "put [the book] together much like a major speech." This was well within the rules of political deceit and did not exceed them until Arthur Krock, turning one last trick for his favorite John, began to lobby for a Pulitzer Prize for the book and its alleged author, the senator from Massachusetts and seeker after the presidency. The Pulitzer judges chose Alpheus Mason's *Harlan Fiske Stone: Pillar of the Law* for the prize, but were overruled by the board, which—denying improper influence—awarded *Profiles in Courage* the laurel, one member of the Pulitzer board making the engaging claim that the board was swayed by his twelve-year-old grandson's enjoyment of the book, which presumably the lad liked better than *Harlan Fiske Stone*. "The incremental touches of glamour were always sought," Wills writes about this prisoner of image. "The unflattering notes were censored. The collision became an attack . . . Reality was all a matter of rearranging appearances for the electorate."

In the Wills version, the lust for image meant a sentence in still another prison, that of charisma. John Kennedy, author/hero, the first president born in the twentieth century, had the

junior line officer's contempt for the general staff, in particular
for that ultimate staff officer, General of the Army Dwight David
Eisenhower. Both as military man and as president, Eisenhower
was the quintessential bureaucratic manager, a delegator of re-
sponsibilities, an advocate of caution who thought of crises in
terms of—and on a scale with—the Normandy landings. His career was predicated on channels and chains of command, which
gave him an intuitive grasp of bureaucracy and an inchoate respect for its procedures. It is a respect shared—hindsight, perhaps—by Wills, who finds bureaucracy the best governor against
the imperial presidency.

The Kennedy concept of leadership was that of a commando
leader (or, more accurately, a PT boat skipper)—lightning strikes
against the forces of darkness, be those forces poverty, Big Steel,
Fidel Castro, or a bunch of obstreperous slopes in the jungles of
Indochina. It was this very impetuosity that the cumbersome bureaucracy tended to thwart, and John Kennedy put that bureaucracy on his administration's hit list; outflank the bureaucrats,
seal them off from the schemes of his government, operate with
mobile tactical squads recruited by and answerable only to the
Oval Office. Here was charisma in action, charisma in the true,
rather than the vulgar, sense of the word. "Insofar as the charis-
matic leader asserts an entirely personal authority," Wills says, "he
delegitimizes the traditional and legal authorities." The Green Be-
rets, the Peace Corps, military advisers to Vietnam—there seemed
no understanding in Camelot that these romantic Chindits, operating outside regular channels of command, would only create
new bureaucracies of their own, outlaw tumors which by their
very dependence on the host body must ultimately metastasize
and adhere to the older bureaucracy.

Kennedy charisma was the cult of personality carried, in a
democracy, to the exosphere: the president as a strong leader in
the Buchan tradition, "willing to administer timely jolts to the
people as a form of therapy." The timely jolt was often a timely

goose. There was a high butch about that Kennedy administration, an obsession with metaphorical genitals. Balls, ballsy, ballsiness, nuts—these were the calibrations of worth, and often of wit. "A Stevenson with balls," Joseph Alsop called John Kennedy, and the *mot* was fondled all the way into the Oval Office. In turn, John Kennedy dismissed the allegedly timid as "holding their nuts" or "grabbing their balls."

The problem with such ballsiness was a constant need to thrust. Crisis was a way to milk the gland, sixteen crises, by Theodore Sorensen's gleeful count, in the administration's first eight months alone. It is this appetite for crisis, particularly the taste for foreign adventurism, that draws Wills's most withering scrutiny. There was of course the Bay of Pigs, a grant from the Eisenhower administration, the hagiographers have advised us, as if the terms of the bequest were binding. "The truth is," Wills writes,

> that Kennedy went ahead with the Cuban action, not
> to complete what he inherited from Eisenhower, but
> to mark his difference from Eisenhower . . . He would
> be bold where he accused Eisenhower of timidity. . . .
> Kennedy was a prisoner of his own taste for crisis, for
> being in the midst of the action. . . . The growing size
> of the invasion army—1,400 men—made the administration hostage to its own agents. Their visibility made
> them an "asset" that had to be used immediately or
> moved in a way that would waste the asset. . . . Once
> again, acquiring a "capability" chained one to its use,
> so that decision became a kind of resignation to the inevitable. . . . Thus do options bind, making "freedom
> of maneuver" a straitjacket for the mind.

Wills believes, contrary to the conventional wisdom of the hagiographers, that the failure of the Bay of Pigs invasion taught

John Kennedy nothing. Rather, John and Robert Kennedy were confirmed in their perception of Fidel Castro as a dagger at the throat, and not, as Senator J. William Fulbright advised, a thorn in the side. Getting rid of him seemed the administration's highest priority. Secret select committees drew up plans and tables of organization—Operation Mongoose and Task Force W and Special Group Augmented and Special Group CI (for counterinsurgency)—and with a nod and a wink from the highest echelons of government the Mob was contacted about whacking Castro out. (John Kennedy, Lyndon Johnson claimed, was running "a damn Murder Incorporated in the Caribbean.") Castro knew what was going on and the missiles he imported from Russia were no more offensive, in the Wills version, than the secret war Washington was waging against him. The very fact of this secret war, Wills contends, punctures any pretense that John Kennedy acted with "restraint" during the Cuban missile crisis; instead the necessity of camouflaging his sordid and shadowy "guerilla strategy" chained him to a policy of high-risk confrontation and bluster.

As with Cuba, so with Vietnam, war on an ad hoc, CI basis. "There was no reluctance to be 'drawn into' Vietnam," Wills writes. "We welcomed it as a laboratory to test our troops. . . . There was no dove position in Kennedy's administration that stood for withdrawal. The doves were for winning the war by gentler methods." Crisis, always crisis, crisis courted, crisis incited: crisis was finally the syphilis of Camelot, and it has infected, in Wills's telling, every subsequent president. "Over and over in our recent history," he writes, "presidents have claimed they had to act tough in order to *disarm* those demanding that they act tough. The only way to become a peacemaker is first to disarm the warmakers by making a little successful war."

Wills's case against the Kennedys, however supple and elegant, is perhaps too clever by half, an extended essay rather than history, and therefore not overburdened by any cargo of facts that might shift and rock the tidy line of argument. At his most graceful and stylish, he is often bracingly mean-spirited, about Eugene McCarthy ("an interesting study in the pride of people trained to embrace humility"), who once stiffed him with a check at Elaine's (dinner for two, plus brandy)—an impolitic thing to do to a writer—and about the more onanistic of the toady courtiers; about Theodore White, who seemed to find sanctifying grace in the Kennedy presence; about Arthur Schlesinger, presented as a tame chaplain ever ready to offer absolution to his mentors from the confessional of history. In the proliferation of honorary Kennedys, layer upon layer around each brother, Wills shrewdly finds a bloated and largely ineffective bureaucracy of sycophants, liabilities where once they were a source of strength, "too many of them now and too few real Kennedys." It was this bureaucracy that sprang into action after Chappaquiddick, crisis managers who managed the solution in such a way that the protagonist was forever scarred.

Wills's John Kennedy is a horror, more Picture than Dorian Gray, a president who "did not so much elevate the office as cripple those who held it after him. . . . Inheriting a delegitimated set of procedures, they were compelled to go outside the procedures too—further delegitimating the office they held." About Robert Kennedy, Wills is ambivalent; in him Wills sees what might have been had he not been his brother's brother, yet had he been the first of the line, would Robert Kennedy ever have been anything more than the nasty piece of work who cozied up to Senator Joseph McCarthy? Toward Edward Kennedy, Wills is patronizing, seeing in him a boozily effective senator condemned to be last keeper of the flame, his life "a permanent floating Irish wake," sorting out friends "according to which brother they accompanied to meet his killer."

The problem with revisionism, however, is that it is too often the mirror image of hagiography, a faith with an orthodoxy of its own. For all its many virtues, *The Kennedy Imprison-*

ment is ultimately unsatisfying, brought down less by its attitude toward the Kennedys than by the Jesuitical rigidity of its premise, its narrative. Narrative is arbitrary and tendentious, useful to the historian only insofar as it throws people and events into an original perspective or relief. The notion of the Kennedys as prisoners—prisoners of legend, prisoners of sex, of family, of image, of charisma, of power—is a romantic idea, a novelist's conceit that Norman Mailer first tried out in *An American Dream*. Mailer had it all and he had it first—the Cardinal and the girls and the Mob and the flunkies and the pet columnists and the spooks and the wartime heroics; his Stephen Rojack was a true prisoner of celebrity.

It is not just that this landscape has already been strip-mined. Part of the fascination with the Kennedys has always been prurient, and Wills is not exempt. The Kennedy administration was sexy, and its sexiness as much as its policies was discussed by the huge army of the knowing. The girls of the thousand days fueled the fantasies of the knowing: Angie Dickinson, Marilyn Monroe, Judith Campbell Exner, who was on loan from Momo Giancana. Wills once studied for the priesthood, which perhaps accounts for what might be called his seminarian's interest in the Kennedys' sexual adventurism. For all his excursions into Montaigne and Chesterton, for all the allusions to Carlyle and Bagehot, it is Mrs. Exner's biography that seems to excite him, and the endless erections and the girls crossed off a list like things to do.

Wills uses Mrs. Exner (who noted that John Kennedy, because of his back, could only perform in the missionary position, with his partner the missionary) and Burton Hersh (whose book Wills never troubles to identify by title) and Mr. and Mrs. Clay Blair the way Mailer used Maurice Zolotow in *Marilyn*—as producers of factoids he can alchemize into meditations. Thus Robert Kennedy could not halt J. Edgar Hoover's crusade against Martin Luther King because Hoover might release information the FBI director had, early in World War II, gathered about a John Kennedy bedmate with Nazi connections. Thus Robert Kennedy could not run forcefully, in 1968, against Lyndon Johnson because Hoover and Johnson knew all about Mrs. Exner and that "damn Murder Incorporated in the Caribbean" and might use it. I have always been impatient with the Hoover factor in the Kennedy equation, and how his secret dossiers allegedly put the brothers at a serious disadvantage that effectively curtailed their freedom of action. Hoover himself did not lead a life free of innuendo. No strangers themselves to muscle and political extortion, the Kennedy brothers could not have been unaware of the stories circulating about the bachelor Hoover and his aide-de-camp, Clyde Tolson, the shared vacations and the lathering of suntan oil each on the other, and the rich possibilities the gossip offered for homosexual blackmail. It need not matter if the stories were true; they could be made to appear so. I suspect that if Hoover had tried to lean on the Kennedys he would have quickly learned that a lecherous philanderer in the White House could play a meaner game of hardball than a putative pansy running the Bureau.

Tumescence as the arbiter of national policy is the plot machinery of trash novels. The imposition of this colorful and vulgar narrative finally makes Wills a prisoner of his own premise, and his book as airless and claustrophobic as the slammers to which he has sentenced the Kennedys. There is no Kennedy success offered, not even an extenuating circumstance. John Kennedy, who did not write *Profiles in Courage*, is compared, to his disadvantage, to Janet Cooke, who made up her Pulitzer Prize-winning *Washington Post* feature. In the Wills telling, there was even some dark purpose in inviting Pablo Casals to the White House; the so-called Kennedy cultural revolution only signified a need to exact an "abject profession of servility" from the Kennedy courtiers.

There is a whiff of the Inquisition here, a high whine from

the pulpit of revisionism, a sermon on every stone, a lesson on every pin. Wills does not accept mitigating evidence and the only defense he allows is the collective sin of the Kennedy forebears. There is no point in arguing that charisma was not invented by John Kennedy, or political deception; no point in claiming that politicians have always acted out of an inflated self-importance and nations out of an unenlightened self-interest, often with beneficial results. This is a kangaroo court and the verdict was in the judge's pocket before the charges on the indictment were read. The end result is that *The Kennedy Imprisonment* becomes just another oddity in the automobile graveyard of Kennedyana, another model, like the Sorensen and the Schlesinger, that future historians can scavenge for parts.

BMOC

It SHOULD be stated at the outset that I have known William F. Buckley, Jr., for twenty-three years, that he published the first free-lance piece I ever wrote (about growing up Irish Catholic in Hartford, Connecticut), that my impending marriage, in 1964, was announced not in *The New York Times* but in the editor's notes column in the *National Review*. In the nineteen years since I last laid eyes on him, we have corresponded fitfully. I count seventeen communiqués from him in my files, many scribbled in haste in red ink ("Pots of love" being his usual valedictory in the 1960s), others typed with the somehow unnerving notation "Dictated in Switzerland, transcribed in New York."

The communications usually arrived with books of his or contained comments on books of mine. Sometimes the comments were trenchant ("Stirring . . . and altogether orthodox," he noted about an admiring book I had written about Cesar Chavez), sometimes generous (adding to his benediction the information that he had recommended the book to someone important like Sol Linowitz), sometimes cagey; he detested the motion picture made from a novel of mine (the one he recommended to Sol Linowitz), but with his voracious generosity of spirit tried to exempt the screenplay, which I wrote, from his good-hearted condemnation of the rest of the exercise.

The last time I saw Mr. Buckley was in 1964 at a Goldwater rally in New York's Madison Square Garden shortly before the Republicans anointed the senator as their presidential candidate against Lyndon Johnson. With various members of his family and functionaries from the *National Review*, Mr. Buckley sat in the $1,000 royal box, conservatism's viceroy regnant, lavishing his dazzling smile on the 18,000 courtiers gathered in the Garden, all of whom, with the possible exception of Senator Goldwater, seemed prepared to kiss the hem of his garment. It was an idolatry that Mr. Buckley gave no sign of thinking either unjust or untoward.

The rally was standard right-wing guff, the level of humor peaking when the late congressman John Ashbrook referred to Walter Lippmann as "Walter Looselippmann." After the rally, there was a party given for the Buckleys and their satraps, one of whom was a genial ex-Communist who could not keep his hands off AWOL servicemen, a situation made unexpectedly poignant by the repeated droll allegations in the Garden that liberals were double-gaited, limp-wristed, and generally so light on their feet they could dance on a charlotte russe. The gentleman in question had stashed his latest find, a youthful marine, in a back bedroom along with the attaché cases, but the gyrene, under the mistaken impression that he was meant to be included in the revelry, kept popping up among the aristocracy of the American right like a stripper jumping out of a birthday cake.

This is the sort of incident for which one will search in vain in *Overdrive*, the latest installment of the long-run Happy Hour that is Mr. Buckley's version of his life. As with *Cruising Speed*, his 1971 excursion along the Buckley Expressway, he sets down the events of a single week, in this instance the Monday to Monday before Thanksgiving 1981. In this eight-day period,

Mr. Buckley gives speeches in Tampa, Toledo, and New York;
tapes two *Firing Line* shows in Louisville; writes three newspaper columns and a piece for *TV Guide* ("Memorable Guests
on *Firing Line*"); attends *Nicholas Nickleby,* a performance of
the New York City Ballet, and a concert by Rosalyn Tureck;
goes sailing twice; gives a luncheon for twenty corporate executives (George Bush, the guest of honor, reneges at the last minute for reasons of state and sends in his stead UN Ambassador
Jeane Kirkpatrick); has David Niven as a weekend house guest;
and decides, in Louisville's Executive West Hotel, to write this
book.

Mr. Buckley set the ground rules: "One, there was to be
no coyness in the matter of who-do-you-know." Construed literally, this charter suggests a narrative propelled only by the charm
of the narrator, and no constitution has ever been given a stricter
construction: Mr. Buckley knows practically everyone* and he
is as discreet as a mother superior. Among those of his huge cast
of characters who are known personally to me there is incidence
of alcoholism, drug addiction, pederasty, pedophilia, adultery,
cuckoldry, and various other manifestations of life's stigmata,
not a hint of which darkens Mr. Buckley's journal. The result
is a truly alarming vision of a life without shadows. In the world
according to Buckley, Gatsby would marry Daisy, Tom Buchanan would find eternal happiness with Jordan Baker, Myrtle
Wilson would open a chic and successful boutique, and Nick
Carraway would become the Republican-Conservative governor
of New York, with William F. Buckley, Jr., as his mentor/
adviser/*éminence blanche.*

The tone is established in the first paragraph:

Gloria brought in my lunch on a tray—two pieces
of whole wheat toast each with tuna fish covered with
some cheese-something my wife Pat had read about

---

* See postscript on pp. 120–122.

somewhere, a salad, a half bottle of Côte Rotie (I remember the wine's name only because it's the one I have in half bottles) and coffee. I leaned back in the big desk chair that reaches to my withers, tucked the napkin under my chin in case bits of tuna oozed out, and looked out at the lawn as I ate.

There is something beguiling about those lines, as there is about much of *Overdrive*. One inhales and becomes giddy on the high octane of Mr. Buckley's personality. He is so sublimely unself-conscious, so "blasphemously happy" with his own life that he wishes to share with his readers what amounts to a 50,000-word advertisement for himself. This is a world stained only by oozings of Pat's tuna thing, a City of God from whence Mr. Buckley dispenses his patronage with almost papal panache.

The art of the published journal, as practiced by Harold Nicolson, say, is that it illuminates the entire social tapestry encompassed by the diarist's personal vision. In Nicolson's diaries, the countless lunches with Sibyl Colefax, Emerald Cunard, and Philip Lothian open up doors that reveal the machinery of abdication and appeasement. What is peculiar about *Overdrive* is that Mr. Buckley does not appear particularly interested in the details of his broad canvas, its vanity fair, or its larger possibilities. *Overdrive* has only one true subject, and that is Mr. Buckley himself. For all his vast acquaintanceship, none of the personalities who crossed his social and psychic horizons that week before Thanksgiving was anything more than a dress extra. Walter Wriston is interchangeable with Huey Newton, Jerry Zipkin with Elmo Zumwalt. Adjectives do the work, rather than incident. "Wonderfully amusing," "marvelously talented," "awesomely sensitive," "young and pretty," "young and resourceful," "young, fresh, enthusiastic and resourceful"—these are the bright, empty phrases of a *Vogue* caption, dropped like a noose around those they are meant to describe.

The spotlight is Mr. Buckley's alone, and he does not blink in its glare. And yet, at stage center, he is really not very giving about himself, except for that sly self-deprecation that comes so easily to the self-infatuated. In his hands, the art of being disarming is a weapon. We learn that he is ambivalent about the ballet, tries to say a rosary before he goes to sleep, has a customized 1978 Cadillac limousine lengthened two extra feet to give him additional leg room, can catnap easily in ten-minute snatches, gives forty-eight lectures a year, loves peanut butter ("I know that I shall never see / A poem lovely as Skippy's Peanut Butter"), has an unlisted telephone number, got paid ($3,000) for his *Playboy* interview, spends every February and March skiing and working in Switzerland. The details are often arresting, but offer no clue about the performer, only about the part he plays.

For what is presented is Mr. Buckley's long-run production of his life, a bus-and-truck show he has perfected over the past thirty years for the country-club constituencies of Louisville and Tampa and Toledo. His stages are the lecture platform, the debater's lectern, the business seminar, the talk show, each perfectly adapted to his style, Henry Higgins as conservative ideologue, all sally and riposte. "It is good to travel aboard a train," he writes about the Orient Express, quoting from a travel piece dashed off for *The New York Times* between midnight and 5 A.M. after a flight from London, "built two years after Lenin died, and fifty-four years after one wishes he had died." He reproves the former editorial-page director of the *Times* for not having a sense of humor, perhaps because he "is understandably melancholy about having to live in a world whose shape is substantially of his own making."

Whereas for most of us the mail is a distraction to be endured, for Mr. Buckley it is a way to keep his trigger finger limber; there is nothing like a gracefully punitive postscript for putting impertinence in its place. He recalls a correspondent from Gettysburg College who had not liked his commencement address, "allowing me to make the obvious reply—namely, that I was hardly surprised, since after all Gettysburg owed its reputation substantially to its historical underestimation of great orations." Always his passion is for the last word. "Sid, the trouble with you is that you find *everybody* innocent," he remarks to Sidney Zion, then a *New York Times* reporter who was claiming someone's innocence. Mr. Zion, no slouch himself at having the last word, seems to have had the tact not to reply, "Except Edgar Smith."

The occasional cloud is wafted off-stage, as if on wires. Mr. Buckley is oblique about his family's difficulties with the Securities and Exchange Commission, which filed a complaint against the Catawba Corporation (owned by Mr. Buckley and his siblings). While specifically exonerating Catawba of fraud, the SEC accepted a consent decree signed by Mr. Buckley's brother acknowledging violations of SEC regulations. "I have a book-length manuscript describing the outrages attendant on my own brush with the SEC," he writes in a letter. "I haven't published the book because my friends tell me it is too goddamn boring, and that part of me which is an editor agrees." He then spends four pages attacking *Time*'s story about the SEC judgment, that part of him which is an editor apparently agreeing that it is never too boring to go after *Time*.

Mr. Buckley is similarly offhand when he recalls once being sentenced to the *Merv Griffin Show* with a bright-eyed young crooner who revealed that he and his wife watched porno movies on their home video recorder. With appropriate irony, he reported this in his column, but since he could not remember the singer's name and was in a rush to get to Fiji and a scuba-diving holiday, he simply called him a "Pat Boone–type." This description earned him a call from Pat Boone's lawyer (the qualifier "type" was lost in transmission to his syndicate, not that it mattered legally; in any case the singer on the show was John Davidson); it cost Mr. Buckley $5,000 to settle. He blithely absolves this libel as an example of "antonomasia" ("the use of a proper name to express a general idea," according to the OED), saying rather too airily that in this instance he meant a "Pat Boone–type" to imply any crooner of the well-scrubbed variety. It is not for Mr. Buckley to admit to an inattentive memory and careless writing when the polysyllabic evasion of "antonomasia" is available.

To recognize such an evasion would be to encourage the self-examination that Mr. Buckley avoids as if it were communism. "I do resist introspection, though I cannot claim to have 'guarded' against it," he writes, "because even to say that would suppose that the temptation to do so was there, which it isn't." Work is introspection's saltpeter. "The search for virtue is probably best drowned out by *commotion,* and this my life is full of. It is easier to stay up late working for hours than to take one tenth the time to inquire into the question whether the work is worth performing."

In the face of all this purposeful commotion, it is instructive to look for literary antecedents. If the Norman Podhoretz of *Making It* can be read as Trollope's arriviste Phineas Finn, with Midge Decter an unlikely Madame Max, then with *Overdrive* we are in the country of *The Good Soldier.* It is a world of surfaces, placid and civilized. The effect is at first glinting and funny, but Mr. Buckley's vision is so hermetically focused on himself that one begins to wonder if under that coat of thin veneer there is anything but another coat of thin veneer. The spontaneous is not valued, because it opens a window of vulnerability. One remembers Mr. Buckley's celebrated television encounter with Gore Vidal. "Crypto Nazi," Mr. Vidal said. "Now listen, you queer," Mr. Buckley replied, spontaneity spurting from him like pus from a boil. "Stop calling me a crypto Nazi or I'll sock you in your goddamn face and you'll stay plastered." This is the true territory of *The Good Soldier.*

Mr. Buckley is an anomaly in American life, a man who

has been made, or who made himself, systematically déclassé. "I never knew I was an Irish Catholic until I ran for mayor of New York," he once told Martin Nolan, then a reporter for the *Boston Globe*. His father made his pile elsewhere, the initial strike in the oil business in Mexico, and having made it set about creating a style. The style was mid-Atlantic patrician, a style that his namesake son further alchemized into patrician celebrity.

Yale was the smithy where this created consciousness was forged. (It is invigorating to speculate how Mr. Buckley might have turned out had he gone to Holy Cross or Seton Hall or any of the more primitive academic stalags of the Irish and the Catholic.) With strenuous Christian energy, he became the quintessential BMOC, the big man on campus, skipping from success to success, from the chairmanship of the *Yale Daily News* (via the minor scandal of a unanimous vote, having cast his own ballot for himself), to Skull and Bones, to *God and Man at Yale*. There always has been a sense of the dominant undergraduate about Mr. Buckley, a triumph of managerial style. His is a BMOC view of life; all good naturally flows to the Bones man.

The undergraduate urbanity never cracks. He is positively jaunty about the suicide of a friend who in life had once threatened to put Yale's first black football captain, Levi Jackson ("amiable and formidable"), on academic probation just before the Princeton game; "I . . . happily assume his tragedy was unrelated to any contrition for what he had done, or almost done, to Levi Jackson and to the Director of Yale Athletics." From John Kenneth Galbraith he dragoons a jacket blurb for his son Christopher's first book, *Steaming to Bamboola*. "Dear Ken," he wires Galbraith. "Tell you what. If you read Christopher's book, I'll take a dive on Thursday" (when Buckley and Galbraith were scheduled to debate Reaganomics). The plug is almost immediately forthcoming, dictated over the telephone by Mr. Galbraith to Mr. Buckley, who then passes it on to his son's publisher. There seems no apprehension that his rendering of this episode might pain either Christopher Buckley or Mr. Galbraith. In the senior society of life, it is what friends are meant to do.

And always he views the world with the amused condescension of the entitled. He drives to Mass with the maids, Rebeca, the "solicitous and fussy Guatemalan," and Olga, "an otherworldly and gay-spirited Ecuadorian," and on the way home discusses with them the mystery of transubstantiation. We are not told how Olga and Rebeca responded to Mr. Buckley, any more than we are told how all those "young, fresh, enthusiastic and resourceful" famous people responded to his ripostes. When it comes to the thoughts of others, Mr. Buckley exercises his droit du seigneur; but the seigneur himself seems distracted and disjointed as he approaches his fifty-eighth birthday. The show has been on the road too long. There have been too many plane trips, too many nights spent in Executive West hotels. Mr. Buckley has spread himself so thin that he has begun to repeat himself, repeatedly. *Overdrive* is *Cruising Speed Redux* as last year's *Atlantic High* is *Airborne Redux*. In the new versions we laugh at the memory of old stories better told. The ambience is "dictated in Switzerland, transcribed in New York." As might be expected, Mr. Buckley is unrepentant. "The unexamined life may not be worth living," he writes, "in which case I will concede that mine is not worth living." He clearly does not believe it, but his is a performance sorely in need of the very examination he refuses to give it.

POSTSCRIPT

MORE OR LESS in order of appearance, the following people turn up in *Overdrive*: Whittaker Chambers, Mortimer Smith,

Evelyn Waugh, Robert Lounsbury, Levi Jackson, William
Sloane Coffin, Jr., Howard Hunt, Charles Frankel, Huey New-
ton, Bernadette Devlin, Harold Macmillan, Jimmy Hoffa, Frank
Stanton, John LeBoutillier, Gordon Liddy, Ronald Reagan,
Nancy Reagan, Ronald Reagan, Jr., Doria Reagan, John Ken-
neth Galbraith, Norman Mailer, Alfred Kahn, Daniel Patrick
Moynihan, Clif White, Marvin Liebman, Ralph Davidson,
Betty Prashker, Hugh Kenner, William Shawn, William Rusher,
John Oakes, A. M. Rosenthal, Punch Sulzberger, James Jackson
Kilpatrick, Allen Weinstein, Rosalyn Tureck, David Oppen-
heim, Merv Griffin, Pat Boone, John Davidson, Norman Lear,
Joe McCarthy, Nelson Rockefeller, Henry Kissinger, Nancy
Kissinger, Carroll O'Connor, Frank Snepp, Stansfield Turner,
Charlton Heston, Frank Shakespeare, Perry Prentice, Estée and
Joseph Lauder, Arlene Croce, Arthur Gelb, Barbara Gelb, Drue
Heinz, Jack Heinz, Ahmet Ertegun, Mica Ertegun, Stringfellow
Barr, Albert Jay Nock, A. Bartlett Giamatti, Irving Kristol, Jef-
frey Hart, James Burnham, David Niven, Queen Elizabeth, the
Duke of Edinburgh, John Simon, Jerry Zipkin, Sidney Zion,
Victor Navasky, Walter Meade, Phil Donahue, Gore Vidal,
Alistair Horne, Gene Shalit, George Will, Sam Vaughan, John
Chamberlain, Schuyler Chapin, Admiral John McCain, Patrick
Buchanan, Roger Fontaine, Elmo Zumwalt, Ellsworth Bunker,
Sam Ervin, Barbara Walters, Roy Cohn, Evan Galbraith, Wil-
frid Sheed, Peter Glenville, Herb Caen, Fernando Valenti,
Michael Novak, Mark Green, Don Hewitt, Louis Auchincloss,
Ralph Nader, Frank Mankiewicz, John Y. Brown, Warren Stei-
bel, Clare Boothe Luce, Thomas Sowell, Spiro Agnew, Robert
Haldeman, Peter Flanigan, Richard Nixon, Dwight Chapin,
Orrin Hatch, Erik von Kuehnelt-Leddihn, Stuart W. Little, the
Prince of Wales, Loel Guinness, Richard Clurman, Shirleykins
(Mrs. Richard Clurman), William Clark, Al Haig, Lee Annen-
berg, Thomas Enders, Edgar Smith, David Belin, Marion Levy,
William Rickenbacker, D. Keith Mano, Martin Nolan, Thomas

Winship, Philip Weld, Carlos Romero Barcelo, Kevin Starr, George Bush, Harvey Shapiro, George Kennan, Pat Brown, Milton Friedman, Frank Borman, Jeane Kirkpatrick, Walter Wriston, Charles Lichtenstein, plus siblings, servants, *National Review* staffers, mother, wife, son, and Rowley the pooch.

New Grub Street

CONSIDER FOR A MOMENT the Richard Avedon photographs of Renata Adler—Adler in a work shirt over a dark turtleneck sweater, a shock of gray hair backlit by the sun, a long braid draped over her right shoulder, the severely planed features of a Renaissance *principessa*. She does not look like a hit woman, but in American literary life today there is no more murderous an adversary. She is not given to equivocation. "Simply, jarringly, piece by piece, line by line, and without interruption, worthless" was her verdict on Pauline Kael's *When the Lights Go Down*. When she was nearing forty, she matriculated at, and graduated from, Yale Law School. "I think it quixotic," I wrote to her after the Kael piece (we have been acquaintances for twenty years; Kael is an aversion we share), "that you go to law school to prepare literary indictments." Attendant to no political theory (*Toward a Radical Middle* is the title she gave an early book), she is obedient in two commandments: Language matters. Words have meaning.

The investigation of an approach to the news in which language matters only insofar as it advances a narrative, in which words have only the meaning that best serves that narrative, is Adler's subject in *Reckless Disregard*, a meditation on the West-

moreland and Sharon libel suits against, respectively, CBS and
Time. The suit by General William C. Westmoreland resulted
from a ninety-minute CBS documentary, *The Uncounted Enemy: A Vietnam Deception*, hosted by Mike Wallace and
produced by George Crile. The broadcast claimed to have discovered, Wallace intoned from the script, "a conspiracy at the
highest levels of American military intelligence"—Westmoreland, having been the U.S. troop commander in Vietnam, took
this to mean himself—"to suppress and alter critical intelligence
on the enemy," the alleged intent being to deceive the public,
the Congress, and Westmoreland's military superiors, up to and
including the commander in chief, Lyndon Johnson. If this be
conspiracy, it is conspiracy at its most sublime.

The Ariel Sharon suit was prompted by a *Time* cover story
on the findings of Israel's Kahan Commission, which investi-
gated the massacres that took place in the Palestinian refugee
camps at Sabra and Shatila after the assassination of Lebanon
president Bashir Gemayel. Implying that its correspondents had
access to an unpublished Appendix B in the Kahan Report,
Time alleged that Sharon, in the magazine's words, "reportedly
told the Gemayels that . . . he expected the Christian forces
to go into the Palestinian refugee camps. Sharon also reportedly
discussed with the Gemayels the need for the Phalangists to
take revenge for the assassination." Now: I am an old *Time*
writer, five years in that salt mine, and my shit detector went
off immediately when I spotted, in two consecutive sentences,
the weasel-word "reportedly," a *Time*-honored hedge against the
possibility that the facts in a given sentence might not hold
up to a reasonably intense scrutiny. To Ariel Sharon, the clear
implication of those sentences was that the Phalangists went
into the camps with his blessing, and that the massacres were
on his hands. He sued.

Adler is not interested in redeeming the reputations either
of Westmoreland, who was perhaps the worst American field

commander since the dawdlers and blunderers who preceded
U.S. Grant, or of Sharon, who carried lightly on his shoulders
thirty years' worth of the most heinous allegations of atrocities
and assorted misbehavior. Rather, she is interested in what happens when a particular kind of story is executed in a particular
kind of way by a particular kind of reporter: the particular kind
of story being one conceived as, and tailored to, a narrative; the
particular method of execution being one that relies on scoops,
confidential sources, and (in Adler's words) "the notion that
what is obtained in secret is most surely true"; and the particular
kind of reporter, one who is perhaps less than entirely compe-
tent, less than entirely honest.

In the manner of I. F. Stone, the reporter she seems most
to admire, Adler goes to the record, nearly 14,000 pages of transcripts from the two trials, plus thousands more pages of pre-
trial depositions, and the records of bench and robing conferences, none of which were generally available until the trials
were over. It is a formidable task to slog through so much documentation, to note the slippages in testimony under oath during
deposition and later in court, to see how a witness's memory
suddenly improves when, under the rule of discovery, his attorneys are ordered to produce, however reluctantly, documents
suggesting the witness was less forthcoming than he might have
been before opposing counsel had access to said documents. Her
style is that of a brief, and at first is all but impenetrable. One
sentence, picked at random, contains a colon, three semicolons,
twenty-three commas, one set of brackets and two pairs of
parentheses. Once mastered, however, the style is lapidary.

Adler is a true hound of heaven. The litany of lies and
evasion from journalists who claim some minimal professional
allegiance to the truth seems to invigorate her. Cravath Swaine
& Moore, the New York law firm that represented both *Time*
and CBS, adopted a litigating strategy of such "mindless ag-
gressiveness," especially in *Sharon,* as to suggest the firm was

well aware it was defending a confederacy of liars. Thomas Barr, who headed the Cravath team defending *Time* against Sharon, was the kind of bullying advocate who in deposition, without a judge present, would try to rattle opposing counsel by calling him "Sonny" and offering such interjections, on the record, as "horseshit" and "Jesus Christ." Once he suggested that a Jewish lawyer's inability to take depositions on Rosh Hashana was "a dodge," a remark that would perhaps pass unnoticed in the Protestant preserves of Meadowcroft Lane in Greenwich, where, according to *Who's Who*, Barr celebrates the Christian holidays.

In Adler's perusal of these details, the two participants who most engage her attention are George Crile and David Halevy, the Israeli correspondent in *Time*'s Jerusalem bureau who provided the source material, such as it was, for *Time*'s allegations about Sharon. Both Crile and Halevy arrived in court with tarnished credentials, each having had his wings clipped, embarrassingly enough, by his own employer. In 1980, *Time* had put Halevy on probation for cooking up a story on Menachem Begin's reputed failing health, a story for which *Time* had to issue a grudging retraction. (In deposition, as Adler notes, *Time* tried to conceal the results of its investigation of Halevy and even that any investigation had taken place, "to a point very near the borderline of legal ethics." Asked if he recalled the contents of Halevy's personnel file, *Time*'s chief of correspondents, Richard Duncan, who had conducted the investigation, swore under oath: "No, I do not," a simple declarative sentence that courts in more fastidious jurisdictions might call perjury.)

CBS, after the Westmoreland broadcast provoked a harsh story refuting its premise and reporting in *TV Guide*, conducted its own internal investigation, directed by the esteemed and very senior Burton Benjamin, an Emmy, Peabody and Overseas Press Club award winner for documentaries he both wrote and produced, as well as former executive producer of the CBS Evening News in the heyday of Walter Cronkite. The resulting Benjamin

Report rebuked Crile for a whole range of distortions and mis-representations, including coaching interviewees who supported the show's thesis, omitting or lying about the availability of those who didn't, and splicing answers onto questions other than those asked.

Adler's portrait of David Halevy, taken from more than eight hundred pages of deposition and six days on the stand, is a comic masterpiece. Halevy is the part Peter Ustinov gets Academy Awards for, the mythic liar who seems to lie for the sheer exhilaration of lying. He had notes, he did not have notes; they were in Manhattan, they were in Israel; he had two prime sources for the Sharon allegation, he had three; he had more than eight secondary sources, he had fewer than fifteen. He lied about his political affiliation, he lied about whether he had ever been involved as a defendant in a criminal proceeding. "A serious newsmagazine, *Time*, and an enormous corporate edifice," Adler writes with awe, ". . . was poised, like an improbable ballerina, on a single toe, David Halevy." Even those *Time* witnesses who had put Halevy on probation now went into contortions to vouch for his bona fides, to the horror, it turned out, of many of his colleagues who had worked with him in the field, but who felt constrained, out of loyalty to their employer, from giving a public and honest evaluation of his trustworthiness. Against her every instinct, Adler seems finally amused by this "rogue witness" and "his apparent readiness to say anything at all, as if factual matters were a thing of barter, or of haggling in a *souk*."

George Crile is another matter. I think it safe to say that Adler sees in him everything she despises in main-chance journalism. On the stand, there was about him, Adler writes, "an aura of the prerogatives of social class"; he was a "derisive, runaway witness," who was "unfazed, even supercilious" when presented with evidence contradicting a prevarication in his testimony. On the days when I watched him testify, Crile reminded me of Tom Buchanan in *The Great Gatsby*, affecting a kind of arrogance so reeking of entitlement that twice the judge was led to reprimand him from the bench. Crile's arrogance seemed misplaced. *The Uncounted Enemy* won him the Benjamin Report; for an earlier CBS documentary, *Gay Power, Gay Politics*, he was censured by the National News Council for editing applause onto a sound track.

"Who *are* those people?" Adler asks about the journalist witnesses in Foley Square. "And why do they consider themselves entirely above the rules?" I can suggest one answer. After watching both trials one day, I told Carl Bernstein that he and Bob Woodward had a lot to answer for, in that Watergate took journalism out of Grub Street, where I suspect it belongs, and made too many journalists into what Adler calls "celebrities bearing facts." The predictable result is that news has slowly alchemized into entertainment. It is easy to blame television for this alchemy, and most print journalists do, even as they aspire to become talking heads on the weekly opinion shows. Far more insidious is the imposition of a narrative line on the news, and in this regard the print media share equal guilt with television. By its very nature, the investigative reporting that became a growth industry after Watergate demands a narrative, with a villain to be brought to account or a conspiracy uncovered. The problem is that news has very few narratives—Watergate was the rare exception—and to wrench events into a dramatic format, with colorful writing and production values, both trivializes and distorts them.

It is ironic that the "villain" in the *Time* case, and the author of the "conspiracy" in the CBS case, emerged from the trials with their tattered reputations enhanced. Westmoreland capitulated in court, but he marches at the head of his forgotten troops in Vietnam parades around the country. In *Sharon*, the jury found *Time*'s story a) defamatory, b) false of the facts, and c) absent malice; because of the absence of malice, it was therefore not per se libelous. But the jury put its distaste for *Time*'s behavior on the record in an extraordinary amplifying statement saying that David Halevy had "acted negligently and carelessly in reporting and verifying the information." "We won, flat-out and going away," Cravath's Barr insisted. I wonder how many such victories *Time* can sustain; any more and the magazine might have to change its name to *Pyrrhus*.

In the meantime, Crile and Halevy have become, in effect, highly paid remittance men, I suspect unemployable except by the corporations that backed them to the limit of the law, even though, on the evidence of internal investigations, neither Crile nor Halevy abided by the standards both CBS and *Time* maintain they require of their staffs. "Better educated than their predecessors," Adler says of Crile and Halevy and their kind, "they were not remarkable for their capacity to reason, or for their sense of language and of the meaning of even ordinary words. Nonetheless, they appeared before the courts not like any ordinary citizens but as though they had condescended to appear there, with their own conception of truth, of legal standards, and of what were to be the rules. . . . What was true and false also seemed, at times, a matter of almost complete indifference to them. Above all, the journalists, as witnesses, looked like people whose mind it had never crossed to be ashamed."

A lethal assessment, and when the book ran, prior to publication, in *The New Yorker*, both *Time* and CBS reacted with fury. "A reckless disregard of the record," George Crile told me. "Orwellian and bewildering." CBS mounted a counterattack in the form of a letter and supplemental memorandum to *The New Yorker*. Prepared by Cravath Swaine & Moore, vetted by George Crile, and signed by Van Gordon Sauter, then president of CBS News, the document accuses Adler of misconduct, misrepresentation, distortion, bias, and personal interest, and suggests that *The New Yorker* "undertake a thorough review of the article," in other words, a Benjamin Report of its own. Under this implied threat of legal action, *The New Yorker* did just that. 'Two things about the CBS-Cravath material were remarkable," Adler wrote in the afterword she prepared for *Reckless Disregard* in response to the CBS demand. "For all their length and characteristically intemperate tone, the memorandum and covering letter did not, upon close examination, find any factual errors at all. . . . The text is virtually identical to what appeared in *The New Yorker*, and the CBS-Cravath harassment did not lead to or require a single change in the manuscript."

What Ader has done in *Reckless Disregard* is to subject the press to the same searching scrutiny it demands the right to focus on others, and the press, or *Time* and CBS, responded in the same way its aggrieved targets usually respond, vide Westmoreland, vide Sharon. The press fervently maintains that issues such as those raised in the two trials should be argued in the court of public opinion. In the abstract, this is a flawless argument, but in reality neither Westmoreland nor Sharon had access to a network or to a mass-circulation magazine. Adler does, and the battle has been joined. The viciousness of the battle gives pause to many: the press is embattled, the press is under siege from an administration and from judges with no particular devotion to the First Amendment—time to circle the wagons; loose lips sink ships. That Adler might have a point is decidedly not the point to make at this time. Which I suspect is precisely the point Renata Adler was trying to make.

Hog Heaven

CLASS HAS ALWAYS BEEN Tom Wolfe's subject. For the past
fifteen years, he has focused his attention on the aristocracies
of the self-made, on the surfers and dopers and car customizers,
on Felicia and Leonard Bernstein, whom he seemed to see as
the first moonwalkers of radical chic. For all his talk about journalism and New Journalism, much of it self-serving, Wolfe has
never really been a journalist. Nor is it meaningful to call him,
as Dwight Macdonald did, a "para-journalist." Reporting to him
has always been a means to a very personal, even unique end.
The novelists he admires—Balzac, Zola, Dickens—were writers
who went out and reported—a socially correct funeral, say, for
Balzac, the infamous Yorkshire boarding schools for Dickens—
and distilled their findings into fiction. Theirs was the method
Wolfe adopted, but not as a novelist. It is perhaps closest to
call him an anthropologist who writes, using reported fact to contemplate the culture and its classes, to note marginal differences
in station and distinction.

To Wolfe's detractors, such scrutiny is a frivolous enterprise in a world under siege from forces, natural and otherwise,
gone out of control. This is the same set of mind that dero-
gates the soft sections of *The New York Times*—"Living" and

"Home" and "Weekend"—as frivolous, entirely overlooking the possibility that the mere presence of these sections suggests at least as much about the society as all those endless column inches on the energy crisis or the opinions on Teddy Kennedy punched out three times a week by the grandees on the Op-Ed page. The clues to a culture are in its style, and Wolfe has always been a creature of style.

As if to make this point unavoidable, he took unto himself a style. There were the white suit and the white socks with clocks and the hat that looked as if it had been lifted from the head of a Marseille gangster. There was the complexion as pale as a loaf of Wonder Bread. In fact he looked like nothing so much as a male Edith Sitwell. He used language not to explain but to distort, to create an illusion, a kind of verbal impressionism, each paragraph a fun-house mirror. "At about the age of thirteen, as I recall," he said at the Hopwood lecture he gave in 1978 at the University of Michigan, "I became intrigued by words that began with 'j.' They looked marvelous to me. 'Jaded.' 'Jejune.' I didn't even know how to pronounce 'jejune'; in fact, to this day I have never heard anyone use the word in conversation, but I put it in every chance I had. . . . Pretty soon it became a noun as well as an adjective. 'The jaded jejune of his hopes,' that sort of thing, and finally it became a verb as well. People were jejuning each other all over the place."

Worse yet, this parvenu refused to be a recipient of received wisdom, another clone of the liberal consensus. Wolfe was a Southerner not burdened by his Southernness, a Southerner who did not wish, as Elizabeth Hardwick, another Southerner, once said she wished, to become a New York Jewish Intellectual. The New York Jewish Intellectual, however, did not escape his attention, and he was not above doing a little jejuning about the New York Jewish Intellectual's habitat. "His is an apartment of a sort known as West Side Married Intellectual," he wrote in "Mauve Gloves & Madmen, Clutter & Vine." "The rooms are big, the layout is good, but the moldings, cornices, covings, and chair rails seem to be corroding. Actually they are merely lumpy from too many coats of paint over the decades, and the parquet sections of the floor have dried out and are sprung loose from one another. . . . The building has a door-man but no elevator man, and on Sundays the door is manned by a janitor in gray khaki work clothes."

With that same cold eye, Wolfe fastened on the new elites of the social frontier. Whatever the endeavor out there on the social ne plus ultra, there were those who did it better, who had the right stuff, the ineffable quality of excellence. Baby Jane Holzer, the girl of the year, was one with Big Daddy Ed Roth, the car customizer, and they were both one with Phil Spector, the first tycoon of teen, and with the margraves and margravines of radical chic. Always Wolfe was interested in why the cream rose to the top. That the stuff may have curdled and soured was of little interest to him. He was an anthropologist who had not lost faith in his method. The tensile strength of molybdenum and the color of the copy paper at *The New Yorker* were for him of equal importance. *Why did things work?* That was always Wolfe's question.

This mechanical engineer of class had the ability to in-furiate, to drive otherwise sane and sensible people clear around the bend. Renata Adler once seriously considered pouring a can of tomato soup over Wolfe's head during a symposium at which they were both panelists, but reticence prevailed over Dada intentions. (Years later I asked Renata Adler how she had pro-posed to open the can. She replied matter-of-factly that she had a can opener in her bag along with the can.)

The question remains why Wolfe was like catnip to so many people. There was of course his instinct for self-promotion, the screeds about the New Journalism and the Death of the Novel. And then he did poach on the sacred burial grounds of *The New Yorker*. And he was in no small part responsible for the social devaluation of the Black Panther Party. But all these social irritants beg the question. The answer is, I think, simple: Wolfe has never sought a passport, visa, or green card into the literary life. He was an outsider and content to remain one. There lately has been an attempt on the part of his more antic admirers to cloak him in the mantle of an American Céline, an attempt both wrong and misguided. Tom Wolfe is unique. He is also very good.

Which brings me to *The Right Stuff*.

In *The Right Stuff*, Wolfe observes the most rarefied aristocracy of all, that flying fraternity that has skipped through the sound barrier into space, the men who circumnavigated and finally walked on the moon. Theirs was a style he found transcendent, and from it he concocted a theory that bravery can only flourish in a social milieu or context where there is no honorable alternative to it. "Not bravery in the simple sense of being willing to risk your life . . . any fool can do that." No; the bravery that enables a man to sit in a metal firecracker, a roman candle with 367,000 pounds of thrust—and do it again and again and again "with an uncritical willingness to face danger." This truly was "the ineffable quality," the right stuff.

The metaphysics here get a little misty, since, for Wolfe, Baby Jane Holzer and Big Daddy Ed Roth and Phil Spector and Felicia and Leonard Bernstein also had some ineffable quality, the right stuff, but it had to do with style, not bravery. It is on the special style of the astronauts' bravery where Wolfe is most precise, for there he is on that social turf where he has staked his claim. The high priests of the right stuff were the test pilots from whose numbers most of the original astronauts were drawn. They were unknown and underpaid, at peace in a world whose "holy coordinates" were "Flying & Drinking" and "Drinking & Driving" and, when the little woman had her back turned, "Driving & Balling." Wolfe puts everything in its slot, the low pay and the hardscrabble bases and the military housing furnished with the detritus of overseas tours. There is the officer who knocks on the door after a husband has crashed, "a pillar of coolness . . . bearing the bad news on ice, like a fish." There is Charles Yeager, the personification of the right stuff, the first man to break the sound barrier, and he did it with ribs broken in a drunken midnight horseback ride a few days before the flight, and no, he did not bother to tell the flight surgeon, that would have been the wrong stuff.

Wolfe describes it all, even death, with relish. "Burned beyond recognition" was the "artful euphemism" for a pilot who had "crunched" or "augered in," for a body that looked

> like an enormous fowl that has burned up in a stove, burned a blackish brown all over, greasy and blistered, fried, in a word, with not only the entire face and all the hair and the ears burned off, not to mention all the clothing, but also the *hands* and *feet*, with what remains of the arms and legs bent at the knees and elbows and burned into absolutely rigid angles, burned a greasy, blackish brown . . . this *ornamentum* of some mother's eye . . . reduced to a charred hulk with wings and shanks sticking out of it.

It did not seem to matter to these aristocrats that the Navy's actuaries had figured that, given twenty years of military flying with no combat, the chances of a fatal crash were one in four. In their gospel, "the figures were averages, and averages applied only to those with average stuff." Out there on the salt flats and high desert and low-rent coastal barrens where planes were tested, the isolation engendered a certain Junkers mentality. "They looked upon themselves as men who lived by higher standards of behavior than civilians, as men who were the bearers and protectors of the most important values of American life . . . who maintained a sense of honor while civilians lived by opportunism and greed."

It was to these few of the test-pilot fraternity that the call went for volunteers for the Mercury program in 1959. Sputnik was in the air, and so was panic: the phrases "national extinction" and "a race for survival" were abroad in the land. "The Communists," said Lyndon Johnson, the Senate majority leader, "have established a foothold in space." Those picked for the Mercury program would in effect be American kamikazes who would blast the Russians from that foothold—kamikazes because the sad and public fact was that our test rockets kept blowing up on the launch pad, live and in living color.

Many test pilots were skeptical of the whole enterprise, not because of the danger but because each Mercury mission commander would essentially be a "lab rat," not a pilot, controlled by scientists and engineers on the ground; a "redundant component," or what the pilots called "Spam in a can."

> An experienced zombie would do just fine. In fact considerable attention had been given to a plan to anesthetize or tranquilize the astronauts, not to keep them from panicking, but just to make sure they would lie there peacefully with their sensors on and not do something that would ruin the flight. . . . There was very little action that an astronaut could take in a Mercury capsule, other than abort the flight and save his own life. So he was not being trained to fly the capsule. He was being trained to ride in it.

To the true possessors of the right stuff, who perhaps lacked a sense of history, whatever their moxie, this was "a Larry Lightbulb scheme," a job for the second team. On the whole the top test pilots did not volunteer for Mercury. In some inchoate way, the fliers who did volunteer had that sense of history, the sense that their predecessors who had broken the sound barrier were "already the old guys, the eternal remember-whens." The volunteers were rigorously tested, physically and psychically, probed and prodded and scanned. When their sperm needed to be counted, they conjured up breasts and pudenda and belted their members for the United States of America. Their rebellion took the form of a Mexican dinner the night before a stool analysis, which the next morning produced a bolus as hard as a moon rock, studded with jalapeño pepper seeds, neatly tied with a bow.

It is with the seven who were finally chosen—Carpenter, Cooper, Glenn, Grissom, Schirra, Shepard, and Slayton—that Wolfe is at his best. John Glenn set the tone for the seven at the first press conference: God-fearing, family-loving, my country 'tis of thee. However bewildering this characterization might have seemed to the others (Gordon Cooper was separated from his wife and Virgil Grissom was hard put to find the odd weekend to spend at home; Alan Shepard was probably a "stone atheist"), they were quick enough to see that the "halo effect" was what the public wanted, and halos were what the public was going to get.

The press—"that last Victorian Gent"—was more than willing to go along; there was an uneasy feeling that the seven were a suicide squad in the space race, that year's moral equivalent of war. *Life* coughed up $500,000 (the moral equivalent here was Charles Lindbergh selling his story to *The New York Times* prior to his Paris run), and the photograph of the astronauts' wives on the magazine's cover perfectly defined the terms preferred by the press. "*Life* had retouched the faces of all of them practically down to the bone. Every suggestion of a wen, a hickie, an electrolysis line, a furze of mustache, a bag, a bump . . . a rogue cilia of hair . . . had disappeared in the magic of photo retouchings." Marge Slayton's divorce seemed to vanish from the record and Annie Glenn's "ferocious jackhammer" stammer filtered through the machine as "a hesitation in her speech." For the astronauts and their families, there would be no "zits, hickies, whiteheads, blackheads, gopheads, goobers, pips, acne trenches, boil volcanoes, candy-bar pustules."

In short, the astronauts were in hog heaven, and I can

think of no writer in America better equipped than Wolfe to describe hog heaven. There they were, lionized as few pilots in history had been lionized, "beamed upon by every sort of congressman, canned-food distributor, Associated Florists board chairman, and urban renewal speculator, not to mention the anonymous little cookies with their trembling little custards who simply materialized around you at the Cape." The rule at Cape Canaveral was no wives. Instead there were Werner von Braun's Germans "pummeling the piano . . . and singing the 'Horst Wessel Song.'" And the girls, "with stand-up jugs and full sprung thighs and conformations so taut and silky that the very sight of them practically pulled a man into the delta of priapic delirium," toting up the astronauts like notches on a gun.

John Glenn was not amused. He called the others together and told them that with all America watching they had best keep clear of that delta of delirium; Alan Shepard told him to buzz off, not to foist his Sunday school piety on them. At best, behind their public mask of civility, the astronauts were like seven warring nations at a peace conference, and most found John Glenn a little hard to take. He was the favorite of the press, the media's "likely choice" to make the first flight, all those freckles and the Tom Sawyer face covering up "four centuries of dissenting Protestant fervor." He took to the PR and the politicking, even to the point of trying to get Alan Shepard kicked off the first Mercury mission and replaced by himself. He hit the road like an evangelist, gladhanding every spacecraft supplier, and when he got home he would "write cards to workers he had met on the assembly line, giving them little 'attaboys,' as if they were all in this together, partners in the great adventure, and he, the astronaut, would never forget his, the welding inspector's, beaming mug."

No one has described the new career military so well as Wolfe: the resentful wives, the low pay, the sniffing after perks and goodies, the sense of living not in a house but in housing. At Cocoa Beach, Virgil ("Gus") Grissom and Donald ("Deke") Slayton "in their Ban-Lon shirts and baggy pants . . . reminded you . . . of those fellows from the neighborhood . . . as they head off to the Republic Auto Parts store for a set of shock absorber pads so they can prop up the 1953 Hudson Hornet on some cinderblocks and spend Saturday and Sunday underneath it beefing up the suspension."

John Kennedy shows up to co-opt the astronauts, for all the world acting as if Camelot materialized the moment Alan Shepard splashed down safely. Lyndon Johnson sits in a limousine calling his aides "pansies, cows, gladiolas," because they can't get him and the TV boys in to see Annie Glenn, this *housewife,* and the reason Annie Glenn will not let the vice president in is her ferocious jackhammer stammer; she has this storehouse of phrases for public occasions—"Of course" and "Certainly" and "I think so" and "Wonderful"—and after that her face contorts and her tongue is an obstacle course, and not even for Lyndon Johnson will she implode over three networks. Even Sally Rand, as if fresh from the 1933 Chicago World's Fair, turns up to strip for the astronauts at a noontime July Fourth cookout and cocktail party for 5,000 in Houston, her flesh "looking like the meat of a casaba melon in the winter," the Virgin Mary of hog heaven shaking "her ancient haunches . . . in an absolutely baffling blessing over it all."

This is ripe stuff, the right stuff, you might say, and it has about as much to do with space as Wolfe's Panthers piece had to do with civil rights. Wolfe is interested in these astronauts for the same reason he was interested in the Bernsteins and in the surfers and in Baby Jane Holzer and in Big Daddy Ed Roth: because they had a panache, a style that, in the case of the astronauts, gave meaning to the low pay and the fiberboard walls. Wolfe has allowed, in an interview in *The Washington Post,* an essential lack of interest in space itself, and this is clear when he is dealing with the unedited transcripts of flight. His gift depends upon observation, and when he is forced to rely on research he is like a predator without his teeth. He gums the transcripts down all but undigested; the flights pile atop one another, one barely distinguishable from the next. Alan Shepard needs to urinate and is forced to do it in his space suit. Virgil Grissom loses his capsule. John Glenn zips into orbit, and it is tactless to mention that Yuri Gagarin did it first. Scott Carpenter comes down 250 miles off course and is effectively eighty-sixed from the program. A heart murmur scrubs Deke Slayton, Walter Schirra is perfect, and Gordon Cooper's mission is hairy. It begins to seem like one long countdown; hypoxia sets in.

The problem is compounded when Wolfe leaves hog heaven and heads for the real one, when he starts to get mystical about the nature of bravery, invoking God and humanity. Wolfe always has had difficulty with abstractions. His style begins to scratch and strain when he goes after the mystical High C. It is as if he does not trust his eye, as if he must invest his findings with an importance, an Ultimate Truth, beyond what they need to carry. What the right stuff really is, finally, is the Code of the West decked out in a bubble helmet and a space suit, Johnny Ringo at 125,000 feet.

It is an "I've-got-it-you-haven't" conditioned response, one-upmanship at Mach 3, 4, and 5; a style but not a transcendent one. "Courage" and "heroism" and "the nation's need for heroes" are abstractions, and all the abstractions provide here is a somewhat rickety frame on which Wolfe can hang his observations on the details of class and style and the marginal differences of excellence. It is in the details, not the abstractions, that Wolfe finds his subject, and it is one that he owns.

REMFs

MEMORIAL DAY 1986. Laying a wreath at the Tomb of the Unknown Soldier at Arlington National Cemetery, President Ronald Reagan paid special attention, in his remarks, to "the boys of Vietnam . . . who fought a terrible and vicious war without enough support from home. . . . They chose to be faithful. They chose to reject the fashionable skepticism of their time. They chose to believe and answer the call of duty."

Ronald Reagan was adopting for his own ends one of the enduring conservative myths of the Vietnam War, that never were so many betrayed by so few. It has become a commonplace in the conservative canon to compare the combat hardships endured by the troops in the line with the cowardice of the military deserters in the field and the draft resisters at home. The truth, as Lawrence Baskir and William Strauss make painfully clear in *Chance and Circumstance*, is a good deal more ambiguous. In what Lawrence Baskir and William Strauss call the "Vietnam era"—that is, between August 7, 1964, when the Senate passed the Gulf of Tonkin Resolution, and March 29, 1973, when the last U.S. combat forces left Vietnam—26,800,000 American men came of draft age. Of that number, there were 570,000 apparent draft evaders. Another 15,410,000—

or 57.5 percent—were "deferred, exempted, or disqualified," one of whom, on medical grounds, was Ronald Reagan's eldest son.

Class was always the domestic issue during the Vietnam War, never communism. Vietnam was the first conflict in the nation's history—although I doubt the last—fought by the American version of a Hessian class, a constituency of the dispossessed from the skid rows of the national dream, from the Appalachian hollows and the exhausted farms and the red-lined areas on the urban maps. What is astonishing about the social history of the Vietnam War is not how many people avoided it, but how many could not and did not.

At the peak of the conflict, draftees were getting killed at twice the rate of enlistees, with the result that avoiding the draft became the preoccupation of an entire male generation, or at least that part of it which had the means and the wit to manipulate the Selective Service System to its advantage. Three years after the pullout of American combat troops, Baskir and Strauss conducted a survey, under the auspices of the Ford Foundation and Notre Dame University, of 1,586 men who had been eligible for the draft during the war. "Three quarters of those who never served admitted they had tried to avoid the draft," their study showed. "A majority—55 percent—believed the action they took may have been responsible for keeping them out of the military."

Evading military service has a long history in American life. During the Civil War, Union conscripts could buy a substitute for $300; in the South, plantation owners could keep their sons home under the so-called 20-Nigger Law, which exempted one overseer for every twenty slaves. So many registrants had their teeth pulled to avoid induction during World War I that the War Department had to warn dentists publicly that they were liable for prosecution for abetting draft dodging. Only World War II, which mobilized ten million draftees, could by any stretch of the imagination be called a people's war.

The men "who fought and died in Vietnam," write Baskir

and Strauss, "were primarily society's 'losers,' the same men who got left behind in schools, jobs, and other forms of social competition." In other words, a rainbow coalition of black, brown, and redneck who, according to the Notre Dame survey, were "about twice as likely as their better-off peers to serve in the military, go to Vietnam, and see combat." According to a 1966 report, they note, a mentally qualified white male was 50 percent more likely to fail his preinduction physical than his black counterpart.

The documentation presented by Baskir and Strauss, and by Myra MacPherson in *Long Time Passing* is relentless. A survey conducted by Congressman Alvin O'Konski of one hundred draftees in his northern Wisconsin district showed that not one came from a family with an annual income of over $5,000. Another survey, in 1965–66, indicated that college graduates made up only 2 percent of all inductees. Of the 1,200 men in the Harvard class of 1970, only fifty-six served in the military, just two in Vietnam. People disposed toward the war showed no more inclination to serve than those with antiwar attitudes. "A 1970 report showed that 234 sons of senators and congressmen came of age since the United States became involved in Vietnam," MacPherson writes.

> More than half—118—received deferments. Only 28 of that 234 were in Vietnam. Of that group, only 19 "saw combat." Only one, Maryland Congressman Clarence Long's son, was wounded. . . . No one on the House Armed Services Committee had a son or grandson who did duty in Vietnam. Student deferments were shared by sons and grandsons of hawks and doves alike. Senators Burdick, Cranston, Dodd, Goldwater, Everett Jordan and McGhee had sons who flunked the physical.

II-S was the magic classification that guaranteed deferment for college students. In the Vietnam era, male college enroll-

ment averaged 6 to 7 percent higher than in the years immediately preceding. Graduate schools were also II-S draft sanctuaries
until 1968, when the Selective Service lifted this exemption. An
exception was made for divinity schools, which of course in-
stantly transformed theology into a popular graduate academic
discipline. The Harvard Divinity School attracted David Stockman. "Once I went to divinity school I never worried about the
draft that much," Stockman told MacPherson. In 1981, when
he became Ronald Reagan's director of the budget, Stockman
moved to cut, as "a dispensable expenditure," funding for Vietnam Vet Centers, in the process calling Vietnam veterans "a
noisy interest group."

When the potential draftees finally reported for their preinduction physicals, approximately half were rejected, a figure
two to three times the rejection rate for the NATO allies. There
was, among those with sufficient motivation, a virtual pandemic
of asthma, bad backs, trick knees, flat feet, and skin rashes.
Hawks who would later describe the war as a noble cause were
no more immune to this scourge than doves; Patrick Buchanan
had a bad knee, Elliott Abrams a bad back, Congressman Vin
Weber asthma. Other hawks, such as Texas Senator Phil Gramm,
sought academic deferments so that they might learn, and better
warn the nation, about those evil empires threatening the republic; they were quicker, in other words, to pledge allegiance
to the flag than they were to serve it. Congressman Newt Gingrich told Jane Mayer of *The Wall Street Journal* that Vietnam
was "the right battlefield at the right time," but when asked
why he had not served, Gingrich replied, "What difference
would I have made? There was a bigger battle in Congress than
in Vietnam." In fact, Gingrich was not elected to Congress
until 1979, having spent his draft-age years during the war earning a baccalaureate, master's, and Ph.D. at Emory and Tulane,
and teaching at West Georgia College. In 1988, he maintained
that not actively serving in the military during the Vietnam

years was a "prudently patriotic" reaction to the mismanagement of the war by two Democratic administrations. Gingrich, of course, is the moral equivalent of a bowel movement, and his ex post facto concept of prudent patriotism only a particularly aromatic definition, and defense, of cowardice.

"The preinduction examination process," Baskir and Strauss write, "rewarded careful planning, guile, and disruptive behavior." Draft counselors seized on a loophole in the law that gave every registrant the right to choose the site of his preinduction physical. "For most of the war," Baskir and Strauss say,

> Butte, Montana, was considered an easy mark for anyone with a letter from a doctor, and Little Rock, Arkansas, for anyone with a letter from a psychiatrist. Beckley, West Virginia, was well-known for giving exemptions to "anyone who freaked out." . . . By far the most popular place to go for a preinduction physical was Seattle, Washington. In the latter years of the war, Seattle examiners separated people into two groups: those who had letters from doctors and psychiatrists, and those who did not. Everyone with a letter received an exemption, regardless of what the letter said.

For those who did not wish to chance the preinduction physical, however many medical affidavits loaded the dice in their favor, the reserves and the National Guard beckoned. In 1969 and 1970, the reserves and the Guard welcomed 28,000 more college-educated recruits than were enlisted or drafted into all the other services combined. In 1968, the Guard had a waiting list of 100,000 men; one Pentagon study showed that 71 percent of all reserve and 90 percent of all Guard enlistees volunteered in order to avoid the draft. The passage of time, however, has tempered that invigorating display of honesty, especially for those embarking on a career in the public sector. Dan Quayle, scion of an Indiana and Arizona newspaper dynasty—the *Indianapolis Star* and the *Arizona Republic,* among others—joined the Indiana Guard in 1969, with the help of retainers working for the family newspapers who were only too happy to curry favor with their employers. After George Bush picked him to be his vice-presidential running mate, Quayle at first said that he joined the Guard because he wanted to go to law school. When that entertaining notion did not play, Quayle changed his tune to say he had "problems" with the "no-win policy aspect" in the way the war was conducted, presumably by the Johnson administration, a statement that exhibited a devotion to the situation ethics most conservatives profess to abhor. It should also be noted that when Quayle joined the Guard, Richard Nixon was president.

The Guard was, furthermore, a force in which Jim Crow appeared to be the recruiting sergeant; only one percent of the total strength of the Guard nationwide was black. Professional athletes were particularly attracted to the reserves and Guard. While the magnates of professional sports have always had an almost mystical devotion to the flag, this devotion, during the Vietnam War, did not extend to volunteering their athlete assets to get shot in defense of it. Ten members of the Dallas Cowboys were assigned to one National Guard division, the backfield of the Philadelphia Eagles to the same reserve unit. The chances that Lyndon Johnson would mobilize all or most of the 1,040,000 men in the Guard or the reserves were always minimal. These were the sons of the white, the well-to-do, the well educated, and the better connected, Johnson's political core, and to activate them would have brought the war into the very venues whose support Johnson most feared losing. In all, only 37,000 men from this manpower pool were called up, and of these, just 15,000 went to Vietnam.

The army of the underprivileged that fought was abandoned not only by the antiwar left but also, Ronald Reagan's revisionism notwithstanding, by the prowar right, whose rhetorical support for the conflict exceeded its interest in fighting it. The marine platoon on Hill 10, near Da Nang, that William Broyles took command of in November 1969, is a case in point. "I have fifty-eight men," Broyles wrote in his diary at the time. "Only twenty have high school diplomas. About ten of them are over twenty-one." Broyles goes on: "The average age of the infantryman in World War II was twenty-six; in Vietnam it was nineteen. . . . In another platoon there was a lance corporal who was twenty-four. He was called Pops." The service records of Broyles's men on Hill 10 similarly indicate a platoon of the socially disenfranchised: "Address of father: unknown. Education: one or two years of high school. Occupation: laborer, pecan sheller, gas station attendant, Job Corps. Kids with no place to go. No place but here." With some bitterness, Broyles remarks:

> It was not a privilege to be able to fight; it was instead evidence that one had failed to understand how to manipulate the system, as if anyone not smart enough to get a deferment or at least a job in the rear was too dumb to do anything but carry a rifle.

William Broyles is one of the three people I know who served in Vietnam.[1] In his book *Brothers in Arms*, Broyles tries to conjugate his feelings about the war, about the men he fought with, the men he fought against, and the men who did not go. "I was drafted at the age of twenty-four," he writes, "and I had

1. I am aware of only one person who was killed there, Lieutenant Ronald Maclean, a young man I had never met but whose parents I knew slightly, and when I went to the Vietnam Memorial in Washington, his was the only name I could think to look up. I also looked to see if any Dunnes had been killed; there were two, Sergeant Gerard Joseph Dunne from New York, killed at 21 on August 25, 1968, and Corporal Paul Herbert Dunne from Newton, Massachusetts, killed at 22 on November 19, 1969, neither kin as far as I know. That I had to do this is a comment on the middle class and its relation to the Vietnam War.

spent the previous three years doing my best to avoid military service." A graduate of Rice University in Texas, he won a Marshall Scholarship to Worcester College, Oxford. The BBC was his link to Vietnam, the television images from Hue during the 1968 Tet offensive his crucible. "Those boys were like the friends I had grown up with in a small town in Texas," he writes. "They were fighting a war while my friends from college and I went on with our lives. I thought my country was wrong in Vietnam, but I began to suspect that I was using that conviction to excuse my selfishness and my fears."

He took his preinduction physical in Newark, one of four whites and 146 blacks. "The Army was their escape from the Newark ghetto," Broyles writes. "They wanted in, not out." Once in the Marine Corps, he expected, because of his educational advantages, to spend his three-year tour studying Chinese at the language school in Monterey, then translating documents in Washington. Instead he was commissioned as a platoon leader. On his way to Vietnam, he briefly went over the hill, packing away his uniform and leaving Norton Air Force Base, his port of embarkation. He saw his refusal to go as a moral gesture against the war, but on reflection realized this was a pipe dream, that no one would really care. He went back to Norton, put on his uniform, and shipped out to Da Nang, finally landing on Hill 10.

The teenagers in his platoon had no middle-class compunctions about obeying the commands of their new shavetail. "No way, José," a nineteen-year-old Cajun point man responded when Lieutenant Broyles ordered him into a tunnel where an enemy soldier was thought to be hiding. A nineteen-year-old squad leader also refused. Broyles went in himself. "Inside the tunnel poisonous snakes might be hung from the ceiling," Broyles says about this insidious and terrifying underground combat. "A pit might lie beneath the floor, lined with sharpened stakes—perhaps with poison on the tips. . . . In Vietnam the monster really was under the bed, the tunnel really did suddenly open in your bedroom wall."

And yet. "It is well that war is so terrible, or we should grow too fond of it," Robert E. Lee said to General James Longstreet at Fredericksburg. Broyles's fondness is at times palpable. He talks about "the soft, seductive touch of the trigger" and the "aesthetic elegance [of] a Huey Cobra helicopter or an M-60 machine gun. They are without artifice, form as pure function." He is disdainful of napalm:

> Greatly overrated, unless you liked to watch tires burn. Far superior was white phosphorus . . . wreathing its target in intense and billowing white smoke, throwing out glowing red comets trailing brilliant white plumes. . . . It would transform human flesh into Roman candles. . . . I knew that, but I still marveled, transfixed. I had surrendered to an aesthetic divorced from that crucial quality of empathy that lets us feel the suffering of others.

Often it seemed to Broyles that his men were more united against their fellow Americans in the cushier logistical billets than against the enemy they were supposed to be fighting. In 1968, at the height of the American involvement, only 12 percent of the troops in Vietnam were assigned to line units, as opposed to 39 percent in World War II. On Red Beach, near Da Nang, there was an air force base with its own massage parlor, while on another beach GIs drew combat pay as lifeguards. Soldiers ran movie theaters and ice cream parlors, and in Saigon there was a Vietnamese officers' club where girls crouched under every table, available for fellatio. Broyles quickly assumed the combat marine's contempt for anyone not a marine. "If your mission makes sense, you might as well be in the army or a civilian," Broyles writes, "not that the two are all that different." His men quickly taught him who the enemy was. Shortly after his arrival on Hill 10, Broyles received a frantic radio message that the American rear in Da Nang was under rocket attack by the North

Vietnamese. The response from his platoon was not exactly what he expected. They emerged from their hooches, cheering and shouting, "Get those REMFs." REMFs was military slang for "rear echelon motherfuckers."

This was an army of the night, a fact Broyles never forgot. He remains fervent in his belief that "the My Lai massacre was a result of the system of privilege that kept educated young men out of the military. William Calley . . . was a dropout and a loser. He should never have been an officer, and would not have been had his more talented peers been drafted." Nor will Broyles accept the common rationale for Calley's behavior: "Almost every American who fought in Vietnam went through the booby traps, the ambushes, the frustrations of never seeing the enemy—what Calley's platoon had been through before the massacre. With only a handful of exceptions in a long war, they didn't respond by slaughtering unarmed old men, women and children." A marine in Broyles's platoon murdered a Vietnamese pimp because a whore in the pimp's string had given him the clap. Broyles turned the marine over to military authorities. He was tried, convicted, and sent to prison for twenty years.

For those in power, Broyles writes, Vietnam was not a war, "it was a policy . . . an item on the agenda." It was "fought not for a hill or a bridge or a capital, or even for a cause; it was fought to keep score." The grunt in the field was also keeping score, and the score he hoped to reach was 365, or the number of days in-country before he was rotated home to the States. "It didn't matter if the war was going badly or if your unit was in trouble," Broyles writes.

> When your time was up, your war was over. . . . The
> ordinary infantryman reasonably thought that the war
> wouldn't be won in a year, so why try. . . . We had
> our short-timer's calendars. Every night we marked off
> another day. That was our goal. . . . There was no

single goal in Vietnam; there were 2.8 million goals, one for every American who served there. And in the end the nation's goal became what each soldier's had been all along: to get out of Vietnam.

In late 1970, Lieutenant Broyles got out. Fourteen years later, by now a man of affairs who had an entry in *Who's Who* and who had been the editor of *Newsweek* (handpicked for the post by Katharine Graham) and invited to the White House to attend Ronald Reagan's private screening of *E.T.*, Broyles went back. The impetus to return came at the dedication, in 1982, of the Vietnam Memorial. "I went back to Vietnam to answer the question, 'What does it mean to go to war?'" he writes. "I set out to see this long defeat from a different perspective—the winner's." Over the four weeks he was in Vietnam, Broyles traveled nearly three thousand miles, talking to soldiers who had fought, as he had, in the paddies and mountains of the south, and trying to find out from their generals "why they won and we lost."

A certain Occidental hubris remains. Like most Americans, Broyles finds it remarkable that the victors still occupy a landscape he calls "pre-industrial," its beat the rhythm of the rice harvest rather than the demands of technology. The realization slowly takes hold that bombing Vietnam back to the stone age would not have pushed it back all that far. Its mechanisms for confronting the twentieth century tend to bewilder the visiting Westerner. Vietnamese fighter pilots learn to fly jets before they learn to drive a car. At one hospital in Hanoi, cardiologists were using the latest advances in Dutch ultrasound equipment to monitor rare cases of left atrial myxoma, "but there was no blood in the lab refrigerator. The patients lay two to a bed in their own clothes," and "several pieces of simple equipment stood dusty and inoperable." The secret to Vietnam, Broyles is told by Do Xuan Oanh, one of the country's leading experts on America, "is in the songs of the buffalo boys." Broyles asks what the songs are like. "Like Bob Dylan's 'Subterranean Homesick Blues,'" Xuan Oanh replies. Xuan Oanh, who translated *Huckleberry Finn* into Vietnamese, says that his favorite American writers are Mark Twain, Jack London, Ernest Hemingway, and Sidney Sheldon, the last because "he is very good on the excesses of capitalism."

The visitor interested in opinions about the war must first endure the standard responses of the communist liturgy, "more or less like grace before a meal"; they had fought with the people, we had fought against them; their cause was just; ours was not; imperialism was destined to be banished from the earth. Only when the litany was finished were Broyles's questions addressed. In retrospect he came to understand, in a way he never had on Hill 10, that for his former foes "the war was their home." Old soldiers showed him the scars from wounds received at the hands of the Japanese, the French, the Americans. In Phat Diem, he met a Communist Party official who did not see her husband for the nine years he was fighting in the south, and heard from him only once, by letter in 1969. The stories multiplied at every stop, and with them the sense that victory or death had been the only dates on the enemy's short-timer calendars.

"Time was on our side," General Nguyen Xuan Hoang told Broyles. "We did not have to defeat you; we only had to avoid losing." American technological superiority was made irrelevant in a war in which, as Broyles puts it, "our enemies steeled themselves to use men as we used bombs." The demented strategy of the body count played right into the enemy's hand. "Our logic was the logic of the trenches in World War I," Broyles writes. "If you kill enough of your enemy's troops, sooner or later he will have to realize the price is too high and give up. But while the logic might hold true in the rational world of war game theory, it had no appreciable effect on our enemy in this war. In fact, it proved true, but only for us—we got to the point where our losses were too high and we quit." Ho Chi Minh had stated the equation to the French in 1946: "Kill ten of our men and we will kill one of yours; in the end, it is you who will tire." The French tired, and then the Americans, each with nearly 60,000 dead. "We had hundreds of thousands killed in this war," the military correspondent for the Communist Party newspaper in Hanoi told Broyles. "We would have sacrificed one or two million more if necessary."

What Americans would have sacrificed remains a matter of ex post facto patriotism and bravado. "We had *business* being there," Elliott Abrams told Myra MacPherson. "And if it would have required a few thousand American troops stationed there for years in order to prevent this *unbelievably damaging* American defeat, then I think most Americans would have been willing to do it." Nearly 60 percent of those on the draft rolls, including Abrams himself (Harvard '69, II-S and a bad back), were not enthusiastic at the time about being among those few thousand. "The argument has one basic flaw," Broyles writes. "Whatever the price of winning the war—twenty more years of fighting, another million dead, the destruction of Hanoi—the North Vietnamese were willing to pay it."

Because of the price paid, Broyles writes, the "theme of martyrdom is everywhere. The pantheon of Vietnam is filled with heroes who were tortured, dismembered and executed for the fatherland. . . . They have even built 'atrocity museums,' not unlike the Holocaust memorials in Jerusalem and Dachau." Constantly prodded by Broyles about their own atrocities, the Vietnamese are less forthcoming:

> The Communists' massacre of civilians at Hue and at places like Thanh My are now inconvenient, so they have been airbrushed out of history; they no longer exist. The Communists stand in the flood of history and pluck from the water only what serves the State.

It is for the survivors who have managed to escape from Vietnam to provide the details that do not serve the state. Doan

Van Toai was arrested at a concert in Ho Chi Minh City on June 22, 1975, less than two months after the last Americans left Vietnam, and spent the next 863 days in Tran Hung Dao and Le Van Duyet prisons.[2] He was never told what the charges were against him, and until deep in his incarceration his family did not know of his whereabouts, or even if he was still alive. He was a nonperson, guilty of unspecified "suspicious acts" (his arrest may have been a case of mistaken identity, which his captors then did not know how to rectify). He was accused during his periodic interrogations of refusing to "commit himself."

In fact, Toai's father was a member of the Vietminh during the war against the French, while he himself, as a youthful pharmacy student, was tossed into jail several times by the South Vietnamese police for his antigovernment activities. Toai describes himself as something of a fence straddler, an opponent of American imperialism and a supporter of the National Liberation Front, although never to the point of actually becoming a member. Buying his way out of the draft, he managed a bank, kept up his secret contacts with the NLF, and held his finger to the wind. " 'Wait,' I told myself. 'Buy time, the situation will clarify itself.' " He is almost beguilingly self-aware: "Most of all, I wanted the revolution to justify my indecisiveness—to reveal itself as complex and ambivalent, but in essence good and constructive."

In prison, Toai hustled to survive, fast-talking himself into jobs as a barber and a kitchen worker and a doctor's helper, positions that gave him access to much of the inmate population. Amnesty International has called attention to the camps where thousands of Vietnamese arrested in the mid-1970s are still held, some of them, like Toai, opponents of the war who would not "commit" themselves to the victors. But many of Toai's fellow prisoners were old-line Communists jailed on the unarticulated grounds that they might become apostates, or even worse, na-

2. *The Vietnamese Gulag*, by Doan Van Toai and David Chanoff.

tionalists. And yet, like the aging Party hands in *Darkness at Noon*, most still kept the faith, viewing their sentences as time in purgatory until heaven was achieved on earth. Conditions were vile, with overcrowded cells—there were sixty-two prisoners in Toai's—and only a subsistence-level rice diet. Prisoners turned on each other, then were punished by their guards. Jailers beat one prisoner to death after a fight over food; when they realized he had died, they forced the cell leader to sign a statement that the prisoner "committed suicide by swallowing his tongue."

Toai's back talk constantly landed him in trouble. Once he was sent to solitary, "a tall box six feet long by three feet wide by six feet high," where he was unable to move because his right arm was handcuffed to his left ankle, his left arm to his right ankle. Finally, more than two years after he was first picked up, Toai was released, the reason for his release as much a mystery to him as his arrest. He was allowed to leave Vietnam and is now living in California.

ON JUNE 10, 1986, *The New York Times* reported that more than three hundred university-level courses on various aspects of the Vietnam era were offered during the 1985–86 academic year, up from almost none in 1980. Rambo rides the curl of revisionism; a few more with Rambo's resolve and the war might have been won. Diligent researchers point out that Sylvester Stallone spent what would have been his Rambo years with a series of deferments, enabling him to sit out the war first as a coach at a private girls' school in Switzerland, then as an acting student at the University of Miami, and finally, when the conflict was winding down, as the star of a soft-core porno film called *A Party at Kitty and Stud's*. It does not matter; "the will to win" is the phrase of the moment. In a 1984 campaign film called *Ronald Reagan's America*, a homage was paid to "John Wayne, An American Hero." That John Wayne only played American heroes, and was never in the service where he might have become one, was an irony that went unmentioned. His on-screen image seemed to satisfy some atavistic need exacerbated by the defeat in Vietnam.

This need provides the emotional power of the debate in the Congress over contra aid and the Reagan administration's Central American policy. Those who served in the armed forces and who have reservations about the military option look with a certain distaste on those who, as Broyles puts it in an Op-Ed piece in *The New York Times*, "avoided service in Vietnam and were miraculously transformed into hawks as soon as they were past draft age." Congressman Andrew Jacobs (Democrat of Indiana), a former marine, calls them "war wimps." "Chicken hawks" and "white featherbed hawks" are other phrases much in favor. The dialogue is ugly. "With the vote on contra aid," Patrick Buchanan wrote in *The Washington Post*, "the Democratic Party will reveal whether it stands with Ronald Reagan and the resistance—or Daniel Ortega and the Communists." Mark Shields, another former marine and a *Washington Post* columnist, responded to this with the suggestion that a Paul Douglas Brigade be formed, named for the Illinois senator who enlisted in the marines after Pearl Harbor at the age of fifty. "By now it must be clear that the Reagan administration and Congress are fairly brimming with some authentically Tough Customers who, but for draft deferments for graduate school or a trick knee, would have happily donned the khaki and kicked a little Commie tail in 'Nam," Shields wrote. "You have to know if the age and medical requirements were waived for the formation of such a brigade, White House communications chief Patrick Buchanan, Assistant Secretary of State Elliott Abrams, and Assistant Secretary of Defense Richard Perle would all volunteer for service in Central America." Even so civilized a voice as Irving Howe suggested, on the Op-Ed page of *The New York Times*, that "some American hearts might beat a little fast at the sight of right-wingers like William F. Buckley, Jr., and Norman Podhoretz donning fatigues to become contra 'freedom fighters.'"

The question of whether or not one served, or was willing to serve, or would be willing to serve, goes deeper than all the name-calling and the red-baiting and the commie-bashing and the allegations of draft dodging that tainted the *contra* debate, and taint every debate in the Congress about the use of force. At the root of the argument is the way in which war is perceived. "A soldier's best weapon is not his rifle but his ability to see his enemy as an abstraction, and not as another human being," Broyles writes. "The very word 'enemy' conveys a mental and moral power that makes war possible, even necessary." Many people in Washington deal only in that abstraction. When Elliott Abrams airily claims that "most Americans" would agree to having "a few thousand" GIs stationed "for years" in Vietnam as the price of avoiding defeat, he is talking with what Hemingway called "that beautiful detachment and devotion to stern justice of men dealing in death without being in any danger of it." He is certainly not talking about war, rather about war games in the war room, geopolitics; and in the field someone else's children, definitely not little Jacob or little Joseph Abrams. War is Hill 10, and a nineteen-year-old squad leader who point-blank refuses an order to go down into a tunnel. To the officers and men who might have to hold some future Hill 10, Elliott Abrams will always be just another REMF.

THE INDUSTRY

Hessians

A YEAR OR SO AGO, I went to the funeral of a screenwriter in the chapel of All Saints Episcopal Church in Beverly Hills. The deceased had won an Academy Award and been nominated for several others, was a former president of the Writers Guild of America West and a recipient of the Guild's annual Laurel Award for distinguished lifetime service to the art of screenwriting. He had written pictures starring Paul Newman and Jane Fonda and Elizabeth Taylor and Dean Martin and Sidney Poitier and pictures directed by Robert Aldrich and Richard Brooks and Sydney Pollack and George Roy Hill. In life he had stood at the very top of his profession.

All Saints was jammed. Two of the deceased's ex-wives were up front, and in a rear pew, keening rather more loudly than necessary, was the sixteen-year-old he had been romancing the last few months of his life. "He kept worrying," whispered my companion at the funeral, a screenwriter and a cad of international repute, "that his pubic hair was turning gray." The Twenty-third Psalm was read, William Blake's "Jerusalem" was sung, and then the eulogies began. The first eulogist was another former president of the Writers Guild. He reminisced about days at the Guild fighting against the indignities done to screenwriters

by studios and stars and directors and recalled how at one Guild
social function the deceased had come up on stage to accept an
award and had thrown a ream of blank pages out into the audience, a symbolic act meant either (I am not sure which) as a
statement against the auteur theory or as a *tableau vivant* of the
loneliness of the writer's life.

The second eulogist was the ex-husband of a movie star.
The deceased, he said, had been kind and gentle and truthful,
although no boy scout (an admission that seemed an implicit acknowledgment of the sobbing teen), but he had also been a
lonely man. To illustrate the degree of loneliness, he told the
following story: "If I hadn't seen him for a long time, the phone
would ring and a voice would say, 'What's up? Is your sauna un-
occupied?' And he would drive into town and we would go into
the sauna and afterwards we would talk for an hour or two. Only
after he left would I stop and think, He drove all the way in from
Malibu to use my sauna in West Hollywood. And I know there
are a lot of saunas he could have used in Malibu that were a lot
closer than mine in West Hollywood."

It was difficult not to reflect on this funeral while reading
The Craft of the Screenwriter, a collection of John Brady's long
interviews with six screenwriters—the late Paddy Chayefsky, William Goldman, Ernest Lehman, Paul Schrader, Neil Simon, and
Robert Towne. "In the beginning," screenwriters are fond of
saying, "is the Word." Screenwriters in fact are given to such
rhetorical flourishes. "The holy chore of screenwriting," one
called his trade recently in a letter quoted in the *Los Angeles
Times*, while another, James Poe, musing about his screenplay of
They Shoot Horses, Don't They?, which he felt had been brutal-
ized by others (he had been fired as director—it was his first di-
rectorial assignment—and his script then reworked by a consor-
tium of writers, producers, and the new director), complained to
the critic Richard Corliss: "If it had been properly dramatized,
we could have achieved catharsis in the grand tragic sense, the

Aristotelian sense, and the audience would have wept at the finale."

Mr. Brady slips easily into this fancy diction himself, never more so than in his capsule description of his interviewees: Chayefsky, a "pugnacious, poetic wordsmith"; Goldman, whom "Scott Fitzgerald, Nathanael West, and his other literary forebears could only have envied and admired"; Lehman, "a transitional giant"; Towne, who "pursues his own art as the forger of strikingly original screenplays." (I suspect the word "forger" might make Towne a tad uneasy.) Although his curriculum vitae gives no indication that he has ever worked on a picture, Mr. Brady has a theory: auteurism is on the wane, the director is in retreat, "the screenwriter . . . is more powerful than ever before." No longer are writers to be considered as merely overpaid, oversexed underachievers, the protagonists of a hundred bad Hollywood novels, victims of credit-stealing and pedestrian directors, their work gangbanged, their spirits broken. "The road from doormat to . . . dominance on a project," Brady says, "has been long and winding." The millennium has arrived, the Word is supreme, "the era of the screenwriter as superstar is at hand."

This of course is tendentious malarkey, malarkey that Brady can't even get his interviewees to swallow. "The niggers of the industry," Robert Towne (*Chinatown, Shampoo*) calls screenwriters. A screenwriter is a "bastardized thing," says Paul Schrader (*Taxi Driver, American Gigolo*), "half a filmmaker." In the longest and most interesting interview in the book, William Goldman (*Butch Cassidy and the Sundance Kid, All the President's Men*) variously calls screenwriting a "craft," "carpentry," and "shitwork." For Ernest Lehman (*North by Northwest, The Sweet Smell of Success*), with nearly thirty years of screen credits, it is *plus ça change* . . . "I don't think things have changed as much as they appear to have changed," Lehman says. "Marginal improvements at best, mostly in the area of financial rewards."

Despite four generally fascinating interviews (the exceptions are those with Chayefsky and Simon, Simon being more interested in the theater and Chayefsky in maintaining his ego), Brady seems to comprehend neither the realities of screenwriting nor the terms his interviewees accept. "Movies are like wars," Towne says in response to a request for a "short course in screenwriting." "The guy who becomes an expert is the guy who doesn't get killed." The military metaphor runs through all the conversations. These are men who recognize that screenwriters are mercenaries interchangeable even on each other's pictures. Alvin Sargent (*Julia, Ordinary People*) rewrote without credit Goldman's screenplay of *All the President's Men*, Towne rewrote Schrader's script of *The Yakuza* and (also without credit) the ending of Goldman's *Marathon Man*. "I think it's shit," Goldman says of that new ending, although not unsympathetically:

> Let me say again, though, that they [Towne and director John Schlesinger] didn't make it that way because they thought they were doing it wrong. Everybody's under the gun. The pressures of making a movie are tremendous. The writer gets a certain chance at tranquillity because there's nothing until the screenplay is in. But when you are on the floor, the pressures are murderous. . . . So when they came up with that ending, nobody sat around and said, "How can we ruin the ending of this thing?"

Towne in fact made his reputation as an uncredited rewriter, most successfully on *Bonnie and Clyde*, less so on *The New Centurions* and *Missouri Breaks* (for which his pay was a new driveway, the cost of which was buried in the picture's construction budget). "Bob may *think* he was anonymous then, but he wasn't," Ernest Lehman says. "Everybody knew about Bob, everyone. . . . It was almost as though by not having his name on it, they thought more of his effort. . . . If the picture was terrific, it was obvious that Bob had made it terrific. Now, if the picture was no good, nobody was going to blame Bob." It is the freedom from blame that makes rewriting someone else's script so much fun. The problems confronted are usually of a technical nature. An example: some years ago, Sam Peckinpah asked my wife and me to rewrite a trucking picture he was directing. The picture was called *Convoy* and was all blather and nonsense about the dignity of the open road and the shallowness of society, which would give Peckinpah the opportunity to stage some spectacular 18-wheeler stunts. All the rewriting had to be done within existing scenes so that the budget of the picture would not change; there could be no new characters or new locations or added scenes. The leading lady was Ali MacGraw. I knew she had gone to Wellesley, and at our first meeting Ms. MacGraw, not without humor, quickly got to the point of the rewrite: "What is a Wellesley girl with my cheekbones doing on this truck?"

It would be useful at this point to describe (as Brady does not) what a screenplay is, the restrictions under which it is written, and most importantly how it is made into a picture. A screenplay is 120 typewritten pages designed to be a motion picture, 120 pages because the rule of thumb is that one screenplay page accounts for one minute of film time. These 120 pages are broken down into scenes and locations and dialogue and narrative. Because it is so skeletal, so fragmented, a form in which words are secondary to potential images, a screenplay is difficult to read; the better a script reads, the smarter it is to be suspicious of the script. It is also essential to remember that a screenplay exists in a vacuum; it has no life of its own. As such, there is really no such thing as a good screenplay; there are only good pictures. An unmade screenplay is consigned to limbo, which means, reduced to the simplest terms, that the screenplay that is made is a good screenplay.

From the moment he or she is signed, the screenwriter is

subject to limitations that make the holy chore something less than sanctified. The first is the inflexible length; it calls for a pre-determination, a schematic approach that fiction, for example, does not demand. Screenplays are charted as much as they are written—how many scenes, how many pages per scene, how long each scene will play. Time is money. Fifteen extra pages mean fifteen minutes of film time. Since cut and finished film is shot at the rate of approximately two minutes a day, that means seven and a half days at a minimum of $60,000 a day, which does not include the "overages" paid to star actors or take into considera-tion scenes that call for extras, car chases, exteriors (which are subject to the vagaries of the sun, not to mention, if a scene is shot on a city street, the necessity for crowd control), and special effects, all of which are more expensive than a simple two-scene, or two actors talking. The mathematics are staggering: for these fifteen pages, $1 million and up. Which is not to say that a cagey screenwriter will not turn in a 135-page first draft. "That lets ev-erybody be creative when they get it," William Goldman says. "That means that the producer will be able to say, 'Well, we must cut fifteen pages out of this.' "

The limitation inherent in letting "everybody be creative" is an absolute of screenwriting. There is first the producer and then the financing organization and then the director and finally the stars (the director and major actors are called "elements," and most motion picture contracts have "change of element" clauses written into them, which allow the financing organization to hold on to a screenplay it had previously decided not to make if there is a change of element, i.e., a major star or name director who decides he or she wishes to make the picture), and each ele-ment has suggestions, suggestions that have the effect of law un-less the screenwriter is very articulate and quick on his feet. Schrader calls the four distinct versions of his *Hardcore* script "the Milius," "the MacElwain," "the Beatty," and "the Scott" after his producer; the studio executive who bought it; and two stars, Warren Beatty, who wanted to do *Hardcore* but insisted that a daughter who became a porno actress in the script be changed into a wife who became a porno actress, and then backed out of the picture after this change was made, and George C. Scott, who finally did do the script—with the daughter Schrader originally intended.

If a writer produces and/or directs his own script, he circumvents several levels of suggestions, but there is still the studio, which puts up the money, and the star; and if a star wants a daughter rewritten into a wife, the studio will generally back him up, especially if he (or she) is that rare bankable actor whose presence alone guarantees a "green light." Beatty and Woody Allen have come closest to circumventing all suggestions. In Beatty's John Reed picture, *Reds*, he stars, produces, directs, and takes a writing credit. The last phrase is used advisedly; Beatty does not write as much as he supervises, in the manner of an architect, teams of writers who in effect work under the pseudonym Warren Beatty. "A Warren Beatty Film" is a far more accurate credit than "Screenplay by Warren Beatty."

Suggestions are especially prevalent on an adaptation of a novel. Invariably a novel has to be replotted to fit into screenplay form. Scenes must be rearranged in order to create a narrative, characters combined or eliminated, parenthetical statements and modifying or subordinate clauses turned into scenes, a wife transposed into a mother, a funeral into a wedding (because it is easier to introduce characters and get rid of exposition at a wedding than at a funeral, where the audience might be distracted wondering who died). This offers an endless forum for suggestions. The suggestions are not necessarily bad—they are sometimes quite good, or at least practical—but they do tend to take the screenwriter away from that beginning where there was the Word. "You can almost say there are two entirely different versions of any screenplay," Goldman notes. "There's the stuff written before a movie is a go project and there is what's written when the movie is actually going to be shot. And sometimes they have very little to do with each other."

Before a picture is "greenlighted," or a "go project," everything in the screenplay is predicated on seducing another element. My wife and I once worked on a script for Jane Fonda, and when we finished our first draft, Jane asked Sydney Pollack, who had directed her in two previous pictures, for his comments. Jane was also the picture's producer and desperately wanted Paul Newman to play the older of the two men in love with her. A specialist in the psyche of movie stars, and as knowledgeable as anyone in Hollywood about what a screenplay needed to attract them, Pollack had directed Newman in another very successful film, *Absence of Malice*. "If you want Paul," Sydney said after he read the script, "he's got to fuck the girl last." It was the single most astute piece of script direction I have ever received, but Newman still turned down the part even after my wife and I made the appropriate change on the next draft; he was in his sixties, the character was seventy (or what we called "indeterminate middle age" in our stage direction), and he was not willing to make that quantum leap; it is also more than conceivable that he hated the script. A final note about Pollack: one of his main narrative strategies in the development of a screenplay, according to a friend who has worked closely with him, is "Never let the stars fuck too early in the picture, because then you've got no place else to go."

The experienced screenwriter is aware of all these restrictions, of all the choices that will be forfeited down the line, and tries to accommodate them within what Scott Fitzgerald called the "private grammar" of pictures. This grammar is different from the grammar of fiction. "You always attack a movie scene as *late* as you possibly can," Goldman says. "You always come into the scene at the last possible moment. . . . You truncate as much as you can. . . . Get on, get on. The camera is relentless. Makes you keep running."

Rarely does a dialogue scene run more than five pages; five pages equal five minutes, a long time to watch two people talk. Before the technique became a television cliché, exposition was often played against some kind of violence or conflict; Chayefsky used an off-screen narrator for exposition because he thought it saved him twenty minutes of film time. Exposition, however, is usually the first thing to go in the cutting room; a picture moves so fast and is so apparently realistic that the rigor of plot is not always necessary. Towne prefers soft openings. "A splashy beginning to hook an audience," he says, results "with an almost mathematical certainty" in a sag twenty minutes later. "It's been my experience that an audience will forgive you almost anything at the *beginning* of a picture," he says, "but almost nothing at the end." Dialogue is usually functional. The novelist Brian Moore once told me that after working out a scene with Alfred Hitchcock on *Torn Curtain,* Hitchcock would say, "In the old days, Brian, I'd bring in a man now and have him dialogue this in." Structure "is the single most important thing contributed by the screenwriter," says Goldman. "It's a terrible thing for a writer to admit, but in terms of screenwriting dialogue really doesn't matter as much as in plays and books—because you have the camera."

And with the camera comes the director, to screenwriters the most pernicious reality of picture-making. "The weak link in almost every film," Gore Vidal once told *Rolling Stone.* The encomiums roll in from Brady's interviewees. "Pricks," says Towne. "Jealous, petty and frustrated," says Goldman. Ernest Lehman recalls his experiences with Mike Nichols on *Who's Afraid of Virginia Woolf?* with almost palpable pain: "There were a lot of creative conflicts between Mike and me. A lot of give-and-take. He gave and I took."

What of course sets screenwriters' teeth on edge is the auteur theory, the idea that if film is an art, the director is the artist. I confess that I am less unsympathetic to the auteur theory than most screenwriters. I suspect that what upsets screenwriters is not so much the theory as the word. *Auteur.* The tony frenchiness of it plays right into the pretensions and pretentiousness of many directors. Since a number of directors perceive their inability to understand words as the mark of an artist, their embrace of the word "auteur" drives screenwriters mad. (I personally find "film-maker" far more odious, available as it is to every squalid hustler/promotor/producer/executive, many of whom have taken to calling themselves "complete filmmakers," even in one case a "compleat filmmaker.") The captain of the ship theory would be far less provocative; the senior partner theory, the CEO theory.

However grudgingly, screenwriters accept that a director must be in charge when a picture is shooting. "Just another foreman," Stirling Silliphant (*In the Heat of the Night*) says in Brady's introduction. Directing, Silliphant continues, is "an unforgiving routine of administration and traffic control." This is self-serving, and fails to acknowledge that the writer must, by the nature of the medium, cede to the director certain essential writer's functions—pace, mood, style, point of view, rhythm, texture. While it is true, as Goldman says, that there are seven major elements on any picture—writer, director, producer, cameraman, production designer, actors, and editor—the director hires most of them and, more importantly, can fire them if they do not give him what he wants. With the cameraman and the designer, the director controls the look and texture of the picture, with the cutter the pace and the rhythm and the point of view. Imagine a novelist giving up those functions.

A good director—and unfortunately a bad one as well—directs the writer as much as he directs the actors on the set. "On the continuity and story line" of *The Third Man*, Graham Greene wrote in his autobiography *Ways of Escape*, "Carol Reed and I worked closely together when I came back with him to Vienna to write the screenplay, covering miles of carpet each day, acting scenes at each other." Brian Moore and Ernest Lehman each spent months in a room with Hitchcock, working out the scenarios of *Torn Curtain* and *North by Northwest*; Hitchcock always maintained that for him the picture was finished when he was finished with the writer. ("All of Hitchcock's successes were primarily writers' films," Stanley Kauffmann contends breezily in *Living Images*. Not true. He failed to understand that Hitchcock was always the writer of a Hitchcock picture; the credited writers only dialogued it in.) My wife and I once spent fourteen weeks in an office in New York with Otto Preminger, five hours a day broken in the middle by lunch at La Côte Basque. Preminger cherished distractions. Managers would stop by and interrupt script conferences to introduce him to Miss Universe contestants they had just signed to personal service contracts. I met Miss Philippines and Miss Ceylon; Miss Peru was scheduled for Thursday afternoon.

The more politic director always pays lip service to the script. "The script is everything." "It all begins with the script." "There is no film without the script." This has become a litany of the Writers Guild Newsletter. Notice, however, the word "script"; never "scriptwriter." When a director, Alan Pakula, for example, says the script is everything, he means *his* version of the script, the script he must shoot, and will not shoot if it does not meet his specifications. A director once said a script I wrote was a one-span bridge and needed to be a two-span bridge; he meant that the climax came too early and that the screenplay needed another climactic moment closer to the end. He was right. We worked together for six days in a London hotel suite fashioning that second span and all the attendant body work. I wrote every word, but to say that the director's mark was not all over that script would be ridiculous. On the other hand, a less articulate director dunned me so persistently for a "relationship" that I finally said with some asperity that the leading lady was being paid several million dollars to act that relationship and if she could not act it she should be fired; instead I was.

Towne and Schrader, both of whom have directed, say that

having a script rewritten is a director's prerogative. "Everything is and should be rewritten," Towne says. "Movies are not done under laboratory conditions. . . . You are always miscalculating in a movie, partially because of the disparity between what you see on the set and what you see on the screen. No matter how skilled you are in anticipating what the image is going to look like finally, you can still be fooled. So you have to rewrite, and be rewritten—not because the original is necessarily badly *written*, but because, ultimately, if it doesn't *work* for a film, it's bad." This is an admission that most screenwriters, the majority who do not direct, are not willing to make. In a script, everything seems possible; every scene plays, every line sparkles, every actor is perfect for his part. The reality, as Schrader says, is that "every idea goes through a series of diminutions. From the moment an idea is conceived, every step of the process diminishes it. By the time the movie is released, it is a tattered shadow of what you imagined it to be. . . . When you are writing, it is all in the mind."

Where it always works, where the screenwriter is a whole and not half a filmmaker. Sometimes, when a writer of distinction works with a director of distinction, even that half can be quite satisfying. Graham Greene and Carol Reed were the most successful of collaborators in *The Fallen Idol* and *The Third Man;* their skills and outlook and interests not only coincided but were complementary. Raymond Chandler and Billy Wilder detested each other, but out of that friction came *Double Indemnity*. It should be noted, however, that these collaborations produced melodramas, a form particularly suited to motion pictures. It should also be noted that a "writer of distinction" has usually found that distinction in work other than screenwriting.

In the everyday world, professional screenwriters are fated to be chronic malcontents whose value is measured in dollars. "People are going to respect a writer they pay $250,000 to for a script a lot more than a writer they pay $50,000," Schrader says. How true. It is a Hessian ethic, and perhaps the ultimate Hessian is Goldman. His interview is laced with the sour wisdom of the veteran campaigner whose credits are like wound stripes. Rarely has a screenwriter understood so well that there is more to a script than words. In *All the President's Men*, Goldman was faced with the fact that Robert Redford was not only going to play Bob Woodward, he was also the producer, a parlay that would scare off actors of a comparable stature.

"The [Carl] Bernstein part had to not just be *good*," Goldman says, "it had to be . . . as bulletproof as one could make it . . . *appealing* enough to nail Dustin [Hoffman] or Al Pacino." In *A Bridge Too Far*, the problem was that none of the historical figures to be played by the dozen stars had died in the mad dash to capture a bridgehead at Arnhem. "You can't have a war film in which everybody lives," Goldman says. "I mean, I can't have James Gavin dying. He's alive up in Boston, right? Since we had to be authentic, one of the craft problems, in addition to making a dozen star parts, was inventing memorable small characters that I could in fact kill off so that the audience would be moved. The problem is finding air space amid all the material for a three-scene role of someone who can die."

It is this battle-scarred pragmatism that has helped push Goldman's price to a million dollars for an adaptation. He is the definition of, to use Mr. Brady's wretched phrase, "the screenwriter as superstar," a superstar who says, "I don't even have very much respect for anyone who is just a screenwriter in terms of writing." Mr. Brady plunges on, undeterred. What, according to Brady, are the fruits of superstardom? "Acceptance, applause and acclaim . . . more original screenplays, more money and more mention in the movie press."

More mention in the movie press!

In the beginning is the Word indeed.

POSTSCRIPT

I BEGAN THIS PIECE with a funeral. More or less the same funeral turned up a few years later to another point, and with different cast and set decoration, in my novel *The Red White and Blue*. In the later incarnation, I recycled the screenwriter's sixteen-year-old girl friend, his confession that his pubic hair was turning gray, and the eulogist's story of the screenwriter coming in from the beach to use his sauna (the eulogist himself I completely changed). When this piece appeared in *The New York Review of Books*, the screenwriter's last wife asked a mutual friend if I was going to use the scene in a novel. In truth I had never met the screenwriter and had only gone to the funeral out of curiosity, to see who would attend the last rites of an important Hollywood writer. I sat with two friends, one the international bounder I mentioned earlier to whom the deceased had confided about his graying (and who became, in the novel's funeral scene, the model for my dead screenwriter), and the other Gore Vidal, who at one point during the service leaned over and whispered to me, "Are you working?" Again in truth I had no intention of using the scene in a book, and indeed the novel I was working on at the time would not have accommodated it.

Obviously, however, the funeral had made an impression. Early on in *The Red White and Blue*, I needed a set piece that would culminate in the narrator's learning that his brother and his ex-wife had been murdered. As the narrator of the novel was at that point in his life a screenwriter, I thought the set piece should be laid in Hollywood, a gilded venue in sharp and necessary contrast to the fact of the assassinations. I toyed with a number of settings, but kept coming back to the funeral because of the opportunity it presented both for exposition and for laying out the social architecture against which much of the book would be played. So no, I had not planned to use the scene in a novel, but of course yes, it was always there waiting to be retrieved. And the answer to Gore Vidal's question should have been "Always."

Dealing

THIS IS A HOLLYWOOD STORY. It begins in Switzerland. It has stopovers in London and New York. It ends in Burbank and in Brentwood Park. Most of it takes place over the telephone. It is about money and it is about power and it is about pride and it is about vanity. It is about a deal. And it is with a deal, a succession of deals, that a motion picture gets off the ground.

In the fall of 1982, George Roy Hill, the movie director (*The Sting*, for which he won an Academy Award, and *Butch Cassidy and the Sundance Kid*, among others), traveled to Switzerland to meet the English novelist David Cornwell, who is better known under his nom de plume, John le Carré. The reason for George Hill's trip to Switzerland was David Cornwell's recently completed novel, *The Little Drummer Girl*. George Hill had read the new novel in manuscript form, and his enthusiasm was so high that he wanted to make a motion picture from the book. As it happens, the attorney for both George Hill and David Cornwell is Morton L. Leavy, counsel for a Park Avenue entertainment law firm. Morton Leavy was in London on business, and from London he arranged for his two clients to meet.

The meeting in Switzerland was a success. (In spite of Morton Leavy's best efforts, George Hill and David Cornwell had never previously met.) Cornwell agreed that Hill was the director he wanted for *The Little Drummer Girl*, and so Morton Leavy opened negotiations with Warner Bros. to buy the book. Warners was the choice because George Hill's Pan Arts Corporation has a financing and distribution deal with that studio, a deal of course negotiated by Morton Leavy. The package of George Hill and *The Little Drummer Girl* was so appealing to Warners that Morton Leavy was able to conclude a deal quickly. Warners would buy the book and assign it to Pan Arts; and George Hill, with Warners' money, would produce and direct the film.

It was at this point that I received a telephone call from my motion picture agent, Evarts Ziegler of the Ziegler, Diskant Agency in Los Angeles. Among Hollywood agents Evarts Ziegler is an anomaly. He went to Princeton, lives in Pasadena (which in Hollywood is considered as recherché as living in Grosse Pointe Farms), and once, I am convinced, hired a very rich young junior agent only because she had gone to Foxcroft. ("You'll like her," he had told me in the Ivy League drawl he still affects, "she went to Foxcroft," the implication being that he and I, both Princetonians, were perhaps the only two people in Hollywood who had ever heard of Foxcroft.) On the grapevine, Evarts Ziegler had picked up word of the Cornwell-Hill negotiation with Warners, and because the project would need a screenwriter he wondered if we—my wife, Joan Didion, and I—would like to read *The Little Drummer Girl*. He had already talked to George Hill's office and said there was interest at Pan Arts in having us write the screenplay of the book. As *interest* is one of those Hollywood words as slippery as quicksilver—I knew that Evarts Ziegler was interested in our writing the screenplay, but I was less sure how interested George Hill was—I told Evarts Ziegler that I would get back to him. I saw no point in interrupting the novel I had just begun, and the novel Joan was halfway through, to read *The Little Drummer Girl* if there was no real chance of our being asked to do the screenplay.

And so I called Morton Leavy in New York. Again as it happens, Morton Leavy is my attorney as well as George Hill's and David Cornwell's. It is not all that unusual a situation. There are only a handful of good entertainment/literary lawyers, and they are constantly balancing the conflicting concerns of clients who work with each other, who wish to work with each other, who detest each other, sue each other, marry and divorce each other. Morton Leavy is short, round, and benign; he looks, as I have often told him in the fifteen years he has been our attorney, like a Jewish Dr. Dolittle. He is so scrupulous that my wife and I once felt free to leave the country when he agreed to referee a negotiation she was having with her publisher and one I was having with my publisher. The twin negotiations—each for a new novel—needed a referee because my publisher was married to my wife's publisher, a situation further complicated by the competitive strains between my literary agent and my wife's literary agent, each of whom wished to negotiate a better deal than the other. I might add here that Morton Leavy was most aware of these strains as he is also the attorney for both my literary agent and my wife's literary agent. We told him to keep the peace between the two of them, that we did not wish to be played off against each other, but that we also wanted the best deals possible.

Morton Leavy's success as a referee was such that the only real difference between my contract and my wife's contract was that she would receive fifty more free copies of her book when it was published than I would when mine was. Both my publisher and my wife's publisher called Morton Leavy a son of a bitch, which he took as praise for a job well done. I tell you this in such detail only to indicate that I knew Morton Leavy would scrupulously guard the interests of both David Cornwell and George Hill when I asked him if there was more than an outside chance of our writing the screenplay of *The Little Drummer Girl*.

No, Morton Leavy said, the chances were slight. As the lead-

ing character in the novel was an English actress and as much of
the narrative action took place in seedy third-rate English repertory theaters, David Cornwell, who could make such demands
per his contract, was insisting on an English screenwriter familiar
with the theater and provincial repertory companies. It was to
settle on an English writer that George Hill had flown to Europe
to meet with David Cornwell. I thanked Morton Leavy, then
called Evarts Ziegler back and said that we would pass up the
opportunity to read *The Little Drummer Girl*.

Several months passed. Then, early in December 1982, there
was a message on my answering service from Pat Kelley, the
president of George Hill's Pan Arts Corporation. I suspected the
call might have something to do with *The Little Drummer Girl*,
for no other reason than that it had been nine years since last I
had talked to Pat Kelley, and that time over another picture with
which we were both associated, *A Star Is Born*. Pat Kelley was
then president of First Artists Corporation, the company making
that movie, and he had okayed the settlement Morton Leavy
had negotiated to get us out of *A Star Is Born* when Barbra
Streisand and her consort, Jon Peters, wanted us fired off the
screenplay. They also wanted three of our contractual net-profit
points returned, which transformed the firing into a settlement
and made it a very sticky proposition. That settlement negotiation was a triumph for Morton Leavy and a windfall for us, as
ultimately we earned more by being fired and losing those three
points than we would have made if we had remained on the picture under the terms of our original contract. To our surprise,
First Artists had approved all of Morton Leavy's proposals, including a stipulation that we share in the music and record royal-
ties, a clause not previously included in our contract. It turned
out that Pat Kelley was leaving First Artists, and I have often
wondered if his approval of our settlement was perhaps his way
of saying goodbye to the strong and demanding egos of Jon Peters
and Barbra Streisand.

Before returning the call from Pat Kelley, I telephoned Morton Leavy in New York and asked him if *The Little Drummer Girl* might have something to do with the message. Yes, he said. George Hill and David Cornwell had agreed on an English writer acceptable to both, but he was not available until the end of February. As George Hill wanted to start shooting *The Little Drummer Girl* in late summer, the English writer had been ruled out. George needed someone who could begin work immediately. Hence the call.

With this information in hand, I called Pat Kelley back. We exchanged pleasantries for a few moments as if I did not know why he was calling and as if he did not know I knew why he was calling. Then we got down to business. Had we heard that George was going to do *The Little Drummer Girl?* I mumbled that I had heard rumors to that effect. Had I read the book? No. Would I like to read it? Yes. Were we available? To that question I have the standard answer: one could always make oneself available if the project and the personalities were of interest, and the combination of a George Roy Hill production and a John le Carré novel was absolutely intriguing, and the conflict in the Middle East that was the subject of this book was something that touched all our lives every day . . . et cetera and so forth. Pat Kelley had been around long enough to know exactly what that bullshit meant: a definite and enthusiastic *maybe*. He said he would messenger over two copies of the bound galleys of *The Little Drummer Girl* that afternoon. He also said that George was at the Mayo Clinic for his annual checkup and would be in Los Angeles late in the week beginning December 6. If Joan and I liked the book, he said, perhaps we could all meet. It was a conversation of subjunctives with no commitments on either side.

It took us five days to read *The Little Drummer Girl.* Reading a book for adaptation into a screenplay is different from reading for pleasure. It is a relentless, carnivorous read in which the book is reduced to its barest bones; it is from these bones that a screenplay is constructed. One reads slowly, spitting out the fat and the gristle and the extraneous joints. At the end of this five-day read, I was not sure I liked *The Little Drummer Girl* (it is all but impossible to "like" any book read in this fashion), but I was sure there was a movie in it, and I was equally sure that Joan and I knew how to write the screenplay. When George Hill arrived in Los Angeles the end of that week, he called and we agreed to meet at our house in Brentwood over the weekend of December 11 and 12.

Time was now important. One of the attractions of working on the screenplay of *The Little Drummer Girl* for both my wife and me was that we both had a block of time open from mid-December through the end of January 1983, with no conflicting commitments. We were already scheduled to leave on Saturday, December 18, for Barbados, where we were spending Christmas at the house of friends, and where we could work through the holidays. This meant we had to see if we were in sync with George Hill (and he with us) and work out a deal before we flew to Barbados. Joan and I agreed that if a deal could not be worked out by the end of business hours December 17 we would pass on the project. We saw no point in wasting endless infuriating weeks in that Hollywood form of protracted combat: the negotiation.

George Hill arrived at our house promptly at one o'clock on Saturday, December 11. We had known him casually since he made *The Sting*, which was produced by Michael and Julia Phillips, who were friends and neighbors of ours some years before when we had lived in the farthest reaches of Malibu. George comes from a rich Catholic family in Minnesota, graduated from Yale, and also has a degree from Trinity College, Dublin. He served in the marines in World War II and in Korea, and at sixty he still looks like the marine officer he once was—slender, cold eyes, close-cropped hair. Early in his career, he was a stage actor both in Ireland and with Margaret Webster's Shakespeare Repertory Company; I cannot imagine much warmth coming across the footlights. His profit participation in *Butch Cassidy* and *The Sting* has made him millions, but he is famous in the movie business for never picking up a check. His dress can best be described as nondescript, or perhaps janitorial. A producer who once worked on a project with him told me that George would brag that he bought his clothes at an army surplus store in Santa Monica, where he could get khaki pants for under ten dollars; in our brief contacts I never had any reason to doubt this.

Before he came that Saturday, I called two writers who had written pictures for him to find out what George was like to work with. It was as if they were quoting from the same text. Both said he had the best story sense of any director with whom they had ever been associated, both said he was absolutely tenacious about not giving up any point he had settled on but that he would yield if an argument was persuasive enough, both said he thought he was a good writer but was not, both said he could occasionally be a terrible pain in the ass, and both said unequivocally that they would work with him again. I had also taken the trouble to look up all the writer credits on his pictures. Unlike many directors, he does not use multiple writers on a screenplay. One writer works on a script from beginning to end, which meant that George had enormous confidence in his ability to get exactly what he wanted from a screenwriter.

There was almost no preliminary feeling each other out. We settled right into work. What was the book about? What was the line of the movie? What could be eliminated? What was necessary? We continued over an antipasto lunch in the kitchen; Joan and I each had a beer, George had cheap French white wine. By the end of that first day, we were blocking out a possible opening of the picture on a bulletin board. On Sunday the procedure was repeated. Joan had made chili so hot that it made our scalps sweat. More beer, another bottle of $3.49 Château

Thieuley. By late Sunday afternoon we had tentatively blocked out the first forty-five minutes or so of *The Little Drummer Girl* on three-by-five index cards. I do not by any means suggest that this would have been the narrative line of the picture. It only meant that we did seem to be in sync with each other.

George talked about scheduling. He said he would like to begin shooting in late August. We said we would like to work in Barbados over Christmas. He asked if it would be possible for us to work with him for a few days in New York on our way home from Barbados. We said this would be no problem. He asked if we could have a first draft by the end of February. We were thinking the end of January, but we did not tell him that. He said the money people would talk the first thing Monday morning. We kept the index cards when he left. Writers can have meetings with prospective employers, but under Writers Guild rules nothing can be written without remuneration. It looked as if we were going to write the screenplay of *The Little Drummer Girl*. We alerted Evarts Ziegler at his home in Pasadena and Morton Leavy in New York.

But of course we did not write the screenplay of *The Little Drummer Girl*. Money was the ostensible reason the deal fell apart, but the negotiation actually foundered on the twin rocks of Hollywood deal-making—hubris and ego—in equal measure ours and George Hill's. The reason that negotiations take so long in Hollywood—it is common for contracts not to be signed until long after a picture is in release—is that the negotiation establishes the channel of power, the chain of command. Making an individual back down over money in the negotiation process is one quick and clear way to establish that power, to show who is boss. The production company can do this because it has one unassailable advantage: Everyone wants to make a movie. The line is long, the chosen are few, and the chosen learn to suck wind—or someone else is chosen.

It is a situation in which the only leverage my wife and I

have ever had is that we do not particularly care if we ever write another movie. We have a professional life quite independent of motion pictures, and we are not dependent on screenplays for our living. We like writing them, even insofar as the collaboration inherent in moviemaking is antithetical to the very reason one becomes a writer in the first place, but we do not like to suck wind. This attitude encourages intractability, and we were thus set on a collision course with George Hill. A rich former marine who never reaches for a tab and who buys his khaki pants at an army surplus store is the definition of intractable.

That Monday morning, however, everyone was sanguine. Evarts Ziegler said that he would ask for $500,000 guaranteed for us: the picture had to cost over $20 million; George Hill and David Cornwell must be getting $2.5 million between them, so $500,000 for us was not out of line; we had to establish a position. That is how agents think and that is how agents talk. I told Evarts Ziegler he was crazy. We wanted this deal to work; there were only five days to make it work before we left for Barbados; there was no time to waste fishing for a guaranteed five hundred grand. We wanted only what we had received on the last deal he had negotiated on our behalf, a remake of an old classic at another studio: a guaranteed $300,000 for a first draft and one set of changes, against a final fee of $450,000 if there was no shared credit, and a profit participation.

The numbers were staggering, but then so were those accruing to George Hill and David Cornwell, not to mention the millions that any major star would receive for starring in *The Little Drummer Girl*. It deserves to be mentioned here that one purpose of these huge fees is to establish respect; in the constitution of Hollywood, a million-dollar director has half a million dollars more respect than a $500,000 director. This is why the Eleventh Commandment of a motion picture negotiation is Thou shalt not take less than thy last deal. Everyone knows what everyone else makes (this information is passed around like popcorn at a movie), and the person who violates this Eleventh

Commandment is seen not as a model of restraint and moderation but as a plain goddamn fool.

The negotiation was between Evarts Ziegler and a business-affairs lawyer at Warners, but the lawyer was only a conduit for George Hill. After some initial sparring between Evarts Ziegler and Pat Kelley, the Warners lawyer countered with George Hill's offer: a guaranteed $250,000 for a first draft and a set of changes ("a set of changes" is essentially doodling or fixing that can be accomplished in a short specified period, never more than ten working days; a "draft" is a complete rewrite with a whole schedule of remuneration). This guarantee was against a total fee of $450,000 if we received solo credit, with a back-end profit participation to be worked out later. (In a picture as expensive as *The Little Drummer Girl* promised to be, with at least one and probably more elements having a gross participation, the chance of any net profits was practically nil.) Thus at the end of that first day of negotiating, the actual difference between what we wanted and what was offered was the $50,000 in the first-draft guarantee, in Hollywood terms a piddling sum, which is an indication of how far removed the picture business is from the real world. An agreement seemed imminent.

But there was no movement. Monday dissolved into Tuesday into Wednesday. Although that $50,000 would have been made up the next step down the line (that is, in the second draft), George Hill refused to budge, as did we. It was that rarest of negotiations, one in which neither party would give an inch. In retrospect, I am sure the money was irrelevant. George Hill conducts a negotiation as if it were a captain's mast or a summary court-martial. That it was Warners' money and not his that would ultimately be paid was beside the point; price is set by the commanding officer, not by the marketplace or the Eleventh Commandment. I find it an admirable trait, perhaps because I had the means to say bugger off. As the Friday deadline approached, this mutual display of ego and hubris finally caused the negotiation to fall apart.

I sent the two sets of galleys back to Pan Arts with a note saying that as money seemed to be tight, bound galleys were too expensive to keep. Evarts Ziegler could not believe the deal had fallen apart over $50,000, nor could Morton Leavy. "Listen, I will deny ever saying this if you quote me," a Warners executive whispered to me at dinner some weeks later, "but I would never blow a deal for fifty grand." George Hill would, and so would I. It is something perhaps only another pain in the ass would understand.

There is no moral to this story, no lessons to be drawn. It is only the story of a deal, an encapsulated version of every deal. Deals fall apart; the center holds; mere anarchy is not then loosed upon the motion picture industry. Other deals are made. George Hill moved quickly to sign a new writer, Loring Mandel, who is yet another Morton Leavy client. The day after the deal collapsed, we received by messenger a case of wine of such grandeur—six bottles of Château Haut-Brion 1976 and six of Château Lafite Rothschild 1979—that I called the wine merchant to ask its cost. The 1976 Haut-Brion was $80 a bottle; the 1979 Lafite Rothschild, $60 a bottle; the case was $840, less a 10 percent case discount, which brought the price to $756. The card accompanying the wine said only one word: "George." I immediately sent a note to him at his apartment in New York, also with only one word: "Thanks."

The studio insists that the $756 will not be buried in the budget of The Little Drummer Girl, which would be a first in the history of the motion picture business. It is safe to assume, however, that if any of our conversations with George Hill over that weekend in December turn up in the screenplay, the $756 will be a bargain. We then would have worked those two days for approximately one-twentieth of what we would have been paid per day under the deal George had offered. The sad thing is that neither my wife nor I will ever be able to drink a single drop of the Haut-Brion or the Lafite Rothschild. We both have migraines, and red wine is a migraine trigger.

Sam

THE FIRST THING I did when I picked up *Spiegel: The Man Behind the Pictures*, Andrew Sinclair's biography of film producer Sam Spiegel, was look in the index, where I found a listing I was hoping not to find: "Dunne, John Gregory, 131." Immediately I went to page 131:

> Diana Phipps was also at a dinner on the *Malahne* [Spiegel's yacht] with the writers Joan Didion and John Gregory Dunne when Spiegel declared, "I believe I have led the most dissolute life of the four of us." None of the others disagreed.

In fact, I have never been on the *Malahne*, and knew Sam Spiegel but slightly, at the very end of his life, and saw him only in the company of others who knew him better. The dinner took place not on Spiegel's 500-ton yacht in the Mediterranean, but on a Georgian square in London, on a freezing wet spring night, with one of the four people present nursing a high fever and wondering how to get out of a USIA tour to Yugoslavia and Sierra Leone scheduled to begin the end of the week. What Sam actually said was that he had led a more "profligate" life than anyone at the table, "profligate" being a more evocative

and ambiguous word than "dissolute," and even then one had to
hear him say it. His dimensions were those of an altar votive
candle, half melted, the flesh cascading from him like cooled
wax; his voice came from his esophagus, a low rumble, like thun-
der on the horizon, and when he made reference to his "profligate life," drawing the phrase out for what seemed an eternity,
it conjured up priapic adventures that boggled the imagination—
daily doubles, quinellas, and pick-six combinations.

My point here is that *Spiegel* is a genre book, belonging to
what I can only call the literature of anecdote. Anecdotes are
factoids of questionable provenance, burnished to a high gloss,
often set in gilded venues and populated with familiar names as
background atmosphere, purged of subtext in the interest of
keeping the narrative flowing smoothly. Spiegel's allowing to his
own profligacy, or dissolution, plays better on the *Malahne*, an-
chored off the Riviera, with its paneled dining saloon, its seven
staterooms, its crew of twenty-three and annual operating cost,
in port, of $150,000 a year, than it does on a cold night on Con-
naught Square. I might add that when I tell this story (I was
not interviewed by Andrew Sinclair), I always say that I answered, "You don't think you're going to get an argument, do
you, Sam?" In fact, I am not sure I actually said this, or just wish
I had said it, or indeed added it later. This makes the further
point that all anecdote, whether biographical or autobiographi-
cal, is essentially self-aggrandizing, allowing the teller to bask in
his own created, or someone else's reflected, glory; showing his
closeness, or how he humbled him, or whatever it is in his interest to demonstrate.

It is with these caveats that one must approach *Spiegel*.
Stories attached themselves to Sam Spiegel the way lint clings
to a cheap suit, most of them begging for the qualifying adverb
"allegedly," none of them, in *Spiegel*, getting it. "If you woke up
in a motel with a dead whore who'd been stabbed, who would
you call?" Billy Wilder once allegedly asked, and then he an-

swered, "Sam Spiegel." Otto Preminger, who in 1935 fled from Austria with Spiegel, and later fell out with him, once allegedly warned: "Don't turn your back on him, or your hair will be stolen." Once, strolling on a London street with a doxy, Spiegel was allegedly kicked in the rear end by a passerby. Without looking around or breaking stride, he allegedly said, "The check is in the mail."

Winner of three Academy Awards, the producer of *The African Queen, On the Waterfront, The Bridge on the River Kwai,* and *Lawrence of Arabia,* the producer as well of *Melba, When I Grow Up, The Happening,* and many other pictures he preferred to forget he was ever associated with, Sam Spiegel belonged to that dying generation of Middle European buccaneers washed up on the Hollywood shore by the tides of history. He was born in 1901 in Jaroslaw, a Galician market town near the Russian border, the black sheep second son of a tobacco merchant (his elder brother, Shalom Spiegel, a Talmudic scholar, later became the only person in whom Sam ever seemed to take an unequivocal pride). World War I cut short his childhood; German and Russian armies ranged over Galicia, and at war's end Poland's Marshal Pilsudski tried to cut a deal with the Russian Whites. The Red armies counterattacked, and with anarchy in the ascendancy and pogroms in Pinsk and Lvov and Wilno, the family Spiegel decamped from Jaroslaw for the Vienna ghetto.

In Vienna, Samuel Spiegel honed what was to become the habit of a lifetime, the almost daily reinvention of his past. In later years, he would claim a Vienna university degree, but in fact, says Sinclair, his only higher education "was the university of life and hard knocks, his syllabus . . . the syllabus of survival and independence. He learned to avoid war and taxes, to disbelieve governments and stability, to trust only in money and himself." From Austria, Spiegel migrated to Palestine, where he dug ditches and sewer lines in a kibbutz, characteristically up-

grading his labors, in a press release when he was rich and famous, to that of a drainage expert, who reclaimed land in the
desert and assisted in the exploitation of the Dead Sea. He married, and then abandoned his wife and daughter, returning to
Poland, where he recast himself once again, this time as a stock
promoter and cotton broker.

Armed only with charm and a talent for languages—he was
ultimately conversant in nine—Spiegel took on the world, leaving in his path a trail of bad checks, which kept him more or less
constantly peripatetic. In California, sound had come to the
movie business, and when Spiegel crapped out in San Francisco
as a cotton broker, his language skills won him a job at M-G-M
as a scout for European plays and books that might make film
properties; in subsequent publicity, he naturally dolled up his
first film job with the claim that he had been discovered at
Berkeley as a lecturer in European drama. But his paper trail
ultimately caught up with him, and in 1929 he was sentenced to
nine months in the slammer for passing a worthless check; he
served five and was deported to Poland.

In 1930, Spiegel surfaced in Berlin as a factotum in the picture business, part panderer, part promoter, part PR man, a
dubber, cutter, and translator of pictures for the European market. In time he became a minor producer, but fled Germany for
Vienna the day of the Reichstag fire. How he left and under
what circumstances are unclear. In one version, he claimed to
have been warned by his barber, a part-time storm trooper, that
he would be picked up if he returned home; he went from his
shave to the Bahnhof, where he caught a train to Vienna. In
another version, the barber drove his Cord coupe and his clothes
to Vienna; and in still a third, he left with the actor Oscar
Homolka, arriving in the Austrian capital, after changing trains
to avoid detection, with a toothbrush, four marks, and a script
for Homolka. However he arrived, Spiegel's escape would always
subsequently elicit from him the same comment: "These are the

accidents of history that prevent you from becoming a lamp-
shade."

Spiegel stayed in Vienna long enough to have an affair with
Hedy Lamarr, but then in 1935, several months after Austrian
Nazis assassinated Chancellor Engelbert Dollfuss in an abortive
putsch, he headed for Paris with Otto Preminger. Typically the
accounts of this journey differ with the teller. The only fact not
in dispute was that Preminger had a bankroll worth seven thousand dollars, which he was forbidden to take from the country
because of Austria's stringent restrictions on the export of currency. As he was paying for the trip—Spiegel was, needless to
say, broke—Preminger insisted that Spiegel carry the cash in his
coat, and run the risk of arrest if it was discovered. At the border,
in Spiegel's version, he was indeed searched, and then released.
Once safely across the frontier in Switzerland, Preminger demanded to know where the money was. Spiegel said he had in
fact slipped it back into Preminger's own pocket without his
knowing it. I once wrote a screenplay for Preminger, and in his
account of the story—a staple in his repertoire—it was he who
had been stripsearched, but he had succeeded in secretly stashing
the money back in Spiegel's coat on the not unreasonable
grounds that Spiegel would only look innocent if he did not
know he was carrying it.

In Paris, pickings were slim for Spiegel. There were too few
movie jobs for the refugee Jews who were competing for them,
and those who were there had better credentials than he. With
little more than the clothes on his back, Spiegel took himself
to London, where his claim that he had worked for anti-Nazi
youth groups won him the sponsorship of a Jewish film producer.
Hustling every second, he managed to produce a picture with
Buster Keaton, down on his luck and a drunk. But once again
Spiegel financed his extravagances with bad checks, this time
adding a little theft and forgery to the mix. He failed to show
up for his trial at the Old Bailey, deciding to give a champagne

and caviar party at the Dorchester Hotel instead. When the
police arrived to cart him to his prior engagement, he departed
stylishly. "Ladies and gentlemen, please continue to be my
guests," he allegedly announced to the assembled freeloaders. "I
am temporarily a guest of His Majesty's Government."

Spiegel was sentenced to three months in jail and deported.
He seemed to have a past and no future. England and the United
States were now closed to him, and a Europe heading for war
with Nazi Germany was no place for a Jew. As always, his instinct was to keep moving. He hocked the signed first editions
of the collected works of Bernard Shaw lent him by a friend, and
with the proceeds bought himself a ticket to Mexico. There he
indulged in still more financial chicanery, earning himself yet
another brief penance in the pokey. When he got out, he slipped
across the border at Laredo under an assumed name and made
his way to Los Angeles. The date was September 1939; whatever
else might happen, Spiegel this time could not be deported back
to Poland.

He was thirty-eight, with no papers and no prospects, living
on the dole provided by other more successful Middle European
Jews in Hollywood. The founders of the movie business, a gen-
eration older than the refugees from Hitler, came from a veritable Almanach de Ghetto—Louis B. Mayer and the Schenk
brothers from Rybinsk, Samuel Goldfish (later Goldwyn) from
Warsaw, Lewis J. Zeleznik (later Selznick, father of Myron and
David O.) from Kiev, the Warner brothers from Kramaskhilz;
"Poland to polo in one generation," it was said of these pioneers.
Spiegel's first priority was a name, and this three-time jailbird
had the wit to stick with the bird motif, plucking Spiegel into
"S. P. Eagle." The jokes were immediate; Darryl Zanuck claimed
he next would change it to E. A. Gull, while others claimed to
be S. P. Eechless at his gall. But what the jokes meant was that
Sam Spiegel had arrived—that as S. P. Eagle he was finally a
player.

Spiegel operated as he always had. He stole six plots from

six different Hungarian playwrights, reasoning they could not sue him until the war was over, and put together a movie called *Tales of Manhattan*, with Charles Boyer, Ginger Rogers, Henry Fonda, Charles Laughton, and others. His modus operandi was to use one star name to attract another, and then to go back and use the second name to get the first. He bought a house in the Beverly Hills flats, a quasi brothel that insured his social standing. "He'd give a dinner party," Walter Wanger remembered, "and if you didn't take the young lady on your right upstairs between the soup and the entree, you were considered a homosexual."

The movies he made were forgettable, his private extravagance memorable. Five hundred people regularly attended his New Year's Eve parties; the gin rummy games went on around the clock, with girls available if any of the players wanted to take five. "He operated on the edge of financial precipice better than anyone I ever saw," Talli Wyler, wife of director William Wyler said. "I don't know how he did it, but there was always a feeling of lavishness about Sam." Willie Wyler and Billy Wilder, however boon companions, refused to work with him, each employing the nice Hollywood casuistry that friendship with him was too important to be sacrificed to the strains inherent in the making of a movie. He married a young actress named Lynn Baggett, who would sometimes show up at his parties naked under a mink coat, claiming her husband did not give her enough money to buy clothes. His creditors went unpaid, and he reverted to his old habit of passing bad paper. Once again he faced deportation proceedings, on this occasion to Mexico, his last port of entry. This time, however, he had friends, and the fix was in. In hearings redolent of payoff and bribery, Spiegel's past convictions were expunged from his jacket, and he was placed high on the Polish quota for legal entry into the United States, which brought with it the right to apply for future citizenship. The eagle had finally landed.

·   ·

EARLY IN THE 1950s, Spiegel formed Horizon Pictures in partnership with John Huston, an old friend from the days when both were down and out in London. Privately they called the company Shit Creek Productions, and in keeping with that name, Spiegel mortgaged his house in order to scrape together seed money for a picture based on C. S. Forester's novel *The African Queen*. "A story of two old people going up and down a river," Alexander Korda said when he declined to participate in the project. "You will be bankrupt." Spiegel and Huston persuaded Humphrey Bogart and Katharine Hepburn to star in the picture, and then when the financing got shaky, Spiegel was able to renegotiate their contracts so that most of their fees were deferred.

Once the *African Queen* company got to the Ruki River location in the Belgian Congo, where most of the picture was shot, Spiegel had little to do with the production beyond laying on the odd caviar and champagne supper for his principals and arranging for the crew to have expenses paid in the local currency. Huston simply did not want him on the set. In fact it was with Huston in the Belgian Congo where a pattern developed that carried over to all the rest of Spiegel's pictures: he worked best with strong directors. He made four very good pictures, and they were directed by three very tough customers—Huston, Elia Kazan, who did *On the Waterfront*, and David Lean, who directed both *The Bridge on the River Kwai* and *Lawrence of Arabia*, men who would ban him from the set, and bully him as he tried to bully them.

The African Queen made S. P. Eagle rich, and after stumbling with *Melba*, his interest was next piqued by *On the Waterfront*, a Budd Schulberg script about union racketeering on the New York and New Jersey docks that had been around for some time with no takers; Harry Cohn at Columbia Pictures was only interested in the subject if Communists were substituted for gangsters. For nearly a year, Spiegel hectored Schulberg and

Kazan into rewriting the screenplay again and again, all the while trying to line up the money, which was hard to come by because of his insistence that the picture be shot on actual locations on the New York waterfront. Spiegel's most important contribution to *Waterfront*, however, was in persuading Marlon Brando to star in the picture. This was the time of congressional hearings into Communist infiltration of the film business, and Kazan and Schulberg had each purged himself as a friendly witness. Kazan's naming of names had won him the soubriquet "Looselips" and ruptured his relationship with Brando, who he had directed on Broadway in *A Streetcar Named Desire*. At three o'clock one morning, Spiegel, in his version, brought the two volatile men together in a West Side delicatessen, after first allegedly counseling Brando: "Professional is one thing, politics is another; separate them." The actor and the director made their peace and the picture was shot. For his production of *Waterfront*, Spiegel won his first Oscar, but more importantly, he was now so respectable that he could bury S. P. Eagle and professionally disinter the name Sam Spiegel.

The Bridge on the River Kwai and *Lawrence of Arabia* were very much in what was now seen as the Spiegel tradition—pictures with difficult and almost ostentatiously uncommercial subject matter, set in remote locations, and burdened with what seemed insurmountable logistical hardships. Yet somehow he and David Lean, who treated each other, as an observer noted, "with respect and animosity," made them work. It took eight months and $250,000 to build the 90-foot-high, 250-foot-long bridge in Kwai; 45 elephants dragged 1,500 trees through the jungles of Ceylon to the bridge site. "There is no story in *Kwai* without a bridge," Spiegel said, "and the bridge acquires meaning only when it is destroyed. So you build the bridge to illustrate the point. The question of a quarter of a million dollars is only a number on your cost sheet."

For Spiegel, the cost sheet was no longer a problem. He now

had a yacht, bank accounts in various tax havens far from the
prying eyes of the IRS and Inland Revenue, an art collection
begun with four van Goghs, and an FBI dossier, presumably because he used two blacklisted screenwriters, Carl Foreman and
Michael Wilson, on the script of *Kwai.* "Spiegel has in the past
[DELETED]," his FBI file read, "although it was never definitely determined that he was acting as an espionage agent for
the Russians." His work on a picture was essentially done during
pre- and post-production, fighting with his writers over the script,
fighting with his directors over the cut. During the shooting of
Lawrence, he stayed off Aqaba on the *Malahne,* a Galician Jew
who could now entertain King Hussein of Jordan aboard ship.
This ancient mariner, however, was aware of certain proprieties
that still had to be observed with the Hashemite king. When an
unschooled guest on the *Malahne* asked Hussein to explain
Ramadan, Spiegel quickly interrupted (in the version I always
heard), "Dot's our Lent."

After *Lawrence,* Spiegel never again really functioned successfully. He and Lean had a sulfuric falling out, and his mania
for control now meant multiple writers and constant interfer-
ence; strong directors like Mike Nichols pulled out of pictures
(in Nichols' case, *The Last Tycoon*) rather than put up with his
meddling. "Truthfully I would rather make a bad picture and
make it my way than make a good picture and make it your way,"
he told a friend. There was a charm and dignity in this kind of
hubris, but bad pictures had become the rule, a sybaritic life his
last major production. Spiegel married again, but he was now in
his sixties and there was too little time and too many women.
The girls came and went, an alphabet of pudenda: Anne, Brigid,
Charlotte, Dagmar, Eugenie, Francesca, Gretchen, Heather . . .
With women as well as collaborators he could be capricious and
cruel, and a relationship with him was often not without cost.
Lynn Baggett committed suicide, and another girl I knew, a fif-
teen-year-old hillbilly from Tennessee, later tried to kill herself

when another romance ended by breaking all the glassware in her apartment and running, naked and barefoot, over the shards; in London, years later, she was subsequently successful with pills.

With Ann Pennington he had a son, Adam; he adored the child, although he admitted he had little gift for fatherhood, and by her account made the mother's life miserable. In his eighties, he produced *Betrayal*, from the play by Harold Pinter. Told that it was a small picture, he replied: "Is it really? Do you worry in a painting about the size of the canvas?" When he was eighty-two, he took a nineteen-year-old mistress and would spend Thanksgiving with her parents in upstate New York; Sinclair does not record the parents' reaction to their daughter's liaison with a man old enough to be *their* grandfather. (Whenever we saw them together, Sam would invariably introduce the young woman as "Miss So-and-So"; it was not until after he died that we learned her first name.) "I believe in mortality," Spiegel said around this time. "I just don't believe in inflicting it on myself." Finally, on New Year's Eve 1985, he died, alone, in a bathtub at La Samanna, on the Caribbean island of St. Martin. "Give him the kiss of life," the attending physician allegedly said to Peter Ustinov, who was also staying at the resort. "Alive or dead," Ustinov allegedly replied, "I don't kiss Sam Spiegel." After his death, Ann Pennington said, "I feel so relieved, I will never hear his voice on the phone again."

Sinclair runs his compendium of anecdotes together as if he were stringing a necklace. His book is slight, only 162 pages, and even that is padded, full of encyclopedia history and capsule biographies of causes to which Spiegel made monetary pledges he did not honor; twenty of these 162 pages are taken up with index, acknowledgments, and bibliography, and the result reads as if it were written during a coffee break. For the popular biographer, a motion picture producer is not the ideal subject. "A producer," Mike Nichols once said about one of his, "comes on the set and says, 'I don't like the shoes.'" What a producer in fact does is keep a project rolling until it reaches critical mass, that stage when there is so much money involved that the financing organization would find it prohibitively costly to pull out. In this initial stage, the producer must also say no to the writers, do it over. "Producers don't like to think of themselves as glorified production managers, though that's what they are," Larry McMurtry wrote in his book *Film Flam*. "They want to be allowed to participate in the creative act. Keeping a writer handy to talk to every few days convinces them that they are, in fact, participating—it may at the same time drive the writers crazy."

None of this is inherently dramatic. It is difficult to make a libertine, especially an octogenarian libertine, interesting; as the saying goes, you had to be there. To understand the beauty of what Sam Spiegel did it would be necessary to understand the tax codes of the world's condominium governments. If such understanding were forthcoming, it might also be necessary to agree with the assessment of his fellow expatriate, producer Gottfried Reinhardt: "Spiegel was a congenital crook."

What Sam Spiegel did, he did with a certain gorgeous flair. To know him, even slightly, was to appreciate the subtext Andrew Sinclair has not supplied. With the exception of *On the Waterfront*, his great pictures were not entirely to my taste. They were in every sense a producer's pictures, so well prepared that the spark of spontaneity was doused. And yet, Sam belonged to another generation, and when one looks at the pygmies at large in Hollywood today, one can agree with the sentiment expressed by Arthur Schlesinger at his funeral in New York early in 1986. "Sam Spiegel," he said, "was the last of the giants."

Sunkist

1

IN THE MIDST of an argument to some other point, Harry Cohn, the monster responsible for the success and ultimate respectability of Columbia Pictures as a major Hollywood player, once bet his hated brother Jack that he did not know and could not recite the Lord's Prayer. Equally full of bluster, Jack Cohn accepted the wager, and with a certain trepidation, began, "Now I lay me down to sleep . . ." Harry Cohn glowered and shoved his money across the table. "That's enough," he said. "I didn't think you knew it."

Like most stories about Hollywood, this one is probably not true, and certainly not original, its prayerful antecedents going back at least to a book published in nineteenth-century England.[1] Hollywood, however, was not called the dream factory for nothing, its history always more pipe dream than fact, manufactured by generations of flacks, fan magazines, ghostwriters, and those most downtrodden, self-aggrandizing, self-flagellating,

---

1. Otto Friedrich, *City of Nets*, pp. 433 and 464. The nineteenth-century version of the anecdote was told in a book by Angela Lambert, *Unquiet Souls*.

and ultimately most revisionist of the industry's worker bees, the
screenwriters. "Schmucks with Underwoods," Jack Warner, the
most monstrous of the Warner brothers, called screenwriters,
but those schmucks, to whom the words "hack," "overpaid,"
and "undertalented" were usually attached, had the gift of poi-
soned and unforgiving memory. "For their degradation," Neil
Gabler shrewdly writes in *An Empire of Their Own*, "the writers
did exact a small measure of revenge, since it is almost exclu-
sively through writers that we know what we know of the Hollywood moguls. Our whole history of Hollywood is framed by the
writers' prejudices. It is history by retribution."[2]

With such sources, the history is of course anecdotal, and
the anecdotes usually provided by professional storytellers. In
this milieu, truth is not overly valued. "When the legend becomes fact," a character says in John Ford's *The Man Who Shot
Liberty Valance*, "print the legend."[3] In Hollywood, legend and
fact are synonymous. The not altogether unbecoming result is
that most stories about the movies have the shorthand sense of
being scenes from a screenplay, with dialogue, set decoration,
and camera movements. Thus Sam Goldwyn, lying critically ill
in Doctors Hospital in New York, becomes the silent protagonist
of a classical hospital scene, the one in which the female lead
has her big moment.

The time: 1936. Prognosis: Goldwyn has two hours to live
unless new medication works wonders. Conflict: whether or not
to make the final payment of $140,000 for the rights to Sidney
Howard's play *Dead End*. The decision must be made by noon
or all monies previously advanced are forfeited and the option
returned to Howard. With her husband unconscious, Frances
Goldwyn must act, and act she does, with a speech best rendered
in screenplay format:

2. Neil Gabler, *An Empire of Their Own*, p. 325.
3. Andrew Sinclair, *John Ford*, p. 197.

FRANCES

Sam's going to get well. He's going to make
that picture. It will be good. I've got that
faith in God and Sam Goldwyn.[4]

I have no doubt this is how the incident was remembered
and told, but it does have a cutting-room polish to it, with music
cues added in post-production. Even at firsthand, a filmmaker
tends to look at life, not excluding his own, as a series of dramatic moments. The best of them are no more immune to this
tendency than the hacks. John Ford, for example. Early in the
McCarthy era, a reactionary wing of the Directors Guild, led by
the impeccably crypto-fascist Cecil B. De Mille, moved to recall
Guild president Joseph L. Mankiewicz from office because Mankiewicz opposed a mandatory loyalty oath for directors. A special
meeting of the Guild was convened, and for four hours the
liberals opposing the oath and the conservatives favoring it ham-
mered at each other, each side questioning the other's loyalty
and patriotism, one director—George Stevens—even charging
that while he was "up to his ass in mud" at Bastogne, De Mille
was in Hollywood defending his capital gains. Finally Ford, a
man whose own reactionary credentials were beyond dispute,
rose to defend Mankiewicz:

ANOTHER ANGLE—JOHN FORD

rising slowly, chewing on his handkerchief, wearing an
old baseball hat.

FORD

My name is John Ford. I make westerns. . . .

ANGLE ON THE MEMBERSHIP

waiting on Ford's every word.

4. A. Scott Berg, *Goldwyn*, pp. 279–80.

FORD

I don't think there is anyone in this room who
knows more about what the American public
wants than Cecil B. De Mille . . .

ANGLE ON CECIL B. DE MILLE

waiting for the other shoe to drop.

FORD

. . . and he certainly knows how to give it to
them. In that respect I admire him . . .

ANGLE ON THE MEMBERSHIP

Not a sound in the jammed room.

ANGLE ON CECIL B. DE MILLE

an impassive Buddha

ANGLE ON FORD

who waits a beat, staring at De Mille.

FORD

. . . but I don't like you, C.B. I don't like
what you stand for, and I don't like what you
are doing here tonight.[5]

It was a moment of sublimely effective kitsch, with the good
guys winning behind the most unlikely of good guys, the reactionary turned libertarian, a great director of a hundred movies
starring in a scene with dialogue perfected over those same hundred pictures. "My name is John Ford, I make westerns" comes
from the "Go ahead, make my day" school of screenwriting,

5. Sinclair, pp. 157–58.

punchy and to the point. If you doubt kitsch, however, try to imagine Claude Monet rising in the Académie Française to quiet a controversy: *"Je m'appelle Claude Monet, je peins les fleurs."*

2
___

Envy has always informed any contemplation of Hollywood. "Through its star system," Kevin Starr has written,

> Hollywood took ordinary Americans—which by and large the stars were, in terms of talent and frail humanity—and endowed them with a quality of transcendence that flattered star and audience alike. They touched ordinariness with a glamour of appearances and possibilities for which each individual in the audience of millions secretly yearned.[6]

Frailty, to be sure, often compounded by the grubby sexual adventurism the unlettered and undereducated were forced to expend as capital; Merle Oberon was a $100-a-night whore before her star rose,[7] and Clark Gable, according to director George Cukor, a homosexual himself, hustled the meaner streets of Hollywood prior to his being dusted by the starmakers. It was indeed Cukor's contention that Gable had him fired as director of *Gone With the Wind* because he remembered Rhett Butler as a one-trick pony.[8] Inversion, however, was not on the menu

6. Kevin Starr, *Inventing the Dream*, p. 320.
7. Berg, p. 256.
8. Ethan Mordden, *The Hollywood Studios*, p. 100.

when Hollywood, especially in the early days, made movies about itself. In all the precursors to A *Star Is Born*—long-forgotten silents such as *Inez in Hollywood, The Runaway, Hollywood,* and *The Legend of Hollywood*—decency, talent, and hard work were all it took to turn, as it were, the trick.

What the movies offered was the first new way to tell a story since the invention of the printing press, technology as an art form, an art form bankrolled and nurtured moreover by men about whom it was said, in a quote whose provenance has long since been lost, "knew only one word of two syllables, and that word was 'fillum.' " Not that this unfamiliarity with the language was a barrier: the early pictures were silent. Intuitively the founders seemed to understand that the reaction to film was visceral and not intellectual, requiring no verbal agility. They could not articulate this thought; they just knew it. "Enjoyment of motion pictures demanded no special literary abilities or preparation," Starr writes: "Film spoke directly to the cognitive and subconscious self with next to no dependence on the apparatus and language of formal culture."[9]

By 1926, the movies were America's fifth-largest industry, a $1.5 billion-a-year business that accounted for 90 percent of the world's pictures.[10] Hollywood also produced what the rest of American industry could not—a kind of royalty, kings and queens of the screen, not independent with divine rights, but salaried employees at the mercy of their employers' whims. And the employers had whims of steel. Although most of the founders cordially despised each other, they shared certain common traits. They had a need to display how tough they were, how unlettered, uncultured, and foul-mouthed. They had a lust for enemies, as if only through enemies could they define themselves. They were estranged from their children and had Jewish first

9. Starr, p. 310.
10. Ibid., p. 313.

wives who became an embarrassment; Goldwyn, L. B. Mayer, Harry Cohn, and Jack Warner all married shiksas the second time around. Many of them were degenerate gamblers; Sam Goldwyn won $155,000 one week and lost $169,000 two weeks later.[11] Jack Warner once settled a $425,000 gambling debt with Goldwyn by loaning him Bette Davis to star in Goldwyn's production of *The Little Foxes.*

Only the coming of sound threatened the ascendancy of the founders. "It's a fad, it won't last," Adolph Zukor said almost hopefully after an early and primitive demonstration.[12] *The Jazz Singer* dashed that hope. "You ain't heard nothing yet," Al Jolson spoke from the screen. "You want to hear 'Toot, Toot, Tootsie'? All right, hold on." Near panic gripped Hollywood. "Like putting lipstick on the Venus de Milo," Mary Pickford said,[13] and the vacuous gossip columnist Louella Parsons, as always the mouthpiece of management, wrote, "The public has no intention of paying good money to be so annoyed."[14] Uneasy as they were with their adopted language, the founders feared that sound would undermine the hegemony they had fought so hard to establish.

Instead sound allowed them to expand and consolidate. Silent pictures may have been, as the director King Vidor said, "an art form complete unto themselves,"[15] but talkies were a gold mine, and art was never the object. Writers were imported to Hollywood in droves and assigned to a project usually two at a time. With their inchoate distrust of words, many of which they could neither pronounce nor understand, the moguls seemed intuitively to comprehend that while one writer was a possible anarchist, two under harness were only a tame pair on a mule

11. Berg, p. 202.
12. Ibid., p. 165.
13. Ibid., p. 171.
14. Ibid., p. 166.
15. Ibid., p. 172.

team; there were often a dozen mules on the team, fabricating as many as thirty drafts. Ben Hecht and the occasional Broadway playwright—Sidney Howard, say, or Robert Sherwood—were the rare writers allowed to work alone, and Hecht less for his talent than for his speed—he could write a script in two days—a facility that allowed him to make outrageous demands, such as insisting to Sam Goldwyn that for his efforts on *Barbary Coast* he be paid in cash every afternoon.[16] Words mystified the moguls, as indeed did the concept of reading. Even to the present time, film executives rarely use the verb "to read"; the form they prefer is "do some reading," as if reading were a chore, like pushups.

However uncomfortable the founders were with words, the talkies were the means that allowed each studio to evolve a personality of its own. At M-G-M, under L. B. Mayer and Irving Thalberg, the producer was king, the budgets big, the stars the brightest, the director always a subordinate, the stories invariably edifying. Paramount, under Adolph Zukor, was a director's studio where Ernst Lubitsch, Mitchell Leisen, Preston Sturges, and (later) Billy Wilder created a world of surface and sex and double entendre and even abandon in which virtue was not always its best reward. Harry Cohn's Columbia featured the earnest populism of Frank Capra and Robert Riskin, while the Warner brothers made their gangster pictures a metaphor for an underclass that M-G-M, for example, refused to acknowledge.

3

FROM ITS BEGINNINGS, the motion picture business—"the Industry," as its founders insisted on calling it, and as it is still called today—was the only major manufacturing enterprise in the United States that was run almost entirely by Jews. Not Jews

16. Berg, p. 260.

from Middle Europe like the Schiffs and the Kahns, with a taste for finance and a talent for underwriting manifest destiny and wars of conquest, the riches from which were plowed into culture and philanthropy, which brought respectability, if not acceptance by the gentile majority. These Jews looked down in embarrassment on the Jews who would invent Hollywood, coming as the newcomers did from a Baedeker of Polish and Russian pogroms—Warsaw for Sam Goldwyn, Risce in Hungary for Adolph Zukor, somewhere near Vilna for Louis B. Mayer.[17] Most of them were immigrants, illegally so more times than they were willing to admit, uncertain in the language, their first stake earned in the rougher precincts of retailing—hardware, ready-to-wear, and cheaper by the dozen. Their philanthropy, such as it was, extended only to themselves.

The retail experience in cloaks and suits and gloves and furs and dresses was, in fact, a priceless asset. These early movie magnates came from a discipline in which their economic future depended on their giving the goyim what they decreed, season by season, the goyim would want. A certain restlessness prevailed among them, however, because the market for the rag trade was limited, and they felt the urge to widen their horizons. The early movie business offered that opportunity. Between 1910 and 1912, the nickelodeon audience in America had doubled, from ten to twenty million people.[18] And it was a working-class audience, still largely untapped. So new and still so disreputable was the business, so wanting of the vigor that only ambitious immigrants could provide, that Jews were immediately acceptable without their origins being at issue.

No recounting of that early history of filmdom was complete without reference to the founding moguls as former "fur-

17. Friedrich, pp. 14–15. While the founders were largely immigrants, Leo Rosten, in his study *Hollywood: The Movie Colony*, found that by 1941 nearly 60 percent of the 120 leading film executives had graduated from college and that less than 5 percent came from Poland and Russia.
18. Starr, p. 309.

riers" or "rag merchants." It was an ethnic code, cryptological anti-Semitism. For furrier, read Jew. No, not Jew; the Sulzbergers were Jews, and the Kuhns and Loebs; these unlettered cloak and suiters were nothing but ostentatious parvenu kikes, and there was always a giggle to be had at their pretensions. "Put that finger down," John Barrymore once admonished a magnate. "I remember when it had a thimble on it."[19] Even Dwight Macdonald was not above this ploy. In a piece he wrote in 1933 for *The Symposium,* he managed in the space of a few thousand words to deride the ethnic background of the directors Josef von Sternberg, "who spurns as canard the rumor that he was born Joe Stern of Brooklyn"; Mervyn Leroy, "of whom it is rumored that his real name is Lasky"; and Lewis Milestone, "whose actual name is said to be Milstein."[20]

Not all the anti-Semitism was encoded. The movies, Henry Ford raged in his house organ, the *Dearborn Independent,* are "Jew-controlled, not in spots only, not 50 percent merely, but entirely. . . . As soon as the Jews gained control of the 'movies,' we had a movie problem, the consequences of which are not yet visible. It is the genius of that race to create problems of a moral character in whatever business they achieve a majority."[21]

The moguls reacted to these assaults by embarking "on an assimilation so ruthless and complete," Gabler writes, "that they cut their lives to the pattern of American respectability as they

---

19. Starr, p. 315.
20. Dwight Macdonald, *On Movies,* pp. 120–26. I do not wish to imply that Macdonald was an anti-Semite, but the tactic, in the hands of those who were, had an ugly whiff of nativism. Listing the members of the Committee for the First Amendment on 24 November 1947, Mississippi Congressman John Rankin, a member of the House Committee on Un-American Activities and rabid anti-Semite, said: "June Havoc . . . her real name is June Hovick; John Beal, whose real name is J. Alexander Bliedung; Edward Robinson, whose real name is Emmanuel Goldenberg; Melvin Douglas, whose real name is Melvyn Hesselberg." See Gabler, pp. 371–72.
21. Gabler, p. 277.

JOHN GREGORY DUNNE 209

interpreted it."[22] So absolutely did they reject their pasts that when Danny Kaye was brought to Hollywood, Sam Goldwyn ordered his hair dyed blond, in order to downplay what other Hollywood Jews called Kaye's "sinister," or too Jewish, look.

The founders also embraced America, or the America they conceived, in a ferocious, even pathological manner. Carvel, Idaho, the home of Andy Hardy and his family, became the metaphorical center of the good, the true, and the beautiful. It is interesting to speculate whether, before the days of *le ski*, any Hollywood mogul ever actually visited Idaho, and indeed how this haven was selected as cultural ground zero. There is no sense of the West in this Idaho town, no vast empty spaces; the Carvel now occasionally seen when Andy Hardy visits the cable TV channels is a genteel (and needless to say, gentile) suburb, the facades of its upmarket houses owing far more to Sewickly or Shaker Heights or Grosse Pointe than to the Continental Drift. This was an America, Mordden writes, of "Our Father, Dear Mother, admiring Big Brother, razzing Sis and understanding Kid Brother."[23] And the Hardys, he continues, a family of "dreary white Protestants who make one feel good to be single, Jewish, or an axe murderer."[24]

Of course the moguls would have regarded that kind of talk as subversive. An affinity for reactionary politics was part of their American construct. Except, briefly, for the Warner brothers, whose contrary natures would not let them agree with their fellow moguls on anything, the founders were the most conservative of Republicans. The Warners flirted with Franklin Roosevelt ("Court jester I was, and proud of it," Jack Warner declared), but the flirtation did not outlast FDR's first term. The administration refused to quash a lawsuit against Harry Warner, even after Jack interceded with the president, which led Harry Warner

22. Gabler, p. 4.
23. Mordden, p. 148.
24. Ibid., p. 153.

to call Roosevelt an ingrate; the Warners had scratched his back, but FDR had not scratched theirs in return, in the Industry the unforgivable sin. Louis B. Mayer thought Roosevelt a Communist and hung an oil portrait of Francis Cardinal Spellman, in ecclesiastical scarlet, on the wall of his library; Harry Cohn so admired Mussolini that even after the end of World War II he kept Il Duce's photograph in his office.[25]

Reaction's finest hour came in 1934 when the studio chieftains banded together to fight Upton Sinclair when he ran for governor on a platform he called EPIC—End Poverty in California. It was bad enough that Sinclair had once been a Socialist, but he was also perceived as anti-Hollywood as well. With Irving Thalberg leading the way, the studios prepared a series of anti-Sinclair newsreels in which a putative inquiring reporter would ask putative ordinary citizens who they intended to vote for. "Vy, I am foting for Seenclair," claimed a bearded wild-eyed extra in one short. "Vell, his system vorked vell in Russia, vy can't it vork here."[26] The circle had been joined. Eastern European Jews had created the perfect American bogeyman—an Eastern European Jew.

IF THE HOLLYWOOD JEWS were conflicted about their religion and how it affected their place in American society, they had, in Edgar Magnin, the perfect rabbi. For over sixty years, Rabbi Magnin administered to the tonier Hollywood Jews, marrying and burying Irving Thalberg, burying L. B. Mayer with a eulogy praising him as the vigilant enemy of "pseudo-liberals, Reds and pinks."[27] (When Harry Cohn died in 1958, Magnin was asked if he could find something good to say about the deceased and replied, "He's dead.")[28] A member of the Magnin

25. Gabler, pp. 368 (Roosevelt), 285 (Spellman), and 152 (Mussolini).
26. Ibid., p. 314.
27. Ibid., p. 425.
28. Berg, p. 484.

family that founded the retailing empire in San Francisco—for Jews always the most assimilated of American cities—Rabbi Magnin saw himself less a spiritual leader than envoy to the goyim and high priest of secularism. "I have no reason to go into the ghetto," Magnin told Robert Scheer in 1977. "One of my grandparents came out of it. I don't want to go back to it. I see these guys in their yarmulkes eating bacon on their salads at the club. They want to become more Jewish, whatever that means. . . . What virtue is there in ethnic emphasis? We have beautiful Jews and we have stinkers, and so does everybody else. Who's kidding whom with all this nonsense? Roots, roots, roots— baloney."[29] This was a language the founding Hollywood Jews, so divorced from their roots, could truly appreciate.

Magnin's arrival in Los Angeles, in 1914, roughly coincided, appropriately enough, with the filming of *The Straw Man*, the first feature length picture produced in Hollywood. His maiden sermon captured the mood that was to prevail, its title "The Stuff Dreams Are Made Of."[30] Magnin took voice lessons, and when he built the Wilshire Temple, he insisted it have the dimensions of a theater, a Grauman's Chinese of Judaism, as it were, seating 1,500 people. He sold religion the way his flock sold their pictures, changing ancient prayers as if they came from the typewriters of hack screenwriters and existed only for him to work his magic. Hillcrest, the Jewish country club across the street from Twentieth Century–Fox, became in effect his second synagogue, a place where he could work the room, schmooz, and establish a consensus. He avoided piety as if it were a sin and refused to be a moral guide, offering his absolution even to the sexual transgressions of the moguls. "Sleeping with a pretty gentile girl made them feel, if only for a few minutes, 'I'm half-gentile,'" Magnin told A. Scott Berg in 1983. "No wonder they

29. Robert Scheer, *Thinking Tuna Fish, Talking Death: Essays on the Pornography of Power*, p. 33.
30. Gabler, p. 270.

made idols out of shiksa goddesses. They worshipped those blue-eyed blondes they were forbidden to have."[31]

In matters of Americanism, Magnin supplied the text, to which the founders adhered religiously, as they rarely did to the Torah. In 1939, Magnin represented the Los Angeles Jewish community at a monster Hollywood Bowl rally honoring God, the flag, and Congressman Martin Dies, chairman of the House Committee on Un-American Activities. (It was at this rally that Irving Berlin's "God Bless America" was sung in public for the first time.)[32] Magnin's line on the Committee, the blacklist, Senator Joseph McCarthy—and indeed on every public issue—was always, Will it help (or hurt) the Jews? "What was interesting was how much the Hollywood Jews' hatred of communism seemed really a fear that Jewish radicals would make all Jews suspect," Gabler writes, "rather than any ideological opposition."[33] For Magnin, even concern over the Holocaust was something American Jews should best leave unemphasized. "All they talk about is the Holocaust and all the suffering," he said. "The goddamn fools don't realize that the more you tell the gentiles nobody likes us, the more they say there must be a reason for it."[34] He was the perfect spokesman for the Quisling mentality of the founders.

31. Berg, p. 164.
32. Scheer, p. 27.
33. Gabler, p. 320.
34. Ibid., p. 349.

4
___

"In two words, im possible."
—SAMUEL GOLDWYN

ACTUALLY THAT WAS an old English music hall gag, refined by Charlie Chaplin, who then attributed it to Sam Goldwyn.[35] Many of Goldwyn's celebrated malaprops were, in fact, manufactured by others, a point that once again underscores John Ford's maxim: "When the legend becomes fact, print the legend." Without the legends, there is a problem with the biography of any Hollywood mogul. The subjects are essentially no more interesting than Alfred P. Sloan or Harlow T. Curtice, each of whose success (or failure) in running General Motors had a more profound effect on the American economy than the output of any given studio chieftain in any given year.[36] What made the moguls interesting was their tyranny and their excess, and legends about their vices and vulgarity and pleasures that grew more outsized with every retelling.

In the strictest sense, they were only CEOs with a penchant for terror. The laws of libel protected the living, taste the dead. Only in fiction do the moguls really come alive, to the point where they have become stock players. The character we remember in Norman Mailer's *The Deer Park* is Herman Teppis, and we remember Herman Teppis mainly because he was fellated in his office by a contract starlet, remember him also for one of the funniest exchanges in any Hollywood novel, Teppis and his daughter's husband, the producer Carlyle Munshin:

" 'The doctor told me you ought to lower your nervous tension,' [Munshin] said.

35. Berg, p. 396.
36. Curtice, in fact, was interesting in that during his tenure as GM's chief executive, his brother was a foreman in a GM plant. Later, in a hunting accident, Curtice blew the head off a close friend.

" 'You're my son-in-law, and you're a pimp,' Teppis burst out."[37]

It is useful to point out that Norman Mailer wrote his first screenplay for Sam Goldwyn;[38] this is one of the few facts that A. Scott Berg fails to mention in all the reverential amplitude of *Goldwyn's* 579 pages. *Goldwyn* is a classic biography of immigrant boy making good, with all the attendant costs, beginning on the first page with the birth of Schmuel Gelbfisz (later Samuel Goldfish, later still Sam Goldwyn) in the Warsaw ghetto, ending on the last, ninety-seven years later, with the death in Beverly Hills, eighteen months after his own, of Goldwyn's second wife, Frances Howard Goldwyn, her last years a descent into alcoholism, loony Catholicism, madness, and senility. Schmuel Gelbfisz left Warsaw in 1895, when he was sixteen, and walked 500 miles to Hamburg, where he learned the rudiments of the glover's trade and somehow managed passage to England. From London he walked another 125 miles to relatives in Birmingham, who anglicized his name to Samuel Goldfish. In 1898, Sam Goldfish embarked to the new world, probably on stolen money, probably to Canada, where he slipped across the border into the United States, finally finding work as a glover in Gloversville, New York.

By 1904, Goldfish had learned enough English both to become an American citizen and to talk himself into a salesman's job with the Elite Glove Company. He was a natural drummer, his territory always expanding, until finally he became Elite's man in New York, a stockholder in the company and a figure in the *schmata* business. In 1910, he became a bridegroom as well, marrying Jesse Lasky's sister Blanche. Jesse and Blanche Lasky had once been in vaudeville, with a cornet act, and eventually Jesse had become a Broadway producer. Via the Laskys, Goldfish had a foot in the show business door.

37. Norman Mailer, *The Deer Park*, p. 247.
38. Friedrich, p. 375.

To Sam Goldfish, a gambler even then, the infant nickelodeon business offered vistas gloves did not have. His idea of the future was not the nickelodeon's staple two-reel quickie but a picture the length of a Broadway play. With Lasky and a mutual playwright friend, Cecil Blount De Mille, Goldfish formed the Jesse L. Lasky Feature Play Company; Lasky was the front man, Goldfish the salesman, and De Mille the creative force. For $4,000, the Lasky company bought the rights to an old Broadway hit, *The Squaw Man*, a love story set in the old West. That none of the partners knew how to make a motion picture was of small moment; with the exception of D. W. Griffith, almost no one else did either. De Mille headed west with his company of players, found Arizona wanting as a location, and continued on to Los Angeles. It was 1914. Hollywood was born.

The Squaw Man was a hit, and Goldfish set on a course from which he did not deviate until the day he died. When he needed partners, he brought them in, when they had fulfilled their usefulness, he discarded them; even his wife Blanche and their daughter Ruth were jettisoned when they became excess cargo. His life was littered with lawsuits and friends turned enemies. He fought with Mayer and with Zukor and with Chaplin and with Mary Pickford and Douglas Fairbanks and with Edgar Selwyn. Selwyn is of interest only in that his partnership with Goldfish was called by the portmanteau name Goldwyn Pictures, Goldwyn the prefix of one surname and the suffix of the other; when the two partners split acrimoniously, Goldfish took the company name legally as his own.

This period of Goldwyn's life reads like, and has as much interest as, a balance sheet. The titles of unremembered pictures are stacked one atop the next: *The Floor Below, Joan of Plattsburg, Thirty a Week, Dodging a Million, The Kingdom of Youth*. Stock is issued, depositions are taken, women chased, real estate purchased, pictures cast, grosses given, plots synopsized, all to the litany of "And then he produced . . ." What was produced was largely dreck, although Goldwyn did manage to commission an official biography, his command of public relations, as always, masterful.

Goldwyn was forty-six when he finally moved full-time to Hollywood with his second wife, Frances Howard, a famous beauty twenty-four years his junior. (Frances Howard was actually in love with George Cukor, a love that went unrequited because of Cukor's homosexuality. They remained friends for life, and when Cukor died in 1983, he was buried, in accordance with the terms of her will, in the same crypt with Sam and Frances Goldwyn.) Without a studio apparatus, Goldwyn was a true independent producer, using the proceeds of one picture to finance the next; he had no program pictures, as did Mayer at M-G-M and Zukor at Paramount, to cushion the losses, no roster of actors and writers and directors to throw into a picture with a release date set. The amazing thing about Goldwyn's success was that he had absolutely no gift for spotting that indefinable "it" that made a movie star; he tried, and failed, with Vilma Banky, Anna Sten, Virginia Mayo, Andrea Leeds, with Farley Granger and Dana Andrews, a veritable minor-league farm team. Indeed an argument could be made that the only first-class talent Goldwyn ever nurtured and kept was neither an actor nor a director, but a cameraman, the incomparable Gregg Toland, the man Orson Welles used to light *Citizen Kane*.

The forgettable pictures blurred into one. "*Condemned* opened at the . . . *Raffles* had been a warhorse of the London stage since . . . *The Devil to Pay* is the story of a . . ."[39]—and these were just three Ronald Colman pictures, made before Colman hit Goldwyn with a lawsuit to get out of his contract. Humiliation was the given in Goldwyn's relations with subordinates; he reduced director Archie Mayo to carrying film cans in hopes that Mayo would quit his five-year contract; Mayo hung

39. Berg, pp. 189, 190, 191.

on. The Goldwyn Girls were hired to add glamour to the larger productions, and some of them became just that—Goldwyn girls. "You really can't resent Sam's vulgarity," Robert Sherwood told Anita Loos, "when he himself doesn't really understand the meaning of the word."[40]

Dinner at the Goldwyns was a hot ticket, and served promptly at eight whether the guests had arrived or not. Cole Porter, Elsie Mendl, William Paley, and the Averell Harrimans were the draws for such local gentry as Katharine Hepburn, Howard Hawks, the Gary Coopers, and Clark Gable, who presumably did not discuss his days as a cruiser with Cole Porter; evenings usually ended with a movie in the Goldwyn screening room. After twenty-four years of seeing pictures in private screening rooms, I am compelled to say that it is the rare night when at least half the guests do not go to sleep, often loudly so; it is entertaining as Nembutal.

HOLLYWOOD IS FULL of enduring and unexamined legends. One is the genius of Irving Thalberg, in large part perpetrated by F. Scott Fitzgerald's portrait of him as Monroe Stahr in *The Last Tycoon*; Stahr was not the man to let contract actresses do him under his desk. Only Lillian Hellman has ever really put Thalberg into perspective. "*The Last Tycoon* was a sentimental view of Irving Thalberg," she wrote in *An Unfinished Woman*. "Scott . . . got all sticky moon candy about a man who was only a bright young producer."[41]

Another equally unexamined legend is what generations of Goldwyn publicity men called, and which Sam Goldwyn himself agreed was, "The Goldwyn Touch." His biographers have trouble explaining exactly what the Goldwyn touch was. " 'The Goldwyn touch' is not brillance or sensationalism," Alva Johnston wrote in *The Great Goldwyn*. "It is something that manifests

40. Carol Easton, *The Search for Sam Goldwyn*, p. 234.
41. Lillian Hellman, *An Unfinished Woman*, pp. 63–4.

itself gradually in a picture; the characters are consistent; the workmanship is honest; there are no tricks and shortcuts; the intelligence of the audience is never insulted."[42] Berg does no better: "Every decision as to which scenes were reshot or included in the picture required Goldwyn's approval; not a word of the script reached the screen without Goldwyn's okay; none of Richard Day's sets was built or Omar Kiam's costumes sewn until Goldwyn permitted."[43] William Wyler, who directed seven pictures for Goldwyn, including the producer's two best, *Wuthering Heights* and *The Best Years of Our Lives*, has the last word. "Tell me," he asked Berg in 1980, "which pictures have 'The Goldwyn Touch' that I didn't direct?"[44]

Berg struggles manfully page after page with an intractable subject, as if trying to wear the reader down by sheer weight of presentation. Whenever possible he tries to invest Goldwyn's invincible vulgarity with dignity, to the point, in the epigraph, of invoking kinship with Ozymandias. Virtue is even made of Goldwyn's never carrying cash because it would spoil the drape of his custom-tailored London clothes; this is the best evidence we have of a Goldwyn touch. Schmuel Gelbfisz, the wandering Jew about whose threads history is scant, is more interesting than Samuel Goldfish, and Samuel Goldfish, the upwardly mobile philandering glover, more so than Sam Goldwyn.

In the end, we remember not Goldwyn's touch but his

42. Berg, p. 268.
43. Ibid., p. 272.
44. Ibid., p. 309. Although he does not address Wyler's rhetorical question in *Goldwyn*, Berg tried to do so in an interview he gave *The New York Times* (March 27, 1989, p. C18). In apparent rebuttal, Berg asked: "Which pictures have the Wyler touch that Goldwyn didn't produce?" The answer is in the titles of the pictures Wyler directed without Goldwyn. There are, of course, the usual clinkers, but among those with some claim to our attention are *Jezebel*, *The Letter*, *Mrs. Miniver*, *The Heiress*, *Detective Story*, *Roman Holiday*, *Friendly Persuasion*, *The Big Country*, and *The Collector*, as well as the World War II documentary *Memphis Belle*. In two words, im pressive.

Goldwynisms, whether his alone or crafted by other hands. "To-morrow we shoot whether it rains, whether it snows, whether it stinks," he said to the director Leo McCarey after weather delays on *The Kid from Spain*. And when Preston Sturges, of course called "Sturgeon," finished his script of Tolstoy's *Resurrection*, Goldwyn congratulated him for his "snappy nineteenth-century dialogue." Claiming he was not sexually squeamish, he said, "I'm no Polly Adler" and one of his paintings he identified as "my Toujours Lautrec" and to no one in particular he said, "You've got to take the bull by the teeth" and "I'm sticking my head in a moose" and "You need Indians, you can get them right from the reservoir." My particular favorite is a limpid plot summary of one of his less worthy pictures, *Edge of Doom:* "This is a simple story of a boy who wants a fine funeral for his mother, so he kills a priest."

5

IN 1967, WHILE DOING a book about a motion picture studio, I was invited to a party the studio gave for its distributors at the Hollywood Hills home of George Cukor. Cukor stayed inside the house out of sight, receiving only the most senior of the studio executives and the few above-the-title stars in attendance. Out-side, the hoi polloi mingled around the pool. The flowers were in bloom, the trees in full fruit. I finally left, and as I waited for the parking boy to retrieve my car, I casually picked a lemon from a potted tree outside Cukor's house. The lemon, I noted as my car appeared, was stamped with the word "Sunkist."

This is the sort of thing always happening to people visiting what Norman Mailer, in *The Deer Park*, called "The Capital," the sort of thing that makes their trip and improves with every retelling. Ridicule has always been a major component in any

discussion of Hollywood, especially of the founding Hollywood
Jews with their intellectual shortcomings and the conspicuous
consumption they confused with glamour. Zapping the vulgarity
was easier than trying to understand the movie earthquake and
its recurring aftershocks, which are still being felt today. Before
Goldwyn, Zukor, Mayer, Cohn, Carl Laemmle, and the rest
heeded Horace Greeley, whom they probably never heard of, and
went west, this country was defined by the East. Everything was
good or bad to the extent that it did or did not coincide with
the eastern norm; the making of cultural rules, the fact of being
the nation's cultural arbiter imbued confidence. The movies were
a severe shock to that confidence, all the more because the images up there on the screen had no apparent editorial bias. That
the moguls were indifferent to the cultural heritage of an East
in which they had never had a stake was taken as evidence of an
indigenous lack of culture, this and their Sunkist lemon trees the
objects of derision.

In a way, Henry Ford was right: they *were* immigrant Jews,
without the credentials to interpret an Anglo-Saxon culture.
What they did instead was invent an America—"an empire of
their own," as Gabler calls it in his estimable and essential book.
"They would create its values and its myths, its traditions and
archetypes. It would be an America where fathers were strong,
families stable, people attractive, resilient, resourceful and decent."[45] Having invented America, they even invented an established moneyed class for this America—an aristocratic "East." It
is the "East" we see today in the windows of Ralph Lauren's
flagship boutique in the old Rhinelander mansion on Madison
Avenue. Look at the studio photographs by George Hurrell, Bert
Six, and others in *Hollywood Glamor Portraits* and *The Image
Makers*—Humphrey Bogart and Cary Grant and Robert Mont-
gomery and Gary Cooper, Joan and Constance Bennett, Kath-

45. Gabler, pp. 5–6.

arine Hepburn, Paulette Goddard. Every imperfection has been airbrushed out, pipe and cigarette smoke billows, ascots are casually knotted, décolletage discreetly displayed. For all the croquet wickets, badminton racquets, and polo mallets in Lauren's windows, he is presenting not a world of old American money, but old American money as dreamed by Adolph Zukor and L. B. Mayer. Another circle closed: the fugitive rag merchants created an idea of American glamour; its custodians today are the contemporary *schmata* moguls, American sabras with names like Lipschitz (Lauren) and Klein.

There was, of course, a down side to this invented America: "Mother Goose platitudes and primitive valentines," as Ben Hecht said. "There are no problems of labor, politics, domestic life or sexual abnormality but can be solved happily by a simple Christian phrase or fine American motto."[46] In other words, the Hollywood Jews invented the imaginary land we have come to know as Ronald Reagan's America, that America in which it was always morning. This was their most enduring and ironic legacy, one perhaps that most notorious of anti-Semites Henry Ford might even applaud.

46. Berg, p. 417.

MANUAL LABOR

NOTE: *This piece was written in August 1987, and was published the following December, the same week that the uprisings began both in Gaza and on the West Bank.*

In Israel—
An Outsider's Journal

1

THIS IS HOW TIGHT the airport security was boarding Lufthansa Flight 686 from Frankfurt to Tel Aviv. The Frankfurt airport has bath and shower facilities for transit passengers facing a long layover between flights. In the men's room, where I cleaned up after the all-night trip from New York, I watched another passenger dressing, as if for a date. He showered, then shaved, lavished cologne on his face, plucked his eyebrows, and trimmed hair from his nose and ears. He put on fresh socks, underwear, and a clean shirt. When he finished dressing, he swirled his hair over a bald spot, fixed a yellow silk handkerchief in his jacket pocket, and finally, just before leaving, bought a package of condoms from a dispenser on the wall and dropped it into his toilet kit. The next time I saw him was in the security line for Lufthansa 686. Every passenger undergoes the same rigorous scrutiny. First you pass through a metal detector guarded by police armed with automatic weapons. Then a second portable metal detector is run up between your legs. Every bag is opened, and every pocket in every bag, and every container in those bags. The dandy from the men's room was directly ahead of me. The security guard took his toilet kit and spread its contents on his table. He squeezed the toothpaste, smelled the cologne, and opened a package of Q-tips. Then he removed the three foil-covered condoms from their box and cracked the foil of each in turn. "For plastique," the man behind me in line whispered. Perhaps, or perhaps only an exercise in egalitarianism on the part of the stone-faced security officer.

I HAD NEVER SEEN so many guards with machine guns. They were all over the boarding area beyond the security checkpoint. Two with a large police dog trained as an explosive sniffer checked the bus that would take us to the plane, an Airbus, which for security reasons was parked out on the tarmac, away from any buildings. The passenger bus was escorted to the plane by a van filled with more armed guards in military khaki. Other soldiers with automatic weapons ringed the plane. Finally, as we taxied out, an armored personnel carrier filled with troops moved along-side us to the takeoff runway, where it waited until we were airborne.

THE QUESTION I had to ask myself was Why was I going to Israel? The Catholic Sisters of Mercy who had been the custo-dians of my religious training at St. Joseph Cathedral School in Hartford, Connecticut, had drilled into me their fantasies of a place they called the Holy Land, a place that in their telling seemed populated only by Jesus, the Virgin Mary, Mary Mag-dalene, the twelve apostles, Barabbas, Pontius Pilate, some Jew-ish high priests, assorted Roman soldiers, a few Arab goatherds, and the odd camel. All I needed to know, I was assured by the nuns, was in the Apostles' Creed: . . . the third day He rose again from the dead; He ascended into heaven . . . from thence He shall come to judge the quick and the dead. As for current events, first there was Israel, then there was Palestine, then there was Israel again. In other words, I was traveling light.

. .

WE—MY WIFE AND I—asked the authorities at Ben-Gurion Airport in Tel Aviv not to stamp our passports when we landed. Our plans called for us to go to Jordan when we left Israel, over the Allenby Bridge, the lower of the two bridges across the Jordan River, the de facto frontier between the Occupied West Bank and Jordanian territory. Had our passports shown a stop in Israel, we would have been denied entry into Jordan. Similarly, we had to have separate airline tickets from Amman to Paris, our next stop, with no extraneous carbons indicating a landing in Tel Aviv; otherwise we would not have been allowed to leave Jordan. Logic dictates that we had to come from somewhere, especially if, as planned, we walked across the Allenby Bridge, but as long as our passports did not indicate that the somewhere was Israel, the Jordanian border authorities could maintain the pretense that we had not been there; the Allenby Bridge was on the West Bank, the West Bank had prior to the 1967 war been under Jordanian control, the Jordanians still considered the West Bank theirs, hence we came not from Israel but from the West Bank. The Israelis simply did not care where we went; they went along with the charade, stamping two blank pieces of paper rather than our passports. It was our introduction to the magic carpet legalities of the Middle East.

WILD MUSTARD ran over the hills on the road to Jerusalem, which is less than an hour's drive from Tel Aviv. In the 1948 war, this road was Jerusalem's lifeline, over which the Haganah trucked supplies and weapons to the beleaguered city. The convoys were like ducks in a shooting gallery, targeted by the Arab troops commanding the heights. Now the hillsides were festooned with the wreckage of those convoys, trucks and armored cars, washed in rust-resistant red paint and left there as memorials. On the outskirts of Jerusalem, a soldier was hitchhiking. He was wearing sweatpants and sneakers and a yarmulke and a T-shirt with the logo of the rock group U-2. His military kit was in a tennis bag slung over one shoulder, and slung from the other was an automatic weapon, from which hung a baseball glove. He was probably an American, our driver indicated, returned to Israel under aliya, or the welcoming of diaspora Jews back to the homeland. As the traffic slowed, our driver told us where we could exchange dollars for shekels at black market rates in East Jerusalem, the Arab section of the city.

WE WERE STAYING at Mishkenot Sha'Ananim, a guesthouse maintained by the city of Jerusalem and the Jerusalem Foundation for non-Israeli visitors involved in the arts. Also in residence were the South African novelist J. M. Coetzee and the English historian Alan Bullock. Our visit had been arranged by our English publisher, Lord Weidenfeld, who is closely associated with both the Foundation and Mishkenot. Not the least of Mishkenot's charms was that our stay was free, save for laundry and telephone calls. We had a five-room suite on two levels—living room, kitchen, bedroom, two baths, and two studies. The veranda outside overlooked the walls of the Old City and the Jaffa Gate. I went out onto the terrace. The valley between Mishkenot and the Old City had been a no-man's-land before the 1967 war. Twice in those days Jordanian artillery had blown off the top of the windmill that dominated the Mishkenot complex, and twice it had been replaced. Though it was warm in the sun outside, the suite itself was frigid enough to refrigerate meat; the stone floors and thick stone walls sealed in the cold. In the kitchen there were kosher and non-kosher dishes and implements. I wondered what would happen if we accidentally placed a non-kosher dish in a kosher cabinet, or vice versa. As I understood the dietary laws, the only way to purify tainted dishes was to bury them in the ground. It seemed simpler to take all our meals out.

As IT HAPPENED, our Friday arrival coincided with sundown and the beginning of Shabat, or the Sabbath. To arrive in Jeru-

salem as the Sabbath is closing in is to experience true claustro-
phobia. We could not, we were told, change money. We could
not, we were also told, get dinner, or even a taxi. Religious laws,
we were told, forbade the conduct of any business. In fact, none
of this is really true, but there seemed a general wish that it
should be true, a punitive intent. That I took this personally was
a function, I thought, of the exhaustion attendant to a thirteen-
hour flight and the vicious cold I had picked up on it; the jet lag
was like a deep bruise between my shoulders. After a few days,
however, when the cold and the jet lag both subsided, I realized
that this punitive attitude was endemic. It was as if every encounter was designed to involve the visitor personally, every minute of every day, in the enduring tensions between religious and
secular rituals, forcing him to come down on one side or the
other. Such is the tone of the place that among the non-ortho-
dox Israelis I was to meet, the non-believers and the non-practic-
ers, there seemed an almost rancorous obligation not to observe
the Sabbath strictures, not for any sybaritic reasons but only to
make a point. I tried to imagine some circumstance that might
lead me to make a point of my own agnosticism, but could not
conceive of any that might possibly arise.

WE HAD DINNER in East Jerusalem that first night, at a restaurant called Philadelphia (named not after the city in Penn-
sylvania but for the Greek word meaning friendship, and also
the Greek word for Amman, the capital of Jordan, which from
1948 until 1967 had authority over East Jerusalem). Because
Shabat closes most of the restaurants in Jewish West Jerusalem,
and because those that remain open are subject to either picket-
ing or attack from the more rigorous and relentless of the orthodox sects, Philadelphia was jammed, both with secular Israelis
and with passengers from hotel tour buses. With my instinct for
the peripheral, I immediately lapsed into the habit of a lifetime,
eavesdropping on a conversation at an adjoining table between
an Israeli businessman and an American travel agent who was

trying to sell him on the economic potential of something he called, hands aloft, fingers making quote marks in the air, "The Jerusalem Triathlon." The deal seemed to be that if the Israeli convinced his backers to buy the concept, the travel agent would make the major bookings for the sponsors and the media and the triathletes and their support personnel, cutting the locals in on his commissions. "Jerusalem," the travel agent said, "is the only place in the world with a climate like Honolulu's."

The assertion seemed to perplex the Israeli. It was cold outside, and pissing rain.

"The Honolulu Triathlon."

The Israeli nodded noncommittally and picked at his chickpea salad.

"Ancillary rights," the American said.

The Israeli asked him to define ancillary rights. Both men had their wives at the table, but the two women neither talked to nor looked at each other. Nor did their husbands pay them any attention. It was as if each wife were sitting alone at a separate table for one.

"T-shirts," the American said. "Hats, goggles, socks, you can merchandise anything, the only limit is your imagination." He was talking too fast and he seemed to realize it. "There is a fortune to be made in"—once more he made quotation marks in the air—"The Jerusalem Triathlon."

The Israeli was not convinced. "The premium is too high."

"Triathletes are people with a commitment," the travel agent said, giving it his best shot. "Like the people of Israel."

The check came. The American said, "Will you study the proposal?"

The Israeli picked up the bill. "It's on me."

A FEW DAYS later I was told by an American diplomat that several years before someone had rolled a hand grenade down the stairs into the Philadelphia. I wondered how enthusiastic the travel agent would have been about The Jerusalem Triathlon had he known that.

Lunch with G, a foreign correspondent, not American, with five years in Israel and Lebanon. I had known him fifteen years and a wife ago. "Israel would not have been created if it had not been for the Holocaust, and Western guilt about not having done enough to stop it," G said. "Hitler was responsible for the Holocaust. Hence Israel, if the equation is followed to its logical extreme, would not have been born if it had not been for Hitler." He smiled. "This is a line of reasoning, needless to say, that infuriates the Israelis."

We were in a restaurant overlooking the Old City. The sky was overcast, the weather cold. I asked about his ex-wife, the one I knew. "She fought the divorce tooth and nail, like the good woman she is," he said equably. He noticed I was having difficulty with my lunch, which seemed composed of cardboard shapes of varying sizes and colors, albeit with a consistency of texture and taste. "You don't," G cautioned, "come to Israel for the food."

I asked him about someone we both knew. "He's a spy, of course," I said. "Asshole deep in Israeli intelligence." The waiter hovered around. G, my wife, and I were the only people in the restaurant. "Everyone knows he's a spook." G's silence should have warned me, but I plowed ahead. "If you have a spook working for you, you know he's going to be a liar. Spies lie."

G asked the waiter in French to check the chill of the white wine. Suddenly I realized that the wine chat was G's way of shutting me up, that Israel was a country where it was best to be discreet when talking about spies, whether they be Mossad, CIA, or others. "Sorry about that," I apologized when the waiter left.

"No harm done," G said smoothly. Then another smile. "Of course you should assume your phone's being tapped."

For the rest of the lunch, whenever we talked of anything more sensitive than wives and ex-wives and children and step-children and real estate and the cost of educating two families, G would say "um" and "ah" and "this chap" and "that chap" whenever the waiter was in the vicinity. Like all correspondents, he was a repository of gossip and only too willing to share it. He mentioned the putative homosexuality of a prominent Israeli. "Queer as a coot, that chap." Then the obligatory demurrer. "Just a rumor, of course." And the putative yen of an Arab leader for his country's television anchorwomen. "This chap's screwed them all," G said. "Just a rumor, of course."

I asked him about the Demjanjuk trial, then going on in Jerusalem and carried live over Israeli radio. John Demjanjuk was a retired Cleveland auto worker, a Ukrainian immigrant who was deported from the United States for falsifying his citizenship application and extradited to Israel. The falsification of citizen-ship papers is a relatively small beer charge. What the U.S. had actually done was honor a request from Israel that Demjanjuk be deported so that the Israelis might put him on trial for war crimes. Specifically, Israel charged that Demjanjuk was the no-torious and sadistic "Ivan the Terrible," a Soviet army conscript and POW turned Nazi torturer and prison camp guard at Tre-blinka, in Poland, where 850,000 Jews were slaughtered in World War II. Demjanjuk's defense was that he was the victim of mis-taken identity, that while he might have falsified the documents necessary to obtain American citizenship, he was not Ivan the Terrible. Why the fascination with the case? I asked G.

"Because it's likely to be the last major war crimes trial," G said. "The survivors of those camps are old now. Even the ones who were children are middle-aged, or late middle-aged. Their memories are faulty and they're not always the best or most reliable witnesses. When someone testifies, as someone did—he was an old man, almost ninety—that in order to appear at Dem-janjuk's deportation hearing he traveled to the United States by train, across the Atlantic by train, then what you have is a shadow of a doubt. But what you also have is this extraordinary recall of the most unimaginable details of horror to which there is only this pool of witnesses that is inexorably drying up. And because these details are so unimaginable they have an absolutely un-impeachable sense of truth." He paused. "For example, when they burned bodies at Treblinka, they stacked women and chil-dren at the bottom, just over the flames, because they burned better than men did. Like kindling."

In the silence that followed, I remembered reading once in the arson chapter of a homicide investigation manual that the uterus of a woman and the prostate of a man were the last organs to be destroyed in a fire. After a moment I asked if Dem-janjuk's defense would hold water.

"There was an Ivan the Terrible," G said. "There's no question about that. The only question is whether Demjanjuk is he. And I'm not sure that it matters." He let this sink in. "The fact is, for the Israeli believers in realpolitik, the best thing would be to have Demjanjuk acquitted. This would show the majesty and magnanimity of Israeli justice to the world community— which at the present time finds it tarnished—and gain the ad-vantage of telling the story of the Holocaust to a whole new generation. This trial is actually a godsend to the European Jews, the Ashkenazim. Many, maybe most, of the Oriental Jews—the Syrians, the Moroccans, the Sephardim—are bored with the Holocaust. The Holocaust was a European experience that did not touch them directly. They had their own pogroms, in Mo-rocco or Syria or wherever they came from, that the rest of the world did not get terribly excited about. And so what this trial does is bring the Holocaust home not just to a new generation but also to that segment of Israeli society, the Sephardic majority, that did not have a grandmother gassed at Treblinka."

In other words, the trial was a teacher's aid, I thought later. A learning tool. The ultimate historical verb wheel.

•   •

THIS FEELING was reinforced when I met L, a professor at the Hebrew University on Mount Scopus. L's thirteen-year-old son had been assigned a theme topic in school: "Is the Demjanjuk Trial Only a Show Trial Arranged by the Government?" An American thirteen-year-old would be in the eighth grade. I tried to imagine an American eighth-grade teacher giving his class a similar theme topic: "Was the Invasion of Grenada a Political and Military Necessity or Only a Public Relations Demonstration That America Was Back?" The children would rebel, their parents would be up in arms, the school board would cave in to protests, the teacher would be fired, and that fat and flatulent little bully Robert Novak would no doubt nominate him for a post in the Sandinista cabinet.

L's son had taken the affirmative: it was a show trial. Because he is an academic with a taste for philosophical discourse, L had taken the negative, an adversary position to test the strength of his son's arguments, and his commitment to them. It was L's contention that most Holocaust trials involved bureaucrats like Adolf Eichmann, not someone who actually killed Jews, who shot and tortured them, as Ivan the Terrible was alleged to have done. Historically, L said, Holocaust trials had been about the banality of evil, evil as a bureaucratic function. We talk about the banality of evil, he said, as if the banality were more important than the evil itself. Ivan the Terrible was evil incarnate, a murderer, not a banal assigner of death.

L's son was not persuaded. Making evil banal, he argued, was a greater crime than the evil perpetrated; the true evil was the banality of evil.

The argument between father and son seemed to have wandered from whether the Demjanjuk trial was only a show trial or not, but as intellectual theater it was not bad. I gave the decision to the son on points.

•   •

K OFFERED to take us on a driving tour of Jerusalem, a prospect I regarded with dread. I hate sightseeing. I dislike churches, shrines, holy places, great houses, tombs, museums, and grottoes. I tolerate battlefields and battlements only if they have some historical relevance to the century in which I live—the Normandy beaches, say, or Anzio, or Château Thierry. Venice leaves me cold. "The rationalist mind has always had its doubts about Venice," Mary McCarthy wrote in *Venice Observed*; I must have a rationalist's mind. Guides and guidebooks fill me with dismay and consternation. I want to drive, walk, come upon things myself, not in the middle of a tour. I had been visiting Paris for ten years before I finally managed to hit the Louvre, and then only to get in out of a sudden thundershower. How much better to come upon the Mona Lisa that way. I had even seen the sewers of Paris and the Canal St. Martin and the slums of Belleville and Menilmontant before I saw the sublime stained-glass windows of La Sainte Chapelle.

In preparation for the Jerusalem tour I dipped into the chapters on the Holy Land in Mark Twain's *Innocents Abroad*, which I had brought with me. "A fast walker could go outside the walls of Jerusalem and walk entirely around the city in an hour," Twain had written in 1869. "I don't know how else to make one understand how small it is." A comforting thought. Our tour of some of the great shrines of Christendom, of Judaica, and the Muslim world would be short.

K was a slight and intense woman with glasses and close-cropped hair. She was an anthropologist at the Van Leer Institute, and I suspect she was no more interested in showing us the sights than we were in making the trip; it was a pro forma duty she undertook for visitors who had been recommended to her. K was active in Peace Now, a loose coalition of Israelis opposed to the new Jewish settlements authorized and constructed by the government on the occupied West Bank, the Old Testament lands of Judea and Samaria wrested from Jordanian control in the 1967 war. There are 60,000 Jews in these settlements, islands in a sea of 800,000 Palestinian Arabs under the strict control of an always harsh and sometimes repressive Israeli military government. It is the contention of Peace Now that these settlements are like carbuncles that will poison the body politic and destroy any chance for peace between Jew and Palestinian.

In the gathering dusk, we journeyed around the walls of the Old City, traveled up to Mount Scopus and Gethsemane and the Mount of Olives, then circled back to K's house in West Jerusalem. K—she is a widow—shares a ground-floor apartment with her seventeen-year-old son, David. Rock music blared from behind David's closed bedroom door. K shouted for David to turn down the volume. Finally the door opened and David emerged, a muscular blond boy, barefoot, and wearing an earring, followed by his girl friend, a sulky teenager with long dark hair who seemed clad only in one of David's oversized shirts. I had the distinct impression that we had interrupted them making love. In fact, wherever we went in Israel, I noticed an overwhelming charge of sexual energy, I thought probably because the garrison state threw the sexes together at such an early age. With both men and women facing mandatory military conscription at the age of eighteen—women for two years, men for three, and the men committed to the reserves until age fifty-five—a roll in the feathers seemed small enough an allowance to allot to children who soon enough would be on the thin red line.

David was scheduled for call-up in the fall, and was already being interviewed by the various services. He wanted to join an elite unit—the commandos or the frogmen or paratroopers. His mother said that the elite units were as class conscious as the Guards regiments in the British army. "What they want," she said, "are blond, blue-eyed Jews like David, with good educations." She shook her head. "This is the class system at work. In a society with putatively no classes."

We had coffee and fruit. David and his sullen and beautiful

girl friend returned to his room to dress for a party. I could see weightlifting equipment on the floor in his room. The girl put a Beatles tape in the cassette player and in a moment "Let It Be" drowned out all conversation. It suddenly occurred to me that in Israel the state had taken the separation anxiety out of the hands of the nuclear family: the military obligation provided an institutional leave-taking, parent from child, child from parent. The child was not exactly leaving, nor was the family exactly pushing the child from the nest.

David reappeared wearing a toga. He's going to something called a toga party, K said. Did I know what a toga party was? John Belushi and *Animal House*, I answered. "At last an educated man," David said, disappearing back into his bedroom. "How did you know that?" his mother asked.

"That's like my asking you what the Wailing Wall is," I said.

Once again David reappeared, a mock laurel on his brow and his face rouged, as if he were a Roman senator at revel. There had been a small problem at school, he confessed to his mother. What kind of problem? K asked. From the bedroom the Beatles were still providing background music. As he adjusted his toga so that it fell naturally, David said that the orthodox Jewish boys at the religious school next door to the secular academy he attended had pelted his school with stones.

"And what did you do?" K asked warily. It was the kind of question to which mothers rarely expect a straightforward answer, or at any rate one that is not put forward as if the transgression admitted is not the only rational response under the circumstances.

"I mooned them," David said.

Whether the stone-throwing took place before David's mooning, or whether the hail of stones was precipitated by it, I thought were questions best not delved into too deeply, and K seemed tacitly to agree. The incident, however, underscored a deep resentment on the part of mother and son of those religious ultra-orthodox Jews who were exempted from serving in the military. This exemption was based not on a set of pacifist beliefs but rather on the opposition of some of the more rigorously orthodox sects to the state of Israel itself, a secular entity whose legitimacy they choose not to recognize. The true Israel, they maintain, will return only with the Messiah, and until then the only laws to which they owe allegiance are the rules of conduct set forth in the Talmud and the Torah. Successive Israeli governments, fearing civil strife and political retaliation, have not pressed the conscription issue on them, with the result that there are 40,000 religious Jews of military age not in the mobilization pool, an enormous percentage in a country as small as Israel, where the total strength of the armed forces, including reservists up to the fifty-five-year-old age limit, is 500,000 men and women.

With this in mind, my wife asked K and David just what the relation of these doctrinaire orthodox Jews was to the state of Israel.

"Leeches," mother and son replied in unison.

WE WERE HAVING DINNER at the YMCA, across from the King David Hotel. There were eight or ten people at the table. The food was terrible; even an omelet was an adventure. I was seated across from Meron Benvenisti, for five years a deputy mayor of Jerusalem, with East Jerusalem his special bailiwick, and now director of the West Bank Data Base Project, a survey funded by both the Ford and Rockefeller foundations and the American Enterprise Institute. Benvenisti had a corona of curly white hair and the dimensions of a retired middle linebacker fighting a losing battle with his weight. He smoked constantly, rolling his own, and I was struck once again, as I was throughout the trip, by the fact that the relation between cigarettes and cancer appeared to have made no impact in the Middle East; every evening was blue with cigarette smoke.

There was something vaguely familiar about Benvenisti. I had the sense of a face on television, younger, but with the same bulldog intensity. Then I had it. "Are you related to Richard Ben Venisti?" He was an assistant special prosecutor on Leon Jaworski's staff during the Watergate days, a young man with the same curly hair and steel-rimmed glasses who aimed questions like a sharpshooter with arsenic-tipped bullets. "My cousin." Benvenisti smiled.

"And now he's defending the same kind of guys he used to throw into the slammer," I said.

Benvenisti laughed. He himself is something of a spokesman, always available when traveling American anchormen or visiting pundits contemplate Israel's intractable social and political problems, the threats from enemies without and enemies within. He is a walking memory drum of statistics on the occupied West Bank, or the "liberated territories," the name preferred by the more radical Jewish settlers and hard-line military administrators on the West Bank. It is Benvenisti's contention that the Jewish takeover of the territories, begun in the aftermath of the 1967 war, is an irreversible process, amounting to de facto annexation. If the situation continues to stagnate, he argues, with neither the Palestinians nor the Israelis moving toward a settlement, the ultimate reality on the West Bank will incorporate the most volatile elements of life both in Northern Ireland and South Africa. Benvenisti's solution is for Israel to annex the territories formally, maintaining that only by a formal de jure annexation can the civil rights of the 800,000 Palestinians on the West Bank be safeguarded.

These views attract enfilading fire from both the fanatical right and the Peace Now left, which once had reason to consider Benvenisti as one of its own. The most extreme movement on the right is Rabbi Meir Kahane's Kach movement, which wants to expel all Arabs not only from the West Bank but from Israel as well. Kahane and his Kach followers are only too well aware

of Israel's inexorable demographics; fifty-three out of every one
hundred births are Arabs, and government statisticians predict
that by the year 2000, 43 percent of Israel's population will be
non-Jews. Kach and Kahane are not subtle. In many Israeli uni-
versities, Kach passes out handbills depicting the Arab male as a
stud who wants to defile Israeli women as a political statement.
"The best way to screw the Jewish state is to screw a Jewish girl
and broadcast the fact as widely as possible" was the way this
fear was parsed by a putative Arab nationalist in one such broad-
side, this one written in English for circulation among American
diaspora Jewish women pursuing their higher education in Israel.
While most Israelis reject, or claim to reject, Kahane's rhetorical
terrorism, they are made profoundly uneasy at the prospect of
near population parity with the Arabs in what they regard as
their own land—as do the Palestinians.

When I asked K about Benvenisti's annexation proposal,
she became quite heated. "It will only lead to a bicultural state,"
she said, "which would profoundly change the state of Israel."
Close down the West Bank settlements, she said, give the Palestinians a homeland, let the Jews who wish to remain there live
there under Arab guardianship. Another Peace Now member,
Avishai Margalit, a professor of philosophy at the Hebrew University and a friend of Benvenisti's since they made organized
and exhausting childhood pilgrimages in the intense desert heat
of the Negev, is even more unsparing. "The belief that once annexation finally takes place the Arabs will be assured their civil
rights seems to me hopelessly naive," he wrote in 1984. "Nothing will prevent the government from accompanying the act of
annexation with revived 'defense regulations' that will, for all
practical purposes, deprive the West Bank Arabs of their rights.
An official annexation, as far as I can see, will make Israel an
official apartheid state."

HERE ARE SOME statistics about the Jewish settlements on
the West Bank compiled by Benvenisti's West Bank Data Base

Project. There are 60,000 Jewish settlers presently living on the
West Bank. Some 20,000 live in bedroom suburbs of Tel Aviv,
another 28,000 within easy commuting distance of Jerusalem or
in Kiryat Arba, near Hebron. "For many outsiders," Benvenisti
wrote in 1983, "the term 'settlement' conjures an image of huts
strewn on a wind-swept barren hill with a group of bearded religious zealots gathering around an Israeli flag. . . . The typical
settler of the 1980s is a figure well-known throughout the Western world—the suburbanite. The man who wants to escape his
cramped apartment in the stifling, polluted city center, and to
make his dreams of a home of his own with a bit of lawn come
true, is not guided by nationalistic ideology. . . . The main demand of these settlers is not to be more than a half-hour's drive
from their places of work and entertainment centers."

"YOU'RE NOT TALKING Masada here," V said to me one
night at the Cinematheque, just outside the walls of the Old
City. V is a young American Jew, an editor suspected by all
camps as not quite trustworthy and yet accepted in all as a conduit for their opinions. The Cinematheque was jumping. A
Hitchcock film had just let out, and the restaurant downstairs
was jammed. A punk rock group was playing more energetically
than well, and Teddy Kolleck, the mayor of Jerusalem, was trying to hold two drinks and wave to some of his constituents at
the same time. It was the first place I had seen in Jerusalem
where young Arabs and young Jews seemed to mingle unself-
consciously. "You're not talking cowboys and Indians out there
in the settlements, John Wayne in The Searchers. It's not Fort
Apache, it's Sweden in San Diego, low-cost government housing
in a nice climate, five rooms in a settlement for what gets you
two rooms in Tel Aviv. Lawyers and doctors and engineers and
insurance men and auto dealers. The wife, the kids, and the dog.
People the Duke doesn't piss on in a John Ford movie. Towns-
people. People who take a government handout, freeloaders
hanging on the government tit. The IDF is their cavalry." The

Israeli Defense Force, the government's highly visible military presence on the West Bank. "The people in the U.S. will give up Social Security before you get these people out of the settlements."

I asked V if it was not corrupting for the whole state of Israel to have this raj in an area where the Jews were outnumbered nearly fourteen to one by the Palestinians.

"That's the Peace Now line," V said over the din. "Next summer Belfast. Or next year. Or before the turn of the century. The fin de siècle blues. That's why people call Peace Now 'the beautiful Jews.' "

IT WAS NOT UNTIL 4:30 the following morning that I realized V had not answered or even addressed my question. I had not been able to sleep, or perhaps been awakened by the muezzin summoning the faithful to early prayers, and had gone out on the terrace to watch the sun come up over the Old City. When I came back into the living room, I picked up the copy of the Jewish quarterly *Tikkun* someone had lent me. In a roundtable discussion, Meron Benvenisti was more straightforward—and troubling—than V had been. "The assumption that the conquest has caused corruption is highly optimistic," Benvenisti said. "It is based on the supposition that evil done in the territories eventually can reach the consciousness and sensitivity of the ordinary Israeli. But the truth of the matter is that the relationship of that Israeli to the situation in the territories is characterized by boredom, pure and simple. The Palestinian problem does not interest anybody, almost anybody."

Of course I could not sleep. "People think so hard here," Saul Bellow wrote in *To Jerusalem and Back*. The intensity of the political dialogue, or monologues, suffuses every day. It is difficult for the visitor to discern exactly where lines are drawn, where allegiances lie. As barriers disappear, new ones materialize. Jerusalem is thus an incredibly wearing city, if the visitor is to do other than shop and sightsee. It is not fun, in the sense that Tuscany and Provence are fun. There is a constant assault of ideas, options, sights, sounds, smells, a sense of being an eyewitness to a bad marriage and the poisonous bickering therein. Spend any time in Jerusalem and you will truly understand the old line— two Jews, three political parties.

2

THE HEADLINES in those weeks before the twentieth anniversary of the 1967 Six Day War reflected the uneasiness of the country at large. In southern Lebanon, Israeli jets showered the population with leaflets containing threats from the IDF area commander. "Remember the events that preceded 1982," the leaflets warned. "Keep terrorists away from your villages" or the people of southern Lebanon "will not be able to live in peace." In the military prisons on the West Bank, Palestinian prisoners went on a hunger strike and their families marched in protest in East Jerusalem. In Ramallah and Nablus, Arab students stoned the cars of Israeli settlers and set fire to their tires. In retaliation, IDF troops moved in and shut down Bir Zeit University, a hotbed of West Bank Palestinian nationalism. Near the new settlement of Alfei Menashe, a Palestinian lobbed a Molotov cocktail at a passing car. (Israelis have white license plates and Palestinians blue plates, so that the cars of either side are easily identified.) A woman passenger was killed in the conflagration and her husband and four children critically burned. Hundreds of Israeli settlers responded by smashing windows and burning fields in a nearby Arab settlement. At Bir Zeit, the IDF shot and killed a protesting Palestinian student.

WE RENTED A CAR. In the car rental agency, there was a poster-sized cartoon in English listing the Israeli rules of the road: "Wear seatbelts—if you have no guts" and "Use your brakes—if your horn doesn't work." We were headed this Sunday for Jericho and the Dead Sea. It is useful to remember just how small Israel is. From our terrace at Mishkenot we could, on a clear day, see the Dead Sea. The Mediterranean was just an hour away by car; from the border of Lebanon to the Sinai border with Egypt is a distance of slightly more than 250 miles.

The Dead Sea was a half hour from Jerusalem, through a landscape entirely familiar to anyone who has lived in the Southwest. For the whole time we were in the Middle East, this extreme familiarity kept dulling my response to the physical place and the message of its antiquities. It was just another desert, and not one with which I had any atavistic connection. Bedouin goatherds and their camels and tent camps offered a flavor of the exotic, but even this was undercut by the passengers from the tour buses along the highway down from Jerusalem, who posed them for photographs, as if they were dress extras. The Dead Sea itself made no more impact on me than the Salton Sea in the Mojave. We drove alongside an electrified chain-link security fence that here blocked access to the Dead Sea until we came to a partially open gate someone had apparently neglected to shut. We turned off the road, down a narrow rutted desert path. A hundred yards or so along the path was a deserted military post, a ghost encampment that I suspected had once been Jordanian, abandoned in the 1967 war. Tumbleweed clung like barnacles to the sides of the empty buildings, which were all shot up, riddled with shell and bullet holes. We did not get out of the car. I did not fancy getting a foot blown off by a piece of unexploded ordnance left buried in the sand for twenty years. This camp was far more vivid to me than the Dead Sea, or the Bedouins.

The road into Jericho branched off the highway to the Dead Sea. It was Sunday and Israeli soldiers on pass, all carrying weapons, were trying to hitch rides back into Jerusalem. At an Israeli military checkpoint, a young woman soldier wearing earrings trained her automatic rifle on us until we passed, even though our car had white Israeli plates; routine procedure we were later told. An Arab car got the full treatment—passengers out, hood and trunk up, documents checked.

Jericho was hot and dusty, and I wondered why, as legend has it, Mark Antony ever promised it to Cleopatra as a gift. We had lunch at the Seven Trees, one of a half dozen open-air restaurants on Ein Sultan Street. The music, a kind of Arabic rock by a group that called itself Goldenband (or so the logo on the amps and the keyboard indicated), was played at such a deafening volume that my ears rang for the rest of the afternoon. Lunch was the usual assortment of Arab salads and required a fairly constant and energetic vigilance to keep the flies off. Children darted among the hibiscus and oleander and coral-colored roses growing between the tables. On the street, youthful Arab boys in old cars slowly dragged the main, a ritual mating call the world over, stopping traffic as they conversed with equally young Arab girls in cars traveling in the opposite direction. The result was absolute gridlock, blaring horns, frayed tempers.

Largely because there are no Jewish settlements there, Jericho is one of the more docile and placid cities on the West Bank. This is not for want of trying on the part of Gush Eminum, or "The Bloc of the Faithful," the most militantly radical of the Jewish settler groups, committed to settling all the West Bank and keeping it forever under Jewish control. In Jericho, Gush Eminum has begun its expansion push with leaflets claiming that Jewish settlement is in the best interests of the Palestinians living there. "Go out and see how settlement and Jewish neighbors have brought you livelihood, homes, television sets, cars, and a standard of living you and your forefathers never dreamed of," the leaflets passed out before one march said. "Every Palestinian Arab has received a gift from us—a longer life expectancy than any Arab in the Middle East. Your infant mortality has ceased because of the Zionist blessing. When we settle in Jericho, you will enjoy blessings and prosperity."

Manifest destiny, Israeli style. The pitch has a strong element of the kind of economic bribery that was more or less the standard rationale for colonialism, certainly as practiced by the British when they ruled Arab and Jew in Palestine under the Protectorate. Neither Arab nor Jew bought the package then, and the Arabs on the West Bank do not buy it now. It runs up against an implacable historical fact: people would prefer a dictatorship by their own rather than the most benevolent occupation by outsiders.

Certainly the Israeli military occupation of the West Bank is more benign than the rule exercised in most states of the Arab world. This however begs the issue. The Palestinians are constantly reminded even in the most minor ways that they are second-class citizens in a land where many of them can trace their roots back to the Crusades—another invasion. One day I asked Mustafa Abdennah Natsheh, the mayor of Hebron until he was removed by the Israelis, how long his family had lived there. "A thousand years," he said. "Before that we were Bedouins in the Sudan."

On the highway to Nablus, the largest city on the West Bank, the Israelis have changed the road signs to identify it by its Hebrew name, Shechem; in Ramallah, a hotbed of Palestinian nationalism, the signs outside the central police station are in Hebrew and English, not Arabic. Minor irritants perhaps, but so was the tea tax in Boston, and irritations have a way of becoming infections. On the West Bank, Palestinians can be summarily detained without a warrant for eighteen days; Israelis cannot be held for more than forty-eight hours. Snap identity checks by IDF patrols are common, especially among young Arab men, and sassing a militia man is an invitation to the slammer. The usual estimate is that better than 50 percent of young Palestinian men have done a turn in an Israeli jail before they are eighteen. Throw a cheeky kid into the clink and the chances are that he will emerge a fire eater. And so it goes. The Israelis can no more cork this nationalist impulse than the Arabs and the British were able to cork Zionist nationalism before the creation of the state of Israel in 1948. The contest is elemental: a Palestinian majority inflamed by all the fevers of the conquered versus a Jewish nationalistic religious movement that claims the West Bank as Israel's by right of might and the Almighty.

"MYTH-FAKING" is what Amos Elon calls the convergence of Jewish theology and expansionist Israeli nationalism, "as when archeology is used to produce symbols of a false 'unbroken' past, a political continuity uninterrupted through the centuries." Amos is an Israeli writer and historian, for years a *Ha'aretz* correspondent in Washington, Bonn, and Paris. I had met him in New York, at an evening when we were both put on display at a black-tie fund-raiser for the New York Public Library. A few nights later we had dinner at the home of Calvin Trillin, a mutual friend. My sole memory of that night is a hangover that lasted for two days. I also had Amos' telephone number, scratched on the back of a breakfast card from the Carlyle Hotel.

A telephone call when we arrived in Jerusalem produced an invitation to a cocktail party Amos and his wife Beth, an American-born literary agent, were having in conjunction with the Jerusalem Book Fair. My own feeling about the Fair was that it was an event to which people came primarily in order to get laid on an expense account. The party was packed with publishers and agents and writers from around the world. As I made my way through the Elons' crowded apartment, I had a distinct sense of a long international snuggle, with liaisons being arranged and terminated in French, Italian, English, Hebrew, German, and other languages I could not recognize.

I found my wife wedged in a corner with the wife of an American diplomat. "The Palestinians," the diplomat's wife whispered, "should have their *Exodus*." For a moment I did not know whether she was talking about the Bible, the boat, or the book. "I don't mean that you would write a book like *Exodus*, but they need a book by an American writer that would legitimize their case in America the way that *Exodus* did for the Jews." It seemed a rather bizarre suggestion for the wife of a senior American official to be making. She quickly changed the subject when her husband came up, with Teddy Kollek in tow. "Think about it," she said, and then drifted into the crowd.

I TOLD THE STORY to Amos when we had tea a few days later at his apartment. He laughed and said he thought the book might be a tough sell in America. This question of how a people legitimizes itself has long engaged Elon. It is his contention that the rhetoric of expansion encourages, and more importantly requires, an inventive reinterpretation of theology in order to justify Israel's takeover of ancient religious sites, as on the West Bank. In his book *The Israelis: Founders and Sons*, he does not mince words about what he regards as the specious use of archeology as a guarantor of contemporary political legitimacy. "Fake myths of the past can produce a fake and sometimes dangerous present," he wrote. "The insistent search for authentic roots in the distant history of the country at times ignores three thousand years of subsequent Jewish history and ethics by reaching directly back to the barbaric Hebrew tribes of ancient times."

AN OBSERVATION: I have never been to a place, including some of the hairier spots in the Third World, where I saw more people carrying guns than I did in Israel. Mostly they were soldiers, both men and women, or reservists on their way to or from military duty, but in the West Bank settlements many men in civilian clothes also carried weapons that looked as if they came from the property department on *Aliens*. I thought this was what Dodge City must have looked like in the days of Wyatt Earp. And I tried to imagine an American community where so sizable a proportion of the young would be allowed to carry this kind of hardware. In an American city, those who weren't sticking up convenience stores would be using their weapons to get a parking space or a better spot in a movie line. Israel is a nocturnal emission for the Bernhard Goetz crowd.

A SECOND OBSERVATION more or less on the same subject: As I was writing this, I was also watching Lieutenant Colonel Oliver L. North testify before the joint congressional committee investigating the Iran-contra affair. What I remember about Lieutenant Colonel North was the fact that he was wearing his green woolen winter uniform. This was in July. In Washington, the District of Columbia. Where the temperature outside the Capitol was ninety degrees Fahrenheit. Where the hearing room was baking under the television lights. Where Lieutenant Colonel North was wearing a green woolen winter uniform with creases intact, and he was not sweating.

I make a point of this only because in all the time I was in Israel I never saw a soldier who looked as sharp as Lieutenant Colonel Oliver L. North. I remember an IDF patrol in Ramallah. The enlisted men called their officers by their first names. Some of the soldiers were middle-aged men with their stomachs hanging out from under their fatigue jackets. Some wore bright red or purple T-shirts under their fatigue jackets. Some had salt-and-pepper mountain-man beards. Some wore fatigue caps, others were bareheaded, still others wore yarmulkes.

This was the rule, not the exception. The personnel of the IDF generally wore dirty, wrinkled uniforms, often with buttons missing. When I was in the army and was discovered with a button unbuttoned, I had to stand in the company square holding my M-1 at arm's length; try it with a beer bottle and see how long you can do it. These soldiers of the IDF reminded me of the Marine Corps commercial on television: "We're Looking for a Few Good Men." A marine DI would shape these sloppy Israelis up quick enough. Boot camp would do wonders for them. They would look sharp, hair clipped to the skull, starch in their fatigues, yes, sir, no, sir, by the fucking numbers. Just the sort of troops who would forget to set up a perimeter defense at Beirut airport. Despite their slovenly demeanor and the familiarity between the ranks that drill instructors say is destructive to fire discipline, the Israelis are not much on losing wars. We have not won one in forty-three years. In Grenada pomp was so favored over circumstances that the Pentagon passed out more medals than there were troops participating in the operation; My Lai was the last major American military victory, body-count-wise.

These are just a few thoughts to suggest why I was not as impressed by the nattiness of Lieutenant Colonel Oliver L. North as I think I was intended to be. He was a sharp dresser, his shoes were polished, he had a neat haircut, he had all those rows of ribbons—and he peddled weapons to the sponsors of those who murdered 241 of his fellow United States Marines at Beirut airport. In nations less fastidious than ours, selling guns to the people responsible for the massacre of 241 of your country's soldiery might be construed as treason. I would have liked to have seen Lieutenant Colonel Oliver L. North try to justify that action at a marine gunnery sergeants' mess. I suspect the gunnies would have had him for breakfast, spit him out for lunch, and thrown his bones to the dog for dinner.

HERE IS A LETTER from an acquaintance, an American Jew from Pittsburgh, my age, who emigrated to Israel fifteen years ago, acquiring both Israeli citizenship and, even though he was then in his late thirties, a military obligation: "I'm a little late in replying, as I'm in the midst of doing a few weeks of army reserve duty at the moment. I'm just home on leave now for 72 hours and catching up on my correspondence. The damn army thing was one of the things weighing on my mind the day we met. I just learned that I'd be serving again in Israel's 'security zone' in Southern Lebanon, something which I am never keen to do, because at my age I do not fancy getting my ass shot off. As it is, I'm posted upon the snowline in the Hemon range

where it is cold but, thank God, quiet. So the worst is my butt
will get frozen—but not ventilated."

"HEBRON ATTRACTS the real crazies on both sides," K said
as we drove there one afternoon. As always in Israel, and especially on the West Bank, history, and the way it is interpreted,
is the reason; "a single piece of real estate," as Amos Elon defines
the issue nationwide, claimed by two conflicting nationalisms (or
"two just causes," a formulation in *The Israelis* that made Elon
the target of abuse from the more rabid sector of the Israeli pop-
ulace). The prophet Abraham, worshiped by both Muslim and
Jew, is thought to be buried in Hebron, along with his wife
Sarah, in the Cave of Machpelah. Over the centuries their resting place has been covered by both mosque and synagogue, and
the city fertilized with blood. In 1929, Arab rioters drove the
small Jewish community from the city, in the process slaughtering several dozen—and giving Jews an imperative to return. Further riots in 1936 impelled the British to remove those few Jews
who had indeed ventured back, and when the city came under
Jordanian rule after the 1948 war, Jews were forbidden either to
live in Hebron or to worship there. In the aftermath of the 1967
war, a small group of Israeli nationalists, under the leadership of
Rabbi Moshe Levinger and his American-born wife Miriam, re-
established a Jewish presence in Hebron, in contravention of the
then stated policy of the Israeli government, and dared the authorities to remove them. The Israeli military finally agreed to a
temporary encampment, which of course became permanent, on
the outskirts of the city. Then the Levingers moved themselves
into the old Jewish quarter, site of the 1929 massacre, just outside the Arab bazaar. With a few other Jewish families, the
Levingers and their eleven children still live there, under round-
the-clock Israeli military protection, their presence a festering
sore to the Arabs, a symbol of triumphant Jewish irredentism to
radical Israeli nationalists.

Hebron is twenty-two miles south of Jerusalem and has a

population of 70,000 Arabs and 5,000 Jews. Most of the Jews live
in Kiryat Arba, the settlement just outside town where the
Levingers and their followers were first allowed squatters' rights
in 1967. The house trailers and frontier make-do of that first settlement have long since vanished. Indeed it was hard to shake
the sense, as we navigated the neat empty streets of Kiryat Arba,
of one of those walled middle-class communities in the San Fernando Valley, that bastion of white Los Angeles. There were
women about and children and tricycles, but only a few men,
and they were mainly old, a sure sign that the family breadwin-
ner was winning his bread at car-pool distance. Each apartment
complex was the same as the one on either side, each street indis-
tinguishable from those it ran into. Even the planting was uni-
formly unattractive. I could not escape the idea that here was the
kind of subdivision—a description that seemed far more appropriate than settlement—where the prevailing sameness would
tend to encourage a garrison mentality, where righteousness
would tend to erase thought and rhetoric achieve the status of
commandment. "I hate to say this about my own people," K said
as we returned to the highway, "but Jews seem to like ghettos."

It took a long time to find a place to park in Hebron itself.
The city was alive with people and traffic jams and screaming
taxis and markets and bazaars. IDF patrols were everywhere, guns
at the ready. Concertina wire lay along the side of the roads,
ready to be kicked into the street, instant roadblocks in case of
trouble. Before allowing us to enter the makeshift museum maintained by Jewish settlers, Israeli soldiers on guard behind a sand-
bag emplacement gave us a thorough checking over—who were
we, where were we from, why were we here. Inside the museum
there were pictures of the Jews killed in the 1929 massacre and
artifacts of the resettlement spearheaded by the Levingers. I
picked up a newsletter, *Hebron Today*, written in English and
aimed at that segment of the American Jewish audience who
would contribute to the building of "a modern city emerging

from the ruins and desecration." On the back page there was a section under the simple heading "Thank You," followed by a list of donors, the amount of their donations, and the uses to which their donations had been put: "MR. AUSTIN SEARS, FILM PRODUCER OF N.Y.—$2,000 toward rebuilding of Beit Hasson. MR. WILLIAM GOLDMAN OF NEWARK, NEW JERSEY—$25,000 for the Minpaunassan Medical Clinic, in memory of his beloved wife."

These American funds, mixed in with allowances from the Israeli government and a dollop of intimidation (tacitly sanctioned by the military authorities), have allowed the settlers to buy out the Arab families in the neighborhood; the bulldozers I saw everywhere were evidence that they intended to stay. There is barbed wire around some of the windows in the Levingers' house, and nearby a guard tower over which flew the Star of David in the blue and white Israeli flag. Miriam Levinger claims the door to her house is never locked—nor would mine be if I had a company of marines bivouacked on the lawn.

A soldier shooed us away from the house and we entered the casbah. It twisted like a snake, with narrow teeming alleys shooting off in every direction. Children darted among sneaker displays set up on the street while vendors shouted from their storefronts. Customers haggled loudly, some of them Jewish women, their heads covered and carrying shopping bags, from the settlement just outside the market. In the butcher shops, camels hung by their hooves, skinned completely except for their heads. All had the long romantic lashes of cartoon dromedaries, and their dead dopey eyes seemed to follow us, in the manner of trick eyes in a bad painting.

K appeared distinctly on edge. This was Arab turf; Jews had been stabbed in the crowded market, their assassins slipping away undiscovered in the network of alleys. Even though K was strongly Peace Now, I had the sense she felt herself one of the oppressor class there in the casbah. Every time we ran into an

IDF patrol, she seemed to relax. Like a child picking petals from a daisy, she would say as the soldiers passed in their full combat gear, "He's one of ours, he's not, he's one of ours, he's not." When I asked what she meant, she said she could tell just by looking which of the reservists might support Peace Now and which probably would not. Those with beards or long hair or flowers in their fatigue jackets would, she said, those wearing yarmulkes would not. It seemed a sweet and futile distinction, one that made me understand, if not appreciate, why V had disparaged Peace Now as "the beautiful Jews."

FIRST ADD HEBRON: In the well-to-do Arab neighborhoods outside town, television antennas are not just television antennas but decorative elements, some crafted to resemble oil derricks, others the Eiffel Tower. The Eiffel Tower antenna was, in fact, a motif replicated all over the West Bank.

SECOND ADD HEBRON: Among the Palestinians there, it is a source of considerable resentment that for all the Israeli claims about the economic advantages the occupation has brought the Arabs, the 5,000 Jews living in Hebron and Kiryat Arba have 4,000 telephone lines, while the 70,000 Arabs only have 700.

LAST ADD HEBRON: The case of Uziah Sharabaf is a perfect example of the intractability of the situation on the West Bank. In 1983, an Arab stabbed a yeshiva student to death in the Hebron casbah. Retaliation was swift. Armed with hand grenades and Kalashnikovs, Sharabaf and two other members of the Jewish underground infiltrated the campus of Hebron's Islamic College. So that they might be mistaken for Arabs, the three wore boldly checked kaffiyehs, of the kind much favored by Yasir Arafat. In a matter of moments, they killed three Palestinian students and wounded thirty-three others. They were captured, tried for murder, and sentenced to life imprisonment. Uziah

Sharabaf is of special interest because he is the son-in-law of Moshe and Miriam Levinger. In an interview with Dan Fisher of the *Los Angeles Times*, Miriam Levinger talked about Sharabaf and his accomplices. "I just felt that my whole world went topsy turvy and I had to work things out," she told Fisher. This is how she worked them out: an eye for an eye, the biblical injunction; the Arabs are trying to annihilate the Jews, the Jews must reply in kind. "They are not murderers," she said about her son-in-law and his cohorts. "Arabs who murder are murderers."

3

OCCASIONALLY THE MOOD lightens, a case in point being the local spin on Jim Bakker's adventures in the skin trade with Jessica Hahn. One of Jim and Tammy Faye Bakker's pet projects was a plan to relocate the East Jerusalem bus station, directly across from the Damascus Gate in the Old City. The station is adjacent to the Garden Tomb, where many fundamentalists believe Christ was buried. This idea "has little claim to authenticity," says F. E. Peters in his book *Jerusalem*, "but it is indeed outside the city and it responds far more directly to some Christian sensibilities about what the tomb of Jesus should have looked like than the present Greek rococo edicule that sits inside the dark and incense-filled Church of the Holy Sepulcher." The dubious provenance was of little import to the Bakkers, PTL, or other Christian evangelicals. Bothered by all the smoke and noise and filthy diesel fumes so near their hallowed site, they talked of financing the removal of the bus station to another location in East Jerusalem and creating a park on the old spot. The Israelis knew a pigeon when they saw one and were quite willing to have this urban redevelopment scheme underwritten by a bunch of American Bible whackers. But then it came to light that Bakker had spread his seed on a hill of Aphrodite not belonging to the former Tammy Faye LaValley. The project is on hold.

A QUIET DAY at the Demjanjuk trial. Attendance had declined as the dramatic testimony of the Treblinka survivors had given way to infighting between prosecution and defense about the validity of the documents identifying John Demjanjuk as Ivan the Terrible. That morning the pertinent exhibit was an identity card handed over to the Israelis by the Soviet Union. The card placed Demjanjuk at a camp called Trawniki, in Poland, where the SS trained Red Army deserters and defectors to be prison camp guards. Demjanjuk's defense team claimed the card was a clumsy forgery, a blatant attempt on the part of the Russians to get revenge on a deserter forty years after the fact, while the prosecution had brought to Jerusalem a Holocaust historian from Germany who would attest to the card's authenticity.

The trial was held at a theater in Binyanei Ha'ooma, a convention center next door to the Hilton Hotel. (That week, the Jerusalem Book Fair occupied the center's main display space.) Near the entrance was a window marked by a sign that said, in English, "Deposit Weapons," where Israeli soldiers, like cowhands in Abilene on a payday Saturday night, checked their automatic heat. Surrounded by soldiers as I waited to pass through the metal detectors and security check, I was struck once again by the way the Israeli military was woven into the country's social fabric. In the United States, most middle-class citizens are socially removed from the armed forces. Soldiers are those weird-looking young men we usually see only in airports, this one with his hair too short, that one with the tattoo and the mottled complexion and the flat hill accent, the black lance corporal here, the Hispanic PFC over there; in other words, no one we know. At the trial that morning, the young soldiers had the sentient mainstream faces so rarely seen in the contemporary American services. A number of them were women, scarcely older than children; the recruitment of women is a policy that tends to reinforce the impression that army duty is a slice of everyone's life, not just someone else's. Directly ahead of me, there was a squad of twelve young female recruits who seemed to be pushing the uniform code to its limit, in the manner of the in-group at some Middletown High, some with their sleeves pushed up, some wearing jewelry, some with elaborate makeup, twelve girls wearing, I could not help but notice, twelve different kinds of shoes.

Once inside, my wife and I each got a headset that enabled us to follow the trial via a simultaneous translation into English; at the end of every session there were also transcripts of that day's proceedings available in a number of languages. In the theater, behind the prosecutor's table, there was a photo mural of a Treblinka diorama, made from memory by a camp survivor, there being no existing photographs of the camp. The defense had tried to prevent the mural from being admitted into evidence, as it was made from memory, and memory was fallible. It seemed to me that the defense might have further objected that the model was not only based on a fallible memory but also served as a decorative backdrop that could be construed as prejudicial to its case.

There was a scattered whispering of boos and hisses when Demjanjuk entered the courtroom from a door at stage right, a barrel-shaped man in a blue suit and an open-necked white shirt. His bullet head was shaved and he was smiling broadly. A Ukrainian translator sat next to him, his son from Cleveland against the wall just behind. Demjanjuk had a three-man defense team, two Americans (one of whom, the lead lawyer, Demjanjuk later fired) and an Israeli named Yorem Sheftel. Sheftel had been a controversial figure in the Israeli bar since his days in law school, when he was a mover in the formation of a lobby called Citizens for Lansky. The Lansky in question was Meyer Lansky, the Mafia financial wizard, who had been trying to evade extradition to the United States by having Israel extend him citizenship. I had seen

Sheftel at dinner the night before at the American Colony Hotel in East Jerusalem. He was wearing jeans, an expensively painted sweatshirt, and the kind of jewelry Sammy Davis, Jr., might envy. He relished notoriety, and his association with the case had won him his share, along with an extra ration of abuse from many Israelis for taking Demjanjuk on as a client. In the courtroom he had not disappointed, at one point comparing the proceedings to Joseph Stalin's show trials in the 1930s.

Throughout the morning, schoolchildren and military personnel were funneled in and out of the courtroom. Each group stayed for fifteen or twenty minutes before being replaced by another, lending credence to the idea that a major purpose of the trial was the government's desire to bring the story of the Holocaust directly to another generation. On the stand was Wolfgang Scheffler, a professor from the Free University of Berlin and a professional expert witness ("I've testified in forty or fifty trials on all aspects of the Holocaust in various countries") whose special field of interest was the bureaucracy of those administering the Final Solution. He talked at length about the makeshift uniforms worn by the Russians being trained as auxiliary guards at Trawniki, the point being to place Demjanjuk in a historical context. "At first they were black," he said. "Later they were earth brown, since they came from Red Army stocks. Berlin never sent the full complement of uniforms."

Listening to Scheffler was to see evil through the eyes of a supply sergeant. He said the Russian POW auxiliaries had never been given arms of their own. If they were sent to help liquidate a Jewish ghetto, he continued, they were issued weapons, but had to hand them back to an SS armory when the action was completed. "There was always an element of distrust of them," he said, "in the eyes of the Germans." The English transcripts of the simultaneous translations had the appalling specificity of banality. ". . . the decision for the so-called final solution was taken between September and October." And again: ". . . right down to those who did the actual incinerating." A question to Scheffler: "The deputy commander of Treblinka, who was in the final stages the commander, what was his [civilian] profession?" And the answer: "A cook."

A cook!

The reply was to understand Hannah Arendt.

A LETTER TO the *Jerusalem Post*, 9 April 1987: "Amongst the many (an understatement) differences of opinion in almost every aspect of Israeli politics and society, I have noticed a rare consensus regarding the Demjanjuk trial. I find this consensus to be a terribly depressing reflection of Israeli's short history. One would think that after almost 39 years of existence as an independent state, Israel could generate a domestic consensus on an issue other than Jewish suffering. It is ironic to me that the Holocaust, as a catalyst to the formation of the state, remains until today the number one, if not the only, subject of national consensus."

L'ENVOI

MEA SHEARIM, the day before we left Jerusalem. Our guide was L, who had grown up in the neighboring Geulah quarter. L's parents had come from Russia; his mother was an anarchist, his father a socialist. When he was a child, during the 1948 war of independence, his neighborhood came under artillery fire and a piece of shrapnel caught him just above the left ankle. "My only wound in four wars," L said, pulling up his pant leg to show the scar. In the 1967 war, he was one of the paratroopers who forced the walls of the Old City at the Dung Gate, the closest to the Wailing Wall. When he was mobilized during the Yom Kippur War, he reported for duty with eight Ross MacDonald novels in his kit. He read them all in a trench on the Suez Canal. "They gave me such a sense of California," he said, "that I had a feeling of déjà vu when I finally went there to teach." His last war was Lebanon, in 1982. He was then in his forties, and too old for the paras; he was assigned instead to a sapper unit, defusing land mines. The idea of a sapper unit as a sedentary posting for a middle-aged man brought a rueful smile; it was, he said, his most dangerous assignment in the military. Nearing fifty, and now a sergeant, he will fulfill the last five years of his reserve obligation teaching logic and ethics to officer candidates.

Mea Shearim is just outside the walls of the Old City, and is the most fanatical religious enclave in Jerusalem. Its forbidding tone is set immediately; above the gate through which we passed was a sign that said, "Please do not antagonize our religious inhabitants by strolling through our streets in immodest clothing." The quarter is both fortress and ghetto, its terraces and windows facing inward, as if to close out the twentieth century and its attendant blasphemies. To walk there is to become a stranger in time; the feeling is of a century in which one was glad not to have lived. Washing hung over the alleys and the silent streets. There are no trees, because the love of nature is idolatrous; to ride a bicycle in Mea Shearim on the Sabbath is to run the risk of being stoned. Many of the men wore black stockings and shin-length black coats; a number of women had their heads shaved, in accordance with the scriptures, and wore wigs covered by scarves. Yiddish is the lingua franca, L said, because the more zealous of the Hasidim think Hebrew too sacred a language for daily use. He translated a sign: "Joining the army is a sin on the order of murder or idolatry." Considering his four wars, I asked if he thought himself a murderer or an idolator. Another rueful smile.

We walked for two hours, ending up finally in Geulah, where the overflow from Mea Shearim had ultimately forced the secular Jews out. The house where L had grown up now be-

longed to an orthodox family, as did the house down the street
where the novelist Amos Oz had grown up. L pointed to the
spot where he had been wounded in 1948. There seemed an element of sadness in him as he wandered his old neighborhood,
now oppressive with orthodox fanaticism; I was reminded of *The
Cherry Orchard*, of something forever lost. In his chapter on
Geulah in his book *In the Land of Israel*, Amos Oz addresses this
sadness, and the attitude of secular agnostics such as he and L,
toward the orthodox zealots. "You cannot permit yourself to
hate them but you cannot avoid detesting them," Oz wrote. And
then bitterly: "In these neighborhoods where I was born and
raised, the battle has been decided: Zionism has been repulsed,
as if it had never been. Or if not repulsed, then banished to the
cellar, a sort of *Shabbes goy* doing for Orthodox Jewry all the
dirty work—collecting the garbage and maintaining the sewer
system (done by Mahmoud and Yussuf from East Jerusalem).
And providing a good standard of living (courtesy of the American taxpayer). Such are the functions of Zionism in these neighborhoods."

DINNER THAT LAST NIGHT in a tiny restaurant on King George
V Street. Again the meal stank. I thought everything is political
in Jerusalem; even the bad food makes a political statement. And
the clothes. I have never seen a place so immune to the notion
of clothes as decoration, clothes as a way of expressing oneself.
Without exception, everyone was badly dressed, something which
may have begun as a political idea but was now a habit, a reflex.
After dinner we went for a walk in the adjacent Ben Yehuda
mall, an area full of tatty camera stores and alfresco coffee bars
and fast food shops. It was jammed, like the Piazza Navona without the majesty of the architecture. The crowd was young and
festive. Parked at either end of the plaza were Israeli military
jeeps; the soldiers on duty seemed to be cruising for girls, and
the girls with whom they were flirting seemed more than recep-

tive. Just behind us a young girl was lavishing the neck of her soldier boy friend with monkey bites. "Shit," he suddenly said in English, and I followed his frozen gaze to a book bag left unattended at an empty table outside a coffee bar. In Israel an unattended bag means a bomb, and the crowd melted away. Then a tourist, a German woman with white stockings and curly blond hair, picked the bag up, examining its contents to make sure everything was still there, chatting away with a companion, blissfully unaware of the instant panic her forgetfulness had caused. The soldier smiled at his girl, and as they walked away, she resumed nibbling his ear.

THE FOLLOWING MORNING, the American embassy in Tel Aviv kindly provided a car to drive us to the Allenby Bridge, the border point just east of Jericho and the Dead Sea where we would cross from the West Bank into Jordan. "Welcome to Allenby Bridge Terminal," the sign at the first checkpoint said, "Judea and Samaria." Several Israeli soldiers, one of them wearing three automatic rifles slung from his shoulders, lounged under the corrugated tin roof of the checkpoint. There seemed to be a problem; we had not been cleared to pass on to the second checkpoint. The Israeli military command in Jericho claimed not to know we were coming, and no one could be roused at the American embassy in Tel Aviv, which was supposed to have arranged for us to enter Jordan over the bridge (the normal way is to fly from Tel Aviv to Cairo or Larnaca, and then on into Amman by air). Nor was there any way of raising the American embassy in Amman; there was no telephone communication between Israel and Jordan; the normal way for the two embassies to communicate was to patch a call through the State Department in Washington.

We waited in the embassy station wagon, with the air conditioner on against the midmorning desert heat and the car radio tuned to a station playing the score from *Kismet*. There was a line of trucks filled with fruit on one side of the road, and on the other cabs and buses filled with Arab travelers. Occasionally the guards would let a bus or a truck through the checkpoint, taking their own sweet time as they inspected the vehicle and its passengers, as if in slow motion. There seemed no pattern to the delays, only an air of the capricious, of the systematic invention of small difficulties. An hour passed, then a second. I had the feeling we were being made to wait for no other reason than that we were there, that a client state reserves for itself the right to get a little uppity at times with the nationals of its primary benefactor.

Finally, with no explanation, we were allowed to pass to the second checkpoint. We paid our exit fee and were driven to the final checkpoint at the bridge. The Jordan was in full flow, with bullrushes growing on its banks, yet narrow enough almost to spit across. The bridge itself is a makeshift affair, a Bailey bridge of the type used in World War II, thrown across the river to replace the permanent structure destroyed in the Six Day War. The Jordanians have refused to agree to the construction of a more permanent bridge, because to do so would be to imply that the Jordan River is an adjudicated international frontier; nor for the same reason does the Jordanian flag fly over Jordan's side of the river. In symbols are statements. I picked up our bags and we walked across the bridge into Jordan.

Laying Pipe

On June 6, 1982, *The New York Times Book Review* asked a number of writers to describe their work in progress. I did not have a work in progress, only a contract for a work in progress, but no matter: if a writer is asked to describe a work in progress, perhaps the work in progress might actually progress. And so for the *Times* I wrote: "This summer I am going to Central America and will be working on a novel called *The Red White and Blue*. The trip and the novel are not related, but who knows . . . All I know about *The Red White and Blue* is that Scott Fitzgerald considered a similar title for *The Great Gatsby*. What will it be about? About 600 pages, I hope."

The result of this fabrication was that my publisher invited me to lunch at The Four Seasons to discuss the work in progress, and the progress I was making on it. The night before the lunch, I sat down at my typewriter in a suite at the Carlyle Hotel that a movie company was picking up the tab for in the misplaced hope that I was paying more attention to the screenplay I was allegedly writing than I was to the novel the producers did not know I allegedly had in progress. In a spasm of fear, I wrote the following sentence: "When the trial began, we left the country." An hour or so later I had reached the point where I could note in my di-

ary the next day, "Lunch w/JE [my publisher]—showed her 1st
3–4 pp RWB." And thus began four years at the factory.

What civilians do not understand—and to a writer anyone
not a writer is a civilian—is that writing is manual labor of the
mind: a job, like laying pipe. Although I had not written a word,
I had in fact thought a great deal about the novel I was meant to
be writing over the course of the preceding year. I knew what the
first sentence was going to be, and I also knew the last—it is a
peculiarity of mine that I always know the last sentence of a book
before I begin. That last sentence I intended to be a line of dialogue, either "No" or "Yes," with the penultimate line its re-
verse, either Yes or No, not in dialogue. It was the six or seven
hundred pages between "When the trial began, we left the country" and "No" (or "Yes") that seemed a desert I could not irrigate.

I also knew the book would have a first-person narrator,
largely because I had never used one before. The narrator I had
in mind was the narrator of Ford Madox Ford's *The Good Soldier*, a commentator on events and actions, some not even wit-
nessed, others at best only dimly understood, events and actions
that in my case the narrator would have to reconstruct through
letters and diaries and videotapes and secondhand accounts and
Freedom of Information files and whatever else came to mind.
"You'll be sorry," my wife, who is also a novelist, said when I told
her my plan, and how right she was.

That summer of 1982 I did go to Central America, and I
saw the possibilities for a section of the book I would not address for another three and a half years; my notes for the trip
were twice as long as the section that eventually appeared in the
manuscript. In September, I cleared away all other commitments
and began concentrating on the book full-time. By the summer
of 1983, I had completed 262 pages—and none of it seemed to
work. Individual scenes played, but the narrative did not hold
together. Narrative, I should explain, is not plot. Plot is "The

queen died, the king died"; narrative is "The queen died, the king died of a broken heart." (I would like to claim that definition as my own, but it is a loose translation of E. M. Forster by way of Vladimir Nabokov.) Because one has written other books does not mean the next becomes any easier. Each book in fact is a tabula rasa; from book to book I seem to forget how to get characters in and out of rooms—a far more difficult task than the non-writer might think. Still I went to my office every day. That is the difference between the professional and the amateur. The professional guts a book through this period, in full knowledge that what he is doing is not very good. Not to work is to exhibit a failure of nerve, and a failure of nerve is the best definition I know for writer's block.

In August 1983, I put the manuscript aside and traveled to France and England, armed with my tattered copy of *The Good Soldier*, which by then went everywhere with me, not so much a book to read as a talisman to hold and touch. I was also accompanied by a photocopy of an interview Philip Roth had given *The New York Times* in 1977. "My own way," Roth had said, "seems to be to write six months of trash—heterosexual trash usually—and then to give up in despair, filing away a hundred pages or so that I can't stand, to find ten pages or so that are actually alive." The despair of another writer is enormously reassuring to one who thinks his own despair is unique.

Back home, I started all over again on page 1, circling the 262 pages like a vulture looking for live flesh to scavenge. I knew the problem. The narrative was too constricted; it was like a fetus strangling on its own umbilical cord. The time span of the book was eighteen years, ranging from California to Vietnam to Central America, from the radical politics of the 1960s to Hollywood in the '80s, and I knew I was moving uneasily among these venues. Knowing the problem, however, is not the same as solving it. The second draft, which I began in euphoria in the fall of 1983, I abandoned seventy-two pages later, again on the outskirts of despair.

I was now in 1984, having worked steadily for nearly two years with almost nothing to show for it except a file box full of pages with typing on them. To clear my head I wrote a long piece for *The New York Review of Books* about a septuagenarian former Hollywood Communist who had come out of the closet of his past, as it were, disguised as a prizewinning young Mexican novelist. I also needed money if I was ever going to finish this damn book, and I agreed to write the screen adaptation of Norman Mailer's novel *The Deer Park.* The fee was simply too high to pass up, and even with taxes and the commissions of agents, lawyer, and accountants deducted, my wife and I would have enough to keep us for approximately another two years.

Death had also intervened. "When the trial began, we left the country," I had written that spring of 1982. Five months later my niece was murdered, and when her killer came to trial in Los Angeles the following summer, my wife and I indeed did leave the country. "I do not understand people who attend the trials of those accused of murdering their loved ones," I had continued in those three or four pages I had shown my publisher at The Four Seasons half a year before any of this happened. "You see them on the local newscasts . . . I watch them kiss the prosecutor when the guilty verdict is brought in or scream at those jurors who were not convinced that the pimply-faced defendant was the buggerer of Jimmy and the dismemberer of Johnny." I wondered for several years if I should retain those lines in the final manuscript, should I ever complete it; in a slightly altered version I did. There, with all its emotional baggage, was the obscenity of coincidence.

On New Year's Day 1985, I began *The Red White and Blue* for the third time. This time it went well from the start. The two failed previous drafts yielded nuggets I had not been able to find before. Those first three or four pages I had written in the spring of 1982 became, in the spring of 1986, the last five pages of a 710-page novel; pages 44–46 in the second draft became pages 304–307 in the third. Slowly the book began to open up.

In a churchyard in the Cotswolds, I found the name of a nineteenth-century churchwarden, Bentley Innocent; I immediately
gave his surname to a character of my own. On that same trip,
the English novelist Bruce Chatwin told me about a *papeterie*
on Rue de l'Ancienne Comédie in Paris that was the only place
left in the city that sold the notebooks he and I both favored; I
set a scene there. In the papers of a dead friend whose literary
executor I had become, I found an instruction sheet from the
Nevada Department of Prisons on how to operate "a lethal gas
chamber" for an execution and how to clean it when the job was
completed. ("After each execution, sinks, plugs, pot and entire
inside of cabinet should be washed down with warm water and
a detergent. Add 2 ounces of agua ammonia to each gallon of water. . . .") Here was a perfect example of bureaucracy gone mad;
it went into the manuscript. "Let's get the cows to Abilene," the
producer of *The Deer Park* had said when the delivery of the
screenplay was delayed; into the manuscript.

I devised stratagems and inside jokes to relieve the clock-
punching tedium of a book that was building by only a page or
a page and a half a day. I named someone after a character in
one of my wife's earlier novels; a corpse received a name I have
now used in four books. Because I believe scores are made to be
settled, I settled a couple of scores in a way that only the person
against whom the score was being settled would ever recognize, if
indeed that person ever read the book. In my last novel, I had
some gratuitous sport with Peter Jennings, the ABC anchorman,
and when a friend of his asked how I could be beastly about
someone I did not know, I replied, "Never be rude to a stranger,
because the stranger may turn out to be a novelist with a long
memory."

January 5, 1986, the first Monday of the new year: I now
had 493 pages of *The Red White and Blue* completed. In the
next three months, I worked seven days a week, taking only one
day off during that entire stretch, seldom going out at night. This

was the magic time that made up for the previous three and a half years of toil and anxiety and suicidal depression. It is like a dream sexual experience. Everything seems to work; the chance encounter, the overheard remark in a restaurant feed into the next day's material, opening up possibilities you had never considered. In three months I wrote 230 pages; in the last two weeks alone, ninety-two. On Sunday, April 6, at 2:19 in the afternoon, I wrote the last sentence: "No."

The book took two months short of four years to write, with another year spent taking notes and thinking about it. In the course of those four years, this is what I also did: I wrote three pieces for *The New York Review of Books* and a second screenplay, an adaptation of Carlos Fuentes' *The Old Gringo*, a meditation by Carlos (a good friend) on what happened to Ambrose Bierce when he went down to Mexico to die. The screenplay, without me, is in another stage of development, but from a biography of Bierce I would not otherwise have read I did get the book's epigraph: "History is an account, mostly false, of events, mostly unimportant, which are brought about by rulers, mostly knaves, and soldiers, mostly fools." Other than these interruptions, only the book. Four years, 1,400 days, 710 pages; prorated, it amounts to half a page, 125 words, a day. Put that way, not much to show for four years. But that is the writer's life. You write. You finish. You start over again.

Critical

HERE IS WHY writers should never respond to their reviews. In 1969, I published a book called *The Studio*. The review in *Time* was generally enthusiastic, except for a comment that I had used a word wrong. The word was "vicissitudes," and the reviewer said I was the sort of writer who thought "vicissitudes" was classier than "ups and downs." I used to work at *Time,* and I am familiar with what Calvin Trillin, another *Time* alumnus, calls "the old *Time* yutz," that jab in the ribs that says to the alumnus, Don't get too big for your britches now that you're publishing books, buster, we knew you when. I should have let it go—I used the word I meant to use and the review was favorable—but instead I wrote not to the reviewer but to the magazine's managing editor, Henry Anatole Grunwald, formerly my editor and later editor in chief of all the Time Inc. publications. Henry was born in Austria and is full of Middle European charm and savoir faire and killer instinct. "Dear Henry," I wrote sweetly, "Actually I don't blame you for this, because English is after all your second language." As sallies go, not bad, but not as good as Henry's reply. "*Lieber Johann,*" his letter began, and continued to its conclusion, in German.

In their single-minded self-absorption, writers have a tendency to think that criticism is peculiar to their line of work. One night several years ago, I put this proposition to a federal judge and to my brother-in-law, who is CEO of a major corporation. I said they had never been called "slime," as I once was in a counter-cultural newspaper. Words, they answered, only words, words that had no substantial effect on my ability to make a living. As opposed, my brother-in-law said, to that one bad quarter that could make him liable to being fired by his board. As opposed, the federal judge said, to having every ruling and every decision subject to reversal either by the Ninth Circuit or the United States Supreme Court.

In fact, when I was younger, I used to think that reviews really mattered; they were the writer's board, his appelate court, the final arbiter of his professional worth. Now, after nine books and five movies, I reckon that I have been reviewed some four thousand times and find that idea egregious nonsense. Of those four thousand reviews, only the tiniest fraction had any commercial or critical relevance. Outside the major metropolitan areas, many reviewers tend to rewrite jacket copy or the publisher's press release or even to steal a notice from a big-city newspaper. Let me give an example: in the daily *New York Times*, Christopher Lehmann-Haupt once reviewed a novel by my wife; a month or so later the exact same notice appeared verbatim in the Sunday book review of a paper in the Pacific Northwest, under the byline of that paper's book editor. And it was a pan, no less, which did seem to stretch the limits of propriety.

One never gets inured to reviews, but scar tissue does form. In the first place, reviews are always disappointing, even when laudatory. I remember a scene in Frederic Raphael's *Glittering Prizes* in which the author read his reviews—generally good—before breakfast, then had to face the day; that's all there was, there was nothing more. This is because there are two separate aspects to the writer's life: writing, which, however painful, is always rewarding, if only to prove to the writer that he can still do it; and being published, which, no matter how lavish the praise, is for the writer only wasting time until he gets back to work. In the second place, only an amateur believes his negative reviews, because then he has to believe the good ones as well, and it is even more pernicious to believe that you are the latest literary wunderkind than it is to believe you are slime.

One does, however, have to suppress the urge to cross-examine one's attacker. In *Reading Myself and Others*, Philip Roth calls unmailed letters to reviewers "a flourishing subliterary genre with a long and moving history, yet one that is all but unknown to the general public." The best advice is to forget it, and novelists, Roth says, "generally do forget it, or continually remind themselves that they ought to be forgetting it during the sieges of remembering." I remember once waking in the dead of night, and in the privacy of my bedroom accusing a woman reviewer of having a face like a dirt road, a face from which, I knew, every zit and pit had been removed in its book jacket and publicity representation by the miracle of airbrushing and retouching, not to mention the sordid demands of vanity. An aggressive reaction, to be sure, and not even a response (except indirectly) to an indictment of me; rather it was predicated on a single observation in the course of a review in which my wife's foot was held to the fire. "My charity does not naturally extend itself," the reviewer had written archly, "to . . . someone who has chosen to burden her adopted daughter with the name Quintana Roo." Up to that moment, I had fastidiously supposed that one's children were off limits, and that whether a child was natural or adopted was not an aspect of one's talent against which points might be scored. In any event, my daughter Quintana, then thirteen, was so burdened by her name that she was already negotiating, in anticipation of her driver's license three years hence, for the vanity license plate QROO.

When attacked, it is also comforting to consider the slings and arrows endured by other writers. In the darkest days of

World War I, George Bernard Shaw published an antiwar pamphlet, "Common Sense and the War," which elicited an infuriated response from a public ready to accuse him of treason and worse. "The hag Sedition was your mother, and Perversity begot you, Mischief was your midwife, and Misrule your nurse, and Unreason brought you up at her feet," a playwright named Henry Arthur Jones wrote in an open letter to Shaw. "No other ancestry and rearing had you, you freakish homunculus, germinated outside of lawful procreation." Of another writer it was said that his "muse is at once indecent and ugly, lascivious and gawky, lubricious and coarse." And again: "You might strike out of existence all that he has written, and the world would not be consciously poorer." Yet again: "an American writer who . . . attracted attention by a volume of so-called poems which were chiefly remarkable for their absurd extravagances and shameless obscenity, and who has since, we are glad to say, been little heard of among decent people." The target of this opprobrium was Walt Whitman, the volume *Leaves of Grass*; the names of most of his accusers are for their sake blessedly lost to memory, or if remembered at all, only as risible footnotes in the Whitman biographies.

There is another reason it is useless to complain: in a way a critic almost never can, the writer knows where "the dry rot" (as Graham Greene once felicitously called it) of a book is actually located, knows all the tricks he used trying to calk it. For all the animus to which a writer is occasionally exposed, I can recall only once being told by a critic something I did not already know about a book of mine. The critic was John Leonard, then of *The New York Times*, and he mentioned to me at a party that he had wanted to review my novel *Dutch Shea, Jr.* because it was so predicated on class hatred. He was absolutely right, but until that moment I had never been aware of it; I wish he had reviewed the book and expanded on that idea, even though he never told me if he liked it or not.

Leonard also told me he knew that in that same book I had taken a gratuitous whack at him and three other critics (although I never named them), in a scene where the protagonist, as he contemplates suicide, watches the *Dick Cavett Show.* I had actually seen this show, and listened while Leonard and the other panelists talked endlessly about the state of American letters. One panelist was a reviewer whose work, all self-promoting butch and blather, I detested, a sentiment I was sure was reciprocated, although to the best of my knowledge he had never reviewed me in the regional journals and the house organ of Euro-trash where he held forth on literature. As my potential suicide watched the show he mused that the unnamed reviewer "looked like Queen Victoria . . . sadly, badly, desperately in need of a diuretic. Naturetin K for bloat." And on and on in similar vein; suicide deferred, although ultimately not even a subsequent and still uncredited appearance by the Victoria clone on yet another PBS show in the novel's last scene could stay the gun my protagonist placed in his mouth, the Empress of India lookalike prattling on-screen even as the trigger was pulled.

Writers are prone to this sort of thing. When he was an editor at the *Partisan Review,* Delmore Schwartz was once unflattering about a short story submitted him by Calder Willingham. In his novel *End as a Man,* Willingham settled accounts by calling a whorehouse Hotel Delmore, later telling a friend of Schwartz that the choice of the name had been deliberate, adding however that he would not have used it had not "Delmore" been so "exactly right from an artistic point of view." Another novelist I know took aim at a daily reviewer for *The New York Times,* an indefatigable ladies' man whose girls seemed to get younger as he got older. The novelist created a scene in a novel just so the reviewer could walk through it unnamed but unmistakable to those who knew him, giving the author a chance to comment on the reviewer's sexual proclivities. And I suppose the ultimate payback came when a writer I know, infuriated by a bad notice, met the reviewer's wife at a party and with malice aforethought seduced her. I might add that the writer in question is my only source for this story.

There are writers who claim not to read their reviews—Saul Bellow comes to mind. The critic Anatole Broyard once scolded Bellow for this stance, saying he might learn something from his critics. What Broyard actually meant, of course, was that Bellow might learn something from the caveats of Anatole Broyard, *maître* to *maître*, as it were, a very slick form of self-aggrandizement. In any event, it scarcely matters if you read your bad reviews, because your friends will tell you what they say anyway. What, after all, are friends for? A few years ago in New York I saw a headline in a hotel magazine stand: JOHN LAHR PUNCTURES THE DIDION-DUNNE BALLOON, and inside there was a caricature of my wife and me. Better a balloon punctured, I thought, than never a balloon at all, and I neither bought the magazine nor read the piece. I had also written enough pieces like that myself to know a dirty little secret: whatever the author's disavowals, whatever his claim to be acting in the service of literature, he is writing for an audience of one—the object of his disaffection— and for that audience of one not to read it is his Zen triumph.

By the time I returned home to Los Angeles, however, I had already received seven copies of Lahr's puncturing, including two from my mother-in-law, mailed in separate envelopes, as if she only trusted the U.S. Postal Service to deliver one of every two pieces of mail. Sticking to Zen principles, I still have not read it, but via friends and family clucking over the unfairness of it all I was made aware ("Why would he say that you are . . .") of each of the sins for which Mr. Lahr claims that my wife and I should do penance. None of them surprised me much; since the late 1970s, we have been a cottage industry for Mr. Lahr, who has detailed our shortcomings, either singly or in tandem, four times by my account, updating the bill of particulars with each new book. I should be flattered. In at least one instance, Mr.

Lahr has shown himself to be a very acute critic of fiction, in that he seems to have abandoned the writing of novels, a discipline in which he demonstrated no discernible gift. Before he became preoccupied with our general inferiority, he did write two novels and sent advance copies of both, each accompanied by a flowery personal entreaty for favorable comment, this before he had sharpened the pin with which to puncture the balloon.

This is not to argue that Mr. Lahr has no right to change his mind (or to imply that the failure to produce jacket quotes caused him to do so). There is, however, a preemptive-strike school that says if I attack you, then you can't attack me, with a statute of limitations that never seems to run out. A district attorney I know calls this the intellectual's version of extortion. One way around this kind of blackmail is to declare an interest. I once reviewed a book by Pauline Kael after she shredded a movie I had written. I disliked her work even before that review (she was, by the way, on the money about the movie in question), indicated in my first paragraph her prior dislike of the picture, and then wrote, "That, for those who wish to get off here, is the record."

Some years later, in *The New Republic*, Henry Fairlie unloaded on one of William F. Buckley's collections of columns, *Right Reason*. In the course of taking Mr. Buckley rather strenuously to task, Mr. Fairlie noted that among the pieces was "an ad hominem attack on me, notable mainly for its misinformation," then continued his bombing run. Mr. Buckley's response was to buy an advertising page in *The New Republic*, where he reprinted in full the charge sheet Mr. Fairlie had mentioned. Mr. Buckley makes a habit of that sort of reply, although usually less expensively. I was less infatuated with his *Overdrive* than he thought I should be, and he responded to *The New York Review of Books* (where my piece appeared) with a letter in which he detailed the people and publications who liked *Overdrive* more than I (Louis Auchincloss, Lance Morrow, and *People*), made an obliquely humorous reference to Salvadoran death squads, considered the failures and repetitions of my own work, and, finally, delivered the kayo punch: "Dunne begins his review by reporting that he and I have had a 'fitful' correspondence over the years. . . . But you see, those notes, while perhaps addressed to the couple, were really directed to his wife, who, of the two, was my friend."

I suspect the reason for this tick is that Mr. Buckley is an enthusiastic dilator on the defects of others, and in my experience enthusiastic dilators are considerably less enthusiastic when someone dilates upon them—"dilate" being Mr. Buckley's verb, from *Overdrive*. He seems not to understand the basic ecology of the literary life, that if you are not sometimes attacked, then you cannot be very good, the attack itself a certification of worth, whether it be Norman Podhoretz on John Updike or Irving Howe on Philip Roth; *vide* also the attacks on Whitman and Shaw. Better to bask in the glow of being one of the world's best fast writers, a gracefully Delphic encomium Mr. Buckley once received from Kurt Vonnegut, and one that has always seemed to me on the level of being called the world's best premature ejaculator, the pleasure enjoyed in inverse proportion to the pleasure given.

Ultimately it is a waste of time to reply directly to your critics; to do so is only a public acknowledgment that the shot hit home, and that your feelings are hurt. What it comes down to is this: Would I rather do what I do, as imperfectly as my harshest critics say I do it, or what they do, as perfectly as they think they do it? The question needs no answer. Only once do I claim to have had the last word with a critic, and that in a way he never knew. The reviewer was John Simon, he who in his quest for the brass ring has made a reputation for himself mainly by lingering on what he perceives as the physical shortfalls of the actresses he sees on stage and screen. The last time I saw Mr. Simon he was having dinner in the billiard room of a thirty-four-room apartment on Park Avenue. Honesty compels me to report, in the interests of those actresses whose tinny voices and pendulous breasts and flabby muscle tone he has maligned, that a giblet of quiche decorated his primary chin, and his teeth, all too visible as he ate, seemed the product either of bad dentistry or a stagnant genetic pool.

Mr. Simon has sampled every dish on the buffet of hustle, from elitism to language to being the spokesperson for one of Claus von Bülow's discarded mistresses. Language was the rack on which he had me stretched this time, in a column he wrote about a piece I had done on movie reviewers, one of whom coincidentally was Mr. Simon himself. Mr. Simon's scrutiny was sufficiently rigorous to have my friend Calvin Trillin send the following letter:

> Dear John Gregory — As one who has looked to you for guidance in these matters, I was naturally distressed to read in John Simon's column that your grammar and syntax are, to use the vernacular, not worth a shit.
>
> Yours,
> Calvin.

As it happened, Calvin's letter arrived in the same mail as a profit check from a very bad but very successful movie I had once helped to write. The check was, if I recall correctly, in the amount of $264,000. I took the check and Calvin's letter and Xeroxed them together on the same piece of paper. Then I mailed this Xerox back to Calvin by return post, with four words typed on the bottom: "Dear Calvin — Fuck syntax."

POSTSCRIPT

JAMES WOLCOTT was the reviewer who reminded the suicidal protagonist in *Dutch Shea, Jr.* of Prince Albert's widow. I reveal his name only because, declaring an interest, he chose to identify himself and have what I am sure he thought his revenge when he reviewed my last book, *Harp*, in *Vanity Fair*. The seven-year wait had brought his vitriol to a splendid boil, and in a three-page diatribe, a jeremiad from Balmoral, as it were, he paused on all my many and varied literary, moral, personal, familial, and physical inadequacies and malefactions, not excluding my veiled allusions to his startling resemblance to Victoria Regina Imperatrix. He got mad, he got even, an attitude I should report he found particularly odious and unattractive in me, but in his case the attitude was rooted, of course, in the most rigorous critical standards, my character defects reflected in the worthlessness of both the book in particular, and the work in general. "Why does Dunne defiantly insist on being so damned unpleasant?" Wolcott asked. "Why should we submit to having his breath pounding in our face [sic]"? He proposed an answer, his playground idea of a knee-zapper remarkably similar to William Buckley's: "It must bother Dunne that his wife is a better writer than he is and his brother sells more copies. It must *drive him to distraction*." (The italics are Mr. Wolcott's). Wow. Heavy. And "wow" and "heavy" again. For all the italicized heavy breathing, however, thin gruel, neither so good nor so original as "you freakish homunculus, germinated outside of lawful procreation."

Mr. Wolcott's career offers a cautionary tale to those embarking on the literary life. He arrived on the scene, as so many before him, with the provincial's scorn and the unforgivingness of youth, all piss and vinegar, the world an oyster to be swallowed. Ambitious and bright as a penny, Mencken surely his model, he became a sassy critic of popular culture, of films and books and even television, with a certain demotic flair, and if not standards at least attitudes that could be confused with them. Here was a path offering easy if limited acclaim and PBS celebrity, those enemies of promise (in Cyril Connolly's elegant phrase) that destroy youth and with it the freedom to learn and be bad in those very disciplines to which the literary journalist secretly aspires, and whose practitioners he publicly disdains. The chariot takes wing, invective becomes a tic, bluster passes as style. No one, I once wrote, sets out wanting to be a critic; it is where one ends up; a truce is made with ambition, an armistice with life. "Psychological sloth" governs (Connolly again, the unsparing laureate of the breed), "short articles for quick returns."

For that sense of worth, in lieu of work, there is always The Interview, with Mencken invoked, of course, and other of the Interviewee's betters. "It's like when Edmund Wilson complained to Nabokov about 'your eagerness to topple major reputations,' and Nabokov said to Edmund Wilson, 'That's what I do, you're just going to have to prepare yourself for the crash,' " Mr. Wolcott told an interviewer in 7 Days. "I feel I'm behind a drum set, this is my drum set, and you know, sometimes I'm just going to really whip the skins. The right you have is the right you take. Nobody gave H. L. Mencken the right. . . ." Notice the implied straight line from Mencken (The American Language, Prejudices, etc.) through Edmund Wilson (To the Finland Station, Patriotic Gore, etc.) and Vladimir Nabokov (Lolita, Pale Fire, etc.) to James Wolcott (   ). It is a harmless enough conceit, even engaging in its bombast and self-inflation, a whistle in the dark, complete with verbal atrocities ("It's like when . . ." and "you know . . ."), but finally the void between the parentheses, the absence of et ceteras, speak volumes that Interviewee twaddle, however entertaining, cannot rationalize.

Fifteen years evaporate, middle age casts its dispiriting shadow, the greedy piper holds out his scabrous hand; and on

the horizon comes marching another generation of the sassy and
biliously ambitious, with sharp elbows and youth on its side, and
time, there but to be mortgaged. The books meant to be written
have not, nor the screenplays; the novel has been set aside, postponed; abandoned? Hark! An announcement on the contributors'
page: ". . . working on a first novel." A month later, a further
update: ". . . working on a novel." Finishing, of course, is the
trick; the world waits. In the everyday, no cheerleading. Tear-
sheets are life's diary, its dismal history. Ahead lies another
screening, another set of someone else's galleys, and as the young,
so polished, so new, so agreeable as ever to the devil's bargain,
push their way to Tina's table, the future holds a place below
the salt, lesser bylines, chancier outlets . . . September . . .
November . . .

Regards

It was 1960, or maybe 1961, the winter, when I first became aware of Barry Farrell. I was a floater at *Time* magazine. A floater is a writer, usually a new young writer, who floats from section to section each issue, sitting in for the regular who is sick or on vacation. I was writing sports that week, and the lead piece in the section was going to be on a West Coast college basketball team, U.C. Berkeley, if memory serves. Now: I happen to detest basketball—bounce ball, Red Smith called it, an attitude that sums up my own—and I was looking forward to the assignment with low dread. The reporter on the piece was not even a staff correspondent but a stringer attached to *Time*'s San Francisco bureau, another cause for alarm. I waited all day Wednesday—filing day for the back of the book—for the file; nothing came in. Thursday A.M., still nothing. Thursday afternoon, nothing. I was in a rage. Then at dinnertime, the first take, More TK. I read; the fury abated. The file was—there is no other word for it—stylish. Not facts—six foot eleven, 19.7 ppg., 2.3 steals, 6.1 assists, that sort of thing—but an appreciation, a love of the game of basketball, a sense of its subtext and the fluid interplay of its personalities so lucidly explained that it almost made me rethink my own antipathy to the sport. There was nothing I had to do except trim to fit. The cable went into that week's magazine virtually as filed—and what a rarity that was at *Time*. I did not even know the name of the stringer until I hit the tag at the end of the file: "Regards, Farrell."

Regards, Farrell. Rarely have two words so perfectly summed up a single human being. Barry Farrell passed through life bestowing his regard as if it was a benediction, a kind of sanctifying grace. Of course he was hired by *Time* as a regular correspondent, and in due course he moved to New York as a staff writer for the magazine. It was there that we became friends, and we remained so until he died nearly twenty-five years later. Writers do not make easy friends of one another; they are professional carpers, too competitive, mean-spirited, and envious for the demands of lasting friendship. With only occasional lapses from grace, Barry and I were an exception to this rule.

How do you describe a friendship of a quarter of a century? You can't really. There is only a blur of images, shards of memory, and with each memory an angle of distortion, my psychic light meter adjusting differently than someone else's. Physical impressions first. He was tall and somewhat stooped, as if to compensate for his height, bearded, strawberry blond with jug ears, and the most extraordinary eyes, the eyes of someone who had seen too much, too many violations of the human contract. The first story he ever covered, as a young police reporter for the *Seattle Post-Intelligencer*, was a homosexual suicide, and then not so much a hanging as an accident, a homosexual who had strung himself up to increase the pleasure of onanism, and then had slipped during climax. Orgasm and strangulation, the ultimate death trip, and an exposed limp dick mocking the authorities who had to cut the body down: A few stories like that and the capacity for surprise is soon lost. I once told him he had the look of a Graham Greene priest; he had heard too much in confession, his pitch for evasion and deceit was too perfect. And yet always he was ready to absolve; it was not for him to cast the first stone.

Women loved him. He was that rare writer who looked the

way a writer should look. I remember once seeing him standing at the elevator at *Time* wearing a trenchcoat and smoking a
Gauloise (another wonderful affect, as was the occasional joint
he would sometimes puff while in conference with the managing
editor, confident in that innocent time that the editor would
think it only some particularly noisome foreign tobacco he had
picked up on his travels). He was on his way to France to romance a movie star. Forget that the movie star in question had
romanced half the Western world; he was the first person I had
ever known who had been in the feathers with an eminence of
the silver screen. I envied his panache, and I wanted to cheer.

He was stylish, but there was so much substance beneath
the style. Those eyes, the voice—Barry was that rare person who
talked in complete sentences, every sentence perfectly parsed,
plural predicates for plural subjects, no dangling participles, every clause modifying what it was supposed to modify, "that"
never confused with "which"—people trusted him, they told
him things they would never tell another reporter. Barry was a
great chronicler of the city, any city. He liked cops and coroners
and city hall bureaucrats, and to him they would confide the
most appalling tales of municipal mendacity. The hostility between the homicide squads of the two police agencies in Los Angeles—the sheriff's office and the LAPD—was a situation made
for him. He would imply to the LAPD homicide cops that the
sheriffs thought they were no good, nothing more than traffic
cops in polyester double knits, and then tell the sheriffs the
LAPD thought they were firemen with police badges, with the
result that both squads could not wait to tell him about the bone-
headed screwups in the other's murder investigations.

Vietnam, the Middle East, Latin America—wherever Barry
went, first for *Time*, then for *Life*, then on his own, his method
was the same: never trust the official version, hang around, per-
severe, work the telephone, anticipate, and of course take advantage of, the unexpected. The spook he caught in a lie was a

source of rare value—someone he then did not have to believe. He was a tenacious questioner, never deflected, following a kind of quiet Jesuitical logic, a holdover from the Catholicism he had long since abandoned, one that allowed him to illuminate dark corners. "Is Gary well hung?" he suddenly asked a jailhouse snitch about the stoolie's former cellmate, Gary Gilmore; it was a startling question, posed without judgment, perfectly evoking a world without women where any member, any orifice might offer opportunity for sexual release. Prison aristocracies intrigued him; "bum bandit" was the term he coined for a cell-block sexual imperialist, and he studied the bum bandits and the punks and all the sub-categories in between with the eye of an anthropologist.

The cruelties of life did not pass him by. His two-year-old son was killed, electrocuted in a freak household accident, and his first marriage fell apart. His daughter Annie lived with her mother, adored and too rarely seen. Then marriage again, to Marcia, and after a time they adopted Joan, named after my wife. He left the warm embrace of the Time-Life Building and moved back to California and the free-lancer's life. In retrospect, it was probably a mistake. Barry always had difficulty making deadlines—remember that first file he sent me—he needed some kind of corporate whiphand, and the possibility of a paycheck withheld. In the free-lance world, his passion for perfection—the perfect word, the perfect image, the perfect example—led to pieces being a week late, then a month, two months, a year. He needed one more fact, there was someone in Reno, a whore in Salt Lake, a narc hiding out in Miami, this will nail it down, another trip was scheduled, another deadline postponed. Happiness was a motel on the Utah sand flats, interviewing Gary Gilmore on Death Row through a filter of lawyers; it was the obstacle that obsessed him, and the adrenaline and the ingenuity needed to overcome it, and if his Gilmore interviews only provided the subsoil out of which grew Norman Mailer's *The*

Executioner's Song, what the hell, he would get back to his own work later, this was a moment in history not to be missed. Mailer had him pegged:

> Someone was always dying in his stories. Oscar Bonavena getting killed, Bobby Hall, young blond girls getting offed on highways in California. One cult slaying or another. He even had the reputation of being good at it. His telephone number leaped to the mind of various editors. Barry Farrell, crime reporter, with an inner life exasperatingly Catholic. Led his life out of his financial and emotional exigencies, took the jobs his bills and his battered psyche required him to take, but somehow his assignments always took him into some great new moral complexity. Got into his writing like a haze.

Pure Norman, true Barry. I would give Barry the Philistine's argument: Finished is better than good. He did not listen, could not heed.

And yet. It was in this period that his best work was done. He and Marcia and Joan lived in a small house in Hollywood, and God, it was fun to go there for dinner. There were actors and NBA basketball players and writers and defendants and vice cops and lawyers and every kind of oddball—I remember one sweet old woman with a wooden leg who designed turn-on clothes for the hookers who worked the legal Nevada whorehouses, outfits with little heart-shaped openings framing the pubic symphysis—a little dope and a lot of booze. He was also teaching now, non-fiction writing, first at U.C. Santa Barbara, and then at colleges around Los Angeles, both to earn a little money and because he genuinely enjoyed it. He did not have students so much as disciples, acolytes who hung on his every word; he was E.T. as whiskey priest, bringing them communiqués from a world they could not believe existed.

Every morning, precisely at 9:15, he and I would talk on the telephone; a natter, he would call it. He had usually been up all night; he was always trying to find the best time to work, some schedule that would allow him to crack his writing block. In the background, I could hear the noises from the mean streets outside his Hollywood office, the wailing sirens and the voices of the dispossessed floating up through the open window. The New York and Los Angeles newspapers would be read by then, and with ribald shrewdness he would give me a close textual exegesis of the morning's news. I would often tell him I wished a tape-recording device could be implanted under his skin to record his conversation, those beautiful sentences, throwing out its tape at the end of the day. That, I said, would solve his writing block. His private life was becoming more untidy: he could not write and drank; he drank and could not write. He looked terrible. And then one day it happened—a minor automobile accident, a stroke, and a massive heart attack; none of the medical attendants on the scene knew which had occurred first. For six months he lay semicomatose in a Veterans Administration hospital not five minutes from my house in Los Angeles. Finally he died. I cannot hear the telephone ring at 9:15 anymore without a frisson. It will not be Barry.

"He has an enthusiasm for tragedy," he once said about a noxious self-dramatizer who had done him harm; I had never heard anyone so effortlessly eviscerated; a simple declarative sentence in six perfectly chosen words; if only writing came so easy. So many times in the years since his death something has happened and he is the only person I wanted to call, the only one who would intuitively understand what was on my mind, what stuck in my throat. Perhaps that is how to define friendship. "Regards, Farrell." Regards, Barry. Regards, regards, and love.

ABOUT THE AUTHOR

JOHN GREGORY DUNNE lives in New York City with his wife, Joan Didion. He is the author of *Harp*, *The Red White and Blue*, *True Confessions*, *Dutch Shea*, *Jr.*, *The Studio*, and other books.